The Value of Debt
in Retirement

The Value of Debt in Retirement

Why Everything You Have Been Told Is Wrong

Thomas J. Anderson

WILEY

Published by John Wiley & Sons, Inc., Hoboken, New Jersey.
Published simultaneously in Canada.

For general information on our other products and services or for technical support, please contact
our Customer Care Department within the United States at (800) 762-2974, outside the United
States at (317) 572-3993, or fax (317) 572-4002.

Wiley publishes in a variety of print and electronic formats and by print-on-demand. Some
material included with standard print versions of this book may not be included in e-books or in
print-on-demand. If this book refers to media such as a CD or DVD that is not included in the
version you purchased, you may download this material at http://booksupport.wiley.com. For
more information about Wiley products, visit www.wiley.com.

Library of Congress Cataloging-in-Publication Data:

Anderson, Thomas J. (Certified investment management analyst)
   The value of debt in retirement : why everything you have been told is wrong / Thomas J. Anderson.
      pages cm
   Includes bibliographical references and index.
ISBN 978-1-119-01998-5 (hardback); ISBN 978-1-119-02001-1 (epdf);
ISBN 978-1-119-02000-4 (epub)   1. Finance, Personal.   2. Retirement—Planning.   I. Title.
   HG179.A5597628 2015
      332.7084′6—dc23

                                                                              2014049407

Printed in the United States.

10 9 8 7 6 5 4 3 2 1

*This book is dedicated to two very special sets of retirees
who have given me the insight and unconditional love
necessary to write this book:
Grandpa John & Grandma Kay Kay
Marty & Julianne Smith*

Contents

Foreword

Y ou have worked hard for your money. You have saved. If you are reading this book, you are likely in retirement, near retirement, or an advisor to those who wish to retire. When it comes to retirement, Charles Dickens said it best: "It was the best of times; it was the worst of times." Boomers are getting pushed and pulled in a lot of directions as they retire or near retirement. They are the sandwich generation—helping their kids, helping their parents. At the same time, many want to enjoy life, take trips, and buy the things they've always wanted. How can retirees balance these conflicting demands and desires?

Tom Anderson has received multiple national awards for his wealth-management expertise and studied at many of the top schools in finance. Wealth management is all he has done and all he has studied. While others were at summer camp, Anderson went to Wall Street Camp. In *The Value of Debt in Retirement,* Anderson shows you some potentially shocking revelations, "tricks" that high-net-worth individuals have used for years. These include:

- Why rushing to pay off your mortgage in the name of being debt-free when you retire may leave you with less liquidity, less tax efficiency, and a profound inability to take advantage of the basic ideas, strategies, and practices in this book.

- How an intriguing combination of selling and borrowing—selling from your IRA and borrowing against what's called an Asset-Based Loan Facility—can provide you with greatly superior, highly tax-efficient results.
- How and why financial advisors, despite their claims that they are not giving you tax advice, could be doing exactly that . . . often in a way that primarily amounts to guessing with *your* future.
- How conventional wisdom is generally flat-out wrong with respect to assumptions that are made regarding taxes, annuities, IRAs, and Roth IRAs.

Helpful guides at the end of the book will help you see how in the current environment you can buy a $100,000 car for $250 per month with no required monthly payment. How to buy a $1 million second home, 100 percent financed, for $2,500 per month, fully tax deductible. You are going to get amazing ideas on better ways to help your kids, help your parents, and leave a bigger legacy for your charities. Along the way you will see how you can be prepared for emergencies and opportunities that come your way.

Increasing return, reducing taxes, and lowering risk—all with a goal of making sure that you do not outlive your money—is what this book is all about. But make no mistake: There is no free lunch. Not everyone will be able to implement these ideas, and they come with many risks. But I can promise you this: Anderson is going to challenge you. He challenges me most every day!

Sarah Anderson
President, Better Debt, LLC
Revolutionizing Debt™
The leading expert in securities-based lending education,
tools, and solutions
www.betterdebt.com

Acknowledgments

There may be some books where somebody sits down, writes on a computer, hits send, and poof!—a book comes out. This isn't one of those books. Writing a book like this would not be possible without an incredible team surrounding it.

My core business would not be possible without Kerry Abdoney, Jon Bancks, Stacey Halyard, Darla Lowe, JoAnn Masters, and Julie Vogt, as well as my many partners throughout the country. I can't tell you how much you have contributed to my ability to do this project and how much I value you. You are all part of my family and I love you.

Rafe Sagalyn, Brandon Coward, and the team at ICM have been excellent agents and facilitated a great relationship with Wiley. I appreciate our long-term partnership and sincerely value your advice and guidance.

Jordan S. Gruber once again was a true partner and able to take my initial ideas and turn them into a publishable manuscript. I can't thank him enough for his efforts. I love how we connect on projects and am excited that we are already working on the next one.

The following readers gave candid feedback that helped refine our initial work: Mike Finn, Karla and Denny Goettel, Jim and Ann Hoffman, David and Pat Knuth, David Lessing, Jim Mohni, Dr. Jerry and Nancy

Shirk, Dean Swinton, Pen Shade, and Marty and Julianne Smith. Randy Kurtz, you are brilliant and you went above and beyond. The comments this group provided on this work were transformative.

Damian Pardo and Robert Espinoza, I am so thankful for the time, energy, and effort you spent in helping me develop the guide for the LGBT community. This is a small start on an important topic, and I hope together we can expand on these ideas in the future.

An absolutely amazing group of people from diverse backgrounds served as a powerful sounding board that helped beta test many of the concepts and related ideas. These individuals include: Simon Algar, Angela Billick, Adam Browne, Gian Cavallini, Corey Chisnell, Chris Claus, Dodge Daverman, Daniel Eckert, Suzanne El-Moursi, Jeff Finn, Maddy Halyard, Chris Harper, Mike Gibbs, Jim Guthrie, Mike Jackson, Bernardo Jorge, Walter Joyce, Paul Krake, Todd Kurisu, Ed Lomasney, Krista LaFrenz, Britton Lombardi, Chris Merker, Carrie Merritt, Paul Mulvaney, Colin O'Brien, Jeff Prochnow, Linhard Stepf, Josh Stein, Anne Stanchfield, and Scott Watenberg. Sarah and I can't begin to thank you enough for your support during this project. We are blessed to consider each of you to be dear friends.

Brittain and Steve Ezzes, I sincerely appreciate your inspiration and contributions.

To my dad, thanks for everything you have taught me over the years, particularly the time we spent traveling to the Iowa farms, raising cattle and learning about agricultural marketplaces. Those experiences helped to shape my world view and create a foundation for a thriving business and fulfilling life.

To John and Patti, thanks for being wonderful readers of the book. Thanks also on a personal note for your unconditional support of Sarah and me, our family, and our businesses. We are so fortunate to have your shining examples inspire our life. We love you!

The charitable giving guide was inspired by a conversation with Jeremy Scarbrough at Washington University. He later gave thoughtful suggestions to make this section be much more robust.

Robyn Lawrence and Stacey Halyard were incredible early editors who synthesized feedback from early readers and made the book much more impactful. Dave Knuth, your math editing skills were exceptional.

Emmons Patzer is a fountain of creative ideas. Importantly, the concepts of Oppressive, Working, and Enriching debt are developed from base material he provided. Emmons has been a true mentor and advisor and friend throughout the project.

Speaking of Emmons, he, along with Bill King, David Lessing, Dr. Mahendra Gupta, Eliot Protsch, and Steve Vanourny have served as an outstanding board of advisors. Your stewardship, passion, and intelligence are stunning.

This leads me to one of my greatest areas of thanks. I am incredibly enthusiastic about the growing partnership with The Olin School of Business at Washington University in St. Louis that is helping further develop some of the academic studies outlined within this book. I would like to highlight the efforts of Dr. Mahendra Gupta, Anjan Thackor, and Charles Cuny. Charles in particular has been an amazing academic advisor and mentor. Hopefully, together we are scratching the surface of what could prove to be some tremendous breakthroughs in personal finance. To be clear, much of the material that is being presented is only at a Phase 1 level of academic rigor and merits much more study, but it is my sincere hope that we will be able to further expand on these ideas together in follow up works.

Wiley has again assigned a top-notch team. I would particularly like to thank Tula Batanchiev, Associate Editor, who continues to be my North Star guiding me. I sincerely appreciate our partnership. Thank you to Helen Cho, Editorial Program Coordinator, and Melissa Connors, Publicity. Steven Kyritz, Senior Production Editor, and Stacey Rivera, Senior Development Editor, were invaluable and I appreciate their skills. Any remaining mistakes are my own.

The team at Timber Wolf Publishing took an idea and ran with it. Bryan Goettel, Lauren Kurtz, Ted Nims, Brandon Swinton, and David Zylstra all contributed to the project and made it Better!! I want to highlight Jaramee Finn, Fred Rose, and Julie Schmidt. They are the honey badgers. This would not have been possible without their incredible efforts, contributions, and attention to detail. They are the shepherds who have not only guided this book, but also vastly contributed to the content and ideas.

Rowan, Rory, and Reid—I could not be more proud of you. You are excellent helpers! I know that you sacrifice a lot and I can't tell you how much I appreciate your support.

Sarah—I know who you are, and you are the smartest, most talented and magical person I know. You are my inspiration and you are my partner. All of my ideas are really just yours said another way. This book is yours. It isn't that "you make this possible"—it literally couldn't happen without you.

Introduction

Retirement is wonderful, but it certainly isn't easy. It brings with it many fears, uncertainties, and doubts. You're concerned about your health and wellness, your family and extended family, your financial resources and ability to live the life you have always dreamed about. It brings questions about inner purpose, fulfillment, and, frankly, even the meaning of life.

While retirement is an adventure that you will experience only one time, I have had the opportunity to vicariously experience thousands of retirements.[1] Using my academic, professional, and personal experiences, I have learned tricks and tools that may help you live the retirement of your dreams. I take strategies that the best companies and the ultra-affluent have been using for years and apply them to specific personal situations to create the best possible outcome for clients and their families.

My goal is to reframe the conversation around debt in general and highlight its potential benefits as well as the potential *risks of being debt free.* I deliver a new way of thinking about your risk tolerance in which your decisions depend on your needs. In doing so you will see why I care virtually nothing at all about your "risk tolerance." *What I do care about are your needs and the best way to accomplish your goals and objectives.* If you need a low amount of income—less than a 3 percent return—from your portfolio, you may not need to embrace a debt strategy. For example, if you have $1 million and need less than $30,000 per year in income from your portfolio, then you may have little need for debt. However, if you need a return between 4 and 6 percent, it's quite likely that you can benefit from debt. If you need a return of more than 6 percent, I recommend that you pay very, very close attention to this book. It may be the only way that you will be able to achieve your goals.

It is my opinion that the investment process traditionally used by professionals and "do-it-yourself" investors alike is broken. It is missing half of the picture! Too many people *guess* with respect to debt—they don't have a strategy. I often find that if they do it isn't well thought out or comprehensive. Generally it is as simple as "pay it all off as fast as possible." It is time that we consider, as companies do, debt to be a tool and open the world to a new approach to wealth management in retirement, one that factors in both sides of the balance sheet as an integrated ecosystem.

Equally important is that regardless of your beliefs with respect to debt, I want you to have a different understanding of the word "risk" and for you to think about risk differently. Many baby boomers have undersaved for retirement and are making decisions that mathematically make it virtually impossible for them to be successful. In this book I put the greatest care in examining trade-offs. I provide you with tools to compare and contrast different risks. For example, it may turn out that being debt free is great for you. It may also turn out that being debt free in fact considerably increases your risk. My goal is knowledge and empowerment around the risks we all face.

Part I of this book lays the foundation and discusses "why" you should consider the use of strategic debt in retirement. I begin with a discussion of the benefits of strategic debt. Chapter 2 provides an overview of conventional wisdom, what authors are currently saying about debt, and why it might be time for a new approach. Chapter 3 outlines the different types of debt—oppressive, working, and enriching—and establishes the seven rules for being a better debtor. It also discusses the impact of longer life expectancy on retirement planning. The longer our expected retirement, the more important it is that our money lasts for us, which means it's even more important that we take a holistic approach to personal financial management that includes both assets and liabilities (debts).

Part II focuses on "what" debt can do for you. I prove that with a proper debt strategy you may be able to virtually eliminate your taxes, increase your rate of return, and reduce your risk (Figure I.1). The more you understand these ideas, the more confident you will feel that you will have sufficient resources throughout your retirement. Confidence about your resources can ease many of the traditional fears, uncertainties, and doubts that come with retirement. This will in turn let you spend more time focusing on family, friends, charities, and maybe even the purpose and meaning of life!

> A proper debt strategy may be able to virtually eliminate your taxes, increase your rate of return, and reduce your risk.

This section could fundamentally change your life! I start out by discussing the importance of getting your numbers right and look at some big mistakes that even professional advisors make every day. I then prove that debt can enhance your rate of return and increase the probability that you will never run out of money.

This section includes one of my most stunning case studies, an individual with a net worth of $5.5 million who spends $20,000 per month after taxes and pays less than $4,000 per year in taxes. More important,

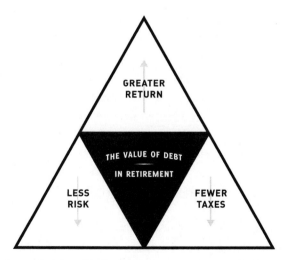

Figure I.1   Strategic Use of Debt in Retirement May Help You

I show you how—regardless of whether your net worth is higher or lower—it may be possible to make these strategies work for you, too!

Finally, I focus on the fact that risk is equally important—if not more important—than return when you are retired and look at the potential role of debt in reducing your risk. You read that right. I prove that it is possible that debt can actually reduce your risk, increase return, and lower taxes.

Part III focuses on the "how." I discuss the risks in detail, outline a glide path on how to embrace these strategies, and conclude by bringing it all together.

It was fascinating to get feedback from early readers. Some people told me that they wanted more detail—and others told me they wanted less detail. Some told me that they wanted to hear more about my experiences with the emotional aspects of retirement; others said stay focused on the numbers. In order to address these conflicting comments this book is laid out differently than most. The nine chapters are written with a big-picture per-spective and are intended to be simple illustrations of the ideas and concepts. In order to address the conflicting comments, I have designed a series of guides and appendices for those who want more detail on specific topics.

The last section of the book is intended to be a customized experience for you and your interests. Think of it as a nonfiction "choose your own adventure." There are three guides. The first is a guide to charitable giving strategies to consider. Here I will give you win-win ideas on how you can protect your needs and leave a legacy. The second guide focuses on things to consider as retirement approaches and how to be mentally prepared. The final guide focuses on the financial aspect of retirement, suggesting better ways to pay for things you want to buy. The goal is that you can use the table of contents to turn to a specific topic that is relevant to you. Finally, I offer a few appendices with helpful information and detail for you to consider as you move forward with implementation of these ideas.

Caution: You Could Burn Your House Down Baking a Cake!

If you read a cookbook it may tell you to chop carrots or to bake some-thing for 30 minutes. Think of all of the risks that these activities include: Chopping with sharp instruments, 350-degree ovens, and maybe an open flame—in your house! Risks range from minor injury to burning the place down. If I had to outline all of the risks with every step of every recipe, each one would likely be (1) impossible to follow and (2) 50 pages long, or longer! Further, a cookbook assumes some basic knowledge, for example, that you know how to operate your oven. A cookbook cannot include an owner's manual for your stove, oven, refrigerator, and dishwasher.

There is a lot of similarity between cooking and the ideas I will be presenting in this book. Risks range from very minor to the serious possibility of burning down your financial house. My goal is to reduce the risk in your life—not to increase it! I will do everything I can to present information in a balanced way and to help identify risks proactively.

Similar to a cookbook, I will not be able to provide an instruction manual for all of the tools in your financial kitchen. The simplest way to look at this book is that the ideas of increasing return and reducing your taxes are based on very basic math facts. To be clear, it is a fact of math that what I am about to outline is possible. However, your ability to accomplish these results depends on so many factors that it is far from certain, and your ability to be successful with these strategies is not a known fact at all. As we will see, all debt is simply a magnifying glass. If you make good decisions they will look better and if you make bad decisions they will be much worse. I will give you some guides to better decision-making but your actual results from using these tools and ideas are indeterminable.

To address risks and to make the book more approachable there is a very important disclaimer at the end of each chapter: "The information in this chapter is to be considered in a holistic way as a part of the book and not to be considered on a stand-alone basis. This includes, but is not limited to, the discussion of risks of each of these ideas as well as all of the disclaimers throughout the book." An entire chapter is dedicated to a discussion of the risks that come with these ideas. The bottom line is that you do need to carefully consider risks before moving forward with any of these ideas. Additionally, it is important to remember all of the examples in this book regarding the use of an asset-based loan facility (ABLF) or securities-based line of credit assume that the loan is in good standing. For the details of these types of loans and the associated risks it is important to review Appendix F and discuss the potential use of these products with your tax, legal, and financial advisors.

The next part of the disclaimer states: "The material is presented with a goal of encouraging thoughtful conversation and rigorous debate on the risks and potential benefits of the concepts between you and your advisors based on your unique situation, risk tolerance, and goals." I chose that language, and I mean what it says. This is not a "how to" book, and the advice should not be considered specific to your situation. This book's goal is to encourage thoughtful conversation and debate at the kitchen table and with your tax, legal, and financial advisors about whether these ideas make sense for you and your situation.

QUICK HOUSEKEEPING ITEM

The elephant in the room is that this book is coming out at a time when interest rates are at or near generational lows in many countries around the world. Therefore it is necessary to share a quick word on interest rates before we dive in.

The ideas and concepts in this book are written to transcend time and geographic boundaries. At the same time I need to use examples in order to make the book topical and relevant. Therefore, the examples in this book are based on interest rates in the United States in early 2015.

It is my fundamental belief that over a long enough period of time interest rates will change. I am also fundamentally concerned that some weird things could happen with rates as a result of some of the policies that are being implemented around the world. We will address these risks in detail throughout the book.

With any luck, reading this book will spur you to consider the merits of not rushing to pay down your mortgage and other "good" debt and instead building up a diversified after-tax portfolio so that you will have more liquidity, more tax flexibility, and the ability to take advantage of these ideas and practices. It may help you increase your rate of return, reduce your taxes, reduce your risk, and increase the chances you will make it through your retirement without running out of money and leaving the legacy you want to leave.

At the end of the day, you will choose whether or not you take advantage of the strategic debt philosophy, ideas, strategies, and practices put forth in this book and its predecessor. And that's exactly my point: Challenge conventional wisdom. I want *you* to have the choice because I believe *you* deserve to be the one who reaps the rewards.[2]

Notes

1. I have been a financial advisor for 15 years. During this time my specialty has been retirement planning and retirement investment management. I have been recognized four times as a *Barron's* top advisor on their state-by-state list and by *On Wall Street* magazine as a member of the "40 under 40" group, which recognized me as one of the largest producing advisors in the industry under 40 years old. Throughout my career I have coached and trained approximately 10,000 advisors on my wealth management process and the benefits of holistic thinking. In the process I have fielded more questions than I can remember and seen more case studies than you can imagine. In addition to my core business, which is made up of hundreds of clients, a large part of my success has been built on direct partnerships with other advisors. These advisors collectively serve well over a thousand additional clients. In addition, I have also served as a sales manager for Merrill Lynch, where I had the opportunity to assist approximately 100 advisors who oversaw well over 10,000 individual client relationships.
2. Author's Note: The information in this chapter is to be considered in a holistic way as a part of the book and not to be considered on a stand-alone basis. This includes, but is not limited to, the discussion of risks of each of these ideas as well as all of the disclaimers throughout the book. The material is presented with a goal of encouraging thoughtful conversation and rigorous debate on the risks and potential benefits of the concepts between you and your advisors based on your unique situation, risk tolerance, and goals.

Part I

BASIC IDEAS AND CORE CONCEPTS

First comes thought; then organization of that thought into ideas and plans; then transformation of those plans into reality. The beginning, as you will observe, is in your imagination.

—**Napoleon Hill**

Chapter 1

A Better Path

The debt we owe to the play of imagination is incalculable.

—**Carl Jung**

The path I am going to outline for a better retirement—how you can retire comfortably, minimize taxes, help your family, and buy the things you have always wanted—is centered around the idea of using the strategic benefits of debt. Give me some time and an open mind, and I will show you some tricks that ultra-high-net-worth individuals have been using for years, including how you may be able to increase your rate of return, minimize taxes, and actually reduce risk by using strategic debt.

Can you—and should you—attempt to benefit from what this book will define and describe as "better" debt? Will a debt-inclusive approach to the entirety of your financial life, including the momentous transition known as retirement, make things better for you and those you love? Or will debt—any debt at all—be the heavy lead anchor that sinks your hopes for achieving happiness now and in your golden years?

It depends. It certainly isn't my belief that all debt is good, nor is it my belief that everybody needs debt. The goal of this book is to offer some perspective, a whole different way of thinking about things, a (w)holistic way that includes both sides of the balance sheet—that is, both your assets *and* your debts. I hope to raise questions worth considering and make suggestions potentially worth implementing. Then I will give you my take on what some of your best next steps might be. I hope to present a realistic case of what's possible, and to guide you in the right general direction. I will offer many everyday examples of how you can obviously, immediately, and substantially benefit from my ideas, while also pointing out pitfalls, obstacles, and dangers along the way.

But honestly, it's an uphill battle. Our culture is replete with fearsome admonitions about all debt being inherently evil, how debt will always make you poorer and worse off, and how the *only* way to retire with peace of mind is to get rid of—ideally, get rid of *all*—your debt, before it's too late. Nobody wants to burden their children with debt when they are gone, right?

Consider Shakespeare's *Hamlet*, in which Polonius tells his son Laertes, "Neither a lender nor a borrower be." Or consider financial author and radio host Dave Ramsey's advice: "You can't be in debt and win. It doesn't work."[1]

Not so fast!

In the first book in this series, *The Value of Debt* (John Wiley & Sons, 2013),[2] I describe a variety of ways that debt can make a huge *positive* difference in the lives of those mentally, emotionally, and financially equipped to take advantage of it. In this book, I will reinforce and expand on the key ideas from the first book and illustrate how with a debt strategy it is possible to increase your returns, reduce your taxes, and reduce your risk, which can increase the chances that you will not outlive your money. I'll also show you ways to pay for the lifestyle you have always wanted to have.

A Successful but Controversial Debut

I was humbled when the first book in this series, *The Value of Debt*, made it onto the *New York Times* bestseller list and was named one of the Top 10 business books of 2013 by WealthManagement.Com, one of the wealth-management industry's most prestigious magazines. *The Value of Debt* begins with the five tenets, or action principles, that anchor a debt-inclusive philosophy and practice, and they are worth repeating here.

FIVE TENETS OF A DEBT-INCLUSIVE PHILOSOPHY

1. Adopt a Holistic—Not Atomistic—Approach
2. Explore Thinking and Acting Like a Company
3. Understand Limitations on Commonly Held Views of Personal Debt
4. Set Your Sights on an Optimal Personal Debt Ratio
5. Stay Open-Minded, Ask Questions, and Verify What Works

Now, would you guess that any of these ideas would be controversial? In fact, to a lesser or greater extent, they all are! To begin with, the idea of a comprehensive, inclusive approach that takes debt seriously was, until *The Value of Debt*, virtually missing from personal-finance literature. You might think that the many promoters of a comprehensive and holistic wealth-management approach would naturally want to include *both* sides of the balance sheet—both assets and debts—but literally none have done so. (It's okay to be comprehensive and holistic, they seem to say, but debt is a special case, and there must be a reason why it has been intellectually and emotionally off-limits for so long, right?) Pointing to such an idea as the central premise for a book naturally raised a good deal of suspicion in certain quarters, both professional and academic.

The second idea, another real shocker, is that individuals and families—especially but not only well-off ones—should consider applying the same sort of thinking and acting with respect to debt that companies utilize. Consider this: The total number of sizeable companies in the United States with zero long-term or short-term debt can literally be counted on one hand.[3] Why? Is it because they can't afford to pay off their debt? No. It's because the well-educated and well-paid CFOs of these companies—who all realize that correctly structured debt actually makes their companies stronger, longer lasting, and more profitable—don't want to be fired. These CFOs all intuitively understand the Indebted Strengths that arise from strategic debt, which we will briefly review in the next section. They also understand why the use of enriching debt available to their organization is both efficient and rational, as we explore throughout this book.

Rooms full of books and studies—including Nobel Prize–winning studies[4]—show how companies benefit from debt. Given this, you might have thought that someone, somewhere, would have applied some of the same principles and mechanisms to affluent individuals and families. You would have been dead wrong. As *The Value of Debt* describes, a careful examination of the available literature found just one academic Scandinavian study that suggested individuals *could* benefit from debt the way companies do . . . and that was all.

Naturally, then, this idea raised quite a lot of suspicion and uneasiness in certain circles. "People aren't companies," I was told, "and people shouldn't take the kinds of risks that companies take, like consciously cultivating a strategic debt practice." It's true, of course, that people aren't companies. But like companies, they need money, and like companies, they can benefit from using better debt—what Chapter 3 defines as working debt and, even better, enriching debt—to access and take advantage of their Indebted Strengths. Also, as we consider in Chapter 3, people are living much longer. Like companies that have long-term economic horizons, they need to more effectively plan for increased life spans—including taking advantage of the better debt organically available to them as a result of the success they have already achieved.

Perhaps most important, I wholeheartedly agree that people are not companies. For example, if Walmart goes bankrupt, that impacts about 1 million people. If my wife and I go bankrupt, it impacts five people— the two of us plus our kids. Therefore, one could argue that I could take more risk than Walmart. Perhaps we should have more debt! But that doesn't seem right to me. Companies are playing a game of probabilities and are in the business of taking risk. People are in the business of surviving first and foremost. For me, nothing is more important than my family. Therefore, in my first book I examine corporate strategies and make them *more conservative* in applying them to the individual household. I believe that if people embraced my ideas, they would be rated close to AAA (the highest rating), something only three companies in America can claim today![5] At worst, individuals would be A rated. I don't want people to have a lot of debt; I want people to consider having the right amount of good debt.

As previously discussed, from Shakespeare to virtually every one of today's most popular books on personal finance and retirement, debt is culturally, linguistically, emotionally, and even religiously and spiritually held to be bad, evil, repugnant, and something to be avoided at all costs and gotten rid of as quickly as possible. I wish I were exaggerating, but the idea that debt is evil is so deeply embedded in our language and culture that it is very rarely questioned and almost never seriously challenged.[6] Similarly, for those who find the idea of personal debt anathema, the idea of having an *optimal personal debt ratio* (debt-to-asset ratio) makes no sense at all.

It's hard to imagine that this would be controversial, as naturally everybody strives to be open-minded, understand things, and find out for themselves whether something works. Well, people will *tell* you that they are willing to examine things in an open-minded way and be open to evidence that contradicts what they already believe and expect, but psychology and simple observation tells us this is often not true.

Consider "confirmation bias"—the tendency to look for and see facts that confirm the outcome one is already expecting or desiring—which is very difficult to overcome. Attempts to describe some of the ways better debt works are often met with counterexamples of a friend or relative who got into an oppressive debt situation that destroyed their financial lives. Well, yes, of course that happens—and better debt concepts are most definitely *not* for people who can't handle having access to any debt. Still, as you will see, many people are already successfully applying a strategic debt philosophy in their lives. Unfortunately, those success stories are filtered out or ignored while debt horror stories are overemphasized.

Bottom line: Nearly everybody will *say* they are open-minded and willing to ask questions to learn what really works, but in reality, few people are actually able to be that way when faced with something new and controversial, especially if it goes against what they've been taught their entire lives. The notion of Indebted Strengths, to which we now turn, is such a concept.

The Fifth Indebted Strength

If you are successful, it is because somewhere, sometime, someone gave you a life or an idea that started you in the right direction. Remember also that you are indebted to life until you help some less fortunate person, just as you were helped.

—Melinda Gates

In *The Value of Debt,* I write a good deal about financial distress—when an individual or family has trouble honoring financial commitments and paying bills, which can lead to bankruptcy if unrelieved—as well as the direct and indirect costs of that financial distress. I also write about both the *impact* of financial distress (which can increase from negligible to moderate to severe to bankruptcy, and then ultimately can create physical survival issues), as well as the *duration* or length of financial distress (a couple of days, several weeks, a few years, chronically ongoing and debilitating). *I then showed how taking on the right kind of debt—strategic debt, smart debt, better debt—can actually reduce your risk!* Let's review why and how this can be true.

This brings four key qualities or Indebted Strengths into play:

1. Increased Liquidity
2. Increased Flexibility
3. Increased Leverage
4. Increased Survivability

As Figure 1.1 shows, the right kind of debt can bring more liquidity. Generally, the more liquidity you have, the more flexibility you have. As you take on debt you gain access to additional leverage, which can increase your overall rate of return. Taken together, all of this ultimately leads to enhanced survivability—the ability to make it without running

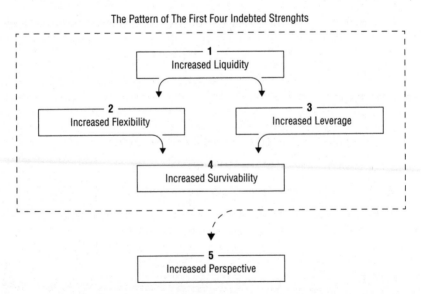

Figure 1.1   The Five Indebted Strengths

out of money! Throughout this book, we will explore these ideas with regard to retirement, showing how the advantages of Increased Liquidity, Increased Leverage, Increased Flexibility, and Increased Survivability can come very directly and personally into play for those planning for, entering, and living in the retirement phase of life.

A *fifth* Indebted Strength that comes into play—especially in retirement—is *Increased Perspective*. This isn't a direct result of debt itself but rather an overall benefit to having a comprehensive philosophy. Those who demonstrate the ability to have an Increased Perspective are able to approach strategic debt with an open-minded attitude and are thus able to implement the strategies.

Increased Perspective is like drawing and painting. People can draw in two dimensions, but the real trick—one that took humanity thousands of years to master—is to use perspective and shading in drawing, so that subjects have depth. Similarly, when you begin to take advantage of strategic debt ideas and consider your situation in terms of both sides of the balance sheet, you are bringing additional depth both to your thinking and potentially to your financial structure. Perspective enables you to see how your whole financial situation fits together and is potentially deeper, more robust, and better able to weather storms than you previously could have imagined.

The final aspect of Increased Perspective is an understanding of our ability to give back to society. No person is an island, and we all have tremendous nonfinancial debts to our parents and those who raised us, our other family members, the organizations and individuals who have made our careers and success possible, and the country we live in. I believe that by embracing these ideas you will not only increase the odds of making it through your retirement, but also will have money left over to leave the legacy you wish!

Who Can Benefit from This Book? Not Only Millionaires! (But They Can, Too)

Debt is part of the human condition. Civilization is based on exchanges—on gifts, trades, loans—and the revenge and insults that come when they are not paid back.

—Margaret Atwood

Are you qualified to adopt—and likely to benefit from—the ideas, strategies, practices, and tools found in this book and on the valueofdebt-inretirement.com website? Ask yourself the following four questions.

Question 1: Do You Have Adequate Resources to Start With?

When I wrote the first book in this series, I was considering promulgating a bright-line rule: For the ideas in the book to be appropriate for you, you need $1 million or more of net worth (outside of your primary residence). I realized later that *anyone with sufficient assets* might be able to benefit because everyone's circumstances vary so greatly. Since that book's release, I have realized this is a bigger, more important topic that applies to everyone's life.

After *The Value of Debt* debuted and people started understanding and implementing some of its ideas and practices, I started getting requests from individuals of every level of net worth who wanted to learn how to make use of strategic debt. For many people, there may not *be* a way to have a successful retirement without embracing these ideas. While it's true that people with greater resources to begin with are in some ways best positioned to make the widest use of the ideas found in this book, these ideas will also work for people with far fewer assets.

Question 2: Are You Psychologically Disposed to Making Wise Use of Better Debt?

Let's face it, we all know people who buy a bunch of stupid things that they can't afford when given money or access to credit. This book is not for them. It's not about buying things that you cannot afford but about better ways to pay for things that you already can afford. I assume you can handle the responsibility associated with this book. This is critical to understand. *If you can't handle debt, then you should in fact put this book down right now.*

Question 3: Are You Truly Open-Minded and Willing to See What Works?

This is the fifth Tenet of Strategic Debt Philosophy: Are you *open-minded*? Are you really willing to take a beginner's mind stance, ask questions, and figure out if what you're thinking of doing is likely to work well for you? Are you willing to invest substantial time and energy and then, if you come to the conclusion that you shouldn't go forward with any debt practices, be willing to let it go?

Question 4: Are You Willing to Put in the Effort to Find and Work with Qualified Experts to Make Sure Your Situation and Circumstances Are a Good Fit?

This question concerns *your willingness and ability to be open-minded with regard to finding a reliable, professional, financial services individual or organization to work with* who can help you understand and assess your situation, give you the kind of objective feedback that you can't give yourself, and help with any implementation. More and more financial advisors and wealth managers are becoming aware of the tremendous value of a debt-inclusive philosophy and practice, and you can also find tools and resources at valueofdebtinretirement.com.

The bottom line is that with sufficient resources, a favorable psychological disposition, general open-mindedness, and a willingness to find an assisting individual or organization, you are far more likely to have a successful and even life-changing experience with better debt. If you can't say yes to one or more of these questions, please slow down and think very carefully before reading any further or making any major changes in your financial affairs.

Everyday Example #1: Immediately Better Credit Card Debt

In this chapter and each of the five that follow, *we will provide one of six Everyday Examples of how people are already successfully using debt-inclusive ideas, strategies, practices, and tools.* The easiest to understand involves bringing better debt practices to your existing credit card debt, as follows.

EVERYDAY EXAMPLE #1: IMMEDIATELY BETTER CREDIT CARD DEBT

After his daughter's wedding, Ted has maxed out his credit card at $25,000 at a 20 percent interest rate. Forgetting for now about minimum payments, paying down principal, compound interest, and other factors that come into play, this means he will owe $5,000 a year in interest on that card, or $416.67 a month ($25,000 × 20% = $5,000, divided by 12 months is $416.67 a month). That's a lot!

Fortunately, Ted also has a qualifying $150,000 investment portfolio and is eligible for a line of credit against it. He may be able to borrow money against the $150,000 at something more like 3 percent interest and pay off his credit card debt. Three percent is better than 20 percent. Let's see how much better:

Instead of owing $5,000 a year, Ted would owe just $750 a year in interest ($25,000 × 3% = $750), which divided by 12 comes out to just $62.50 a month—*a whole lot less than $416.67 a month.*

It gets even better: *Many portfolio lines of credit do not have required minimum monthly payments.* If Ted wants, he can allow the interest to "cap and roll" until he is ready to pay off the interest and then the $25,000 itself.

Of course, Ted has to absolutely keep an eye on how much money he borrows this way, but the reality is that right off the bat he's saving more than $4,000 a year in interest.

This foundational better debt practice is relatively easy to implement, really works, and already has been taken advantage of by many high-net-worth people. It's time for all Americans to be aware of these strategies!

Getting beyond the ABLF and Focusing on Retirement

Although well received, the first book in this series received some criticism for over focusing on tools and in particular the ABLF—asset-based loan facility—that is, the type of credit we made use of in Everyday Example #1. These are also called securities-based lines of credit, and only a small number of investors who are able to put them into place have done so. In fact, my experience suggests that 95 percent of people that are eligible for this type of borrowing do not use it, often because they are completely unaware that it is available to them. I believe this is shortsighted.

These lines of credit are set up against your taxable investment accounts (IRAs and 401(k)s are not eligible). Typically borrowers can borrow around 50 percent of their liquid investable assets. For example, if you have a $300,000 portfolio you can generally borrow up to around $150,000. Some holdings are eligible for lower and higher loan amounts so you will want to check with your financial institution for your exact eligibility.

The benefits of these facilities are that there generally is no cost to set them up, no ongoing fee to have them, and you are paying only interest expense on the amount you borrow, if you borrow at all. Rates on these facilities are typically a bit above or a bit below Prime. At time of this publication Prime was at 3.25 percent. Pricing typically is based on the size of your relationship with the financial institution with lower priced loans going to larger clients.

Generally you will find that these facilities offer incredible flexibility with respect to the terms. Typically there is no amortization and you can pay down any amount at any time you want. What is pretty amazing is that typically there also is no required monthly payment. You can let the interest "cap and roll" which means that it just adds on to your principal balance. As we will see this may or may not be a good long-term strategy but it offers tremendous flexibility for the borrower—in good times and in bad times. Due to the great rates and flexible terms I will occasionally refer to this type of debt as better debt and/or what I will define as enriching debt.

I use the term *asset-based loan facility* to capture what is called margin and securities-based lending products. One of the greatest risks is that your ability to borrow is based off of the value of your portfolio.[7] Therefore, if your assets go down in value, you can borrow less money. This means that you have to always pay close attention to your coverage ratio, which is a way of looking at how much you have borrowed versus your ability to borrow. In *The Value of Debt* I recommend that you never borrow more than 50 percent of your available credit. This means that if you have a $300,000 portfolio I feel that these lines of credit can offer a great liquidity solution for up to $75,000 of borrowing.

These lines of credit typically offer an excellent rate and not only help you to do things like pay down high-interest-rate credit cards, as in Everyday Example #1, but also can also provide a major liquidity cushion in case of disaster or a sudden substantial opportunity. The line of credit will necessarily continue to play a major role in this book, but *the main focus here will be on debt-inclusive ideas, strategies, practices, and tools that relate to or potentially have a substantial impact on retirement.*[8]

AHAs! ADVISOR HIGHLIGHT ANSWERS

The last section you will find in each chapter of this book will be called "Advisor Highlight Answers," or AHAs. These are directed toward professional advisors, industry professionals, and sophisticated investors. They will give you an idea about the questions, problems, fears, and considerations that your clients might have as they become exposed to these materials.

Question #1: I don't think my client has the psychological disposition to handle the ideas in the book. What should I do?

Answer #1: You're most likely right and need to trust your instincts. I start with the premise that people will be rational, smart, and disciplined with these ideas. But as we all know, many people can't handle the responsibility associated with debt. If they start down this path, they may abuse the flexibility, spend too much, and buy a bunch of things they don't need.

The problem on the other side is that many people will not be on track for retirement without these ideas nor will they be able to buy the things they want, minimize taxes, or help their family. In my opinion, balancing these risks is one of the, if not the, most important parts of your job.[9]

Notes

1. Quoted in Chris Carpenter, "The Total Money Makeover: An Interview with Dave Ramsey," www.cbn.com/family/familyadvice/carpenter-daveramsey moneymakeover.aspx.
2. Thomas J. Anderson, *The Value of Debt: How to Manage Both Sides of a Balance Sheet to Maximize Wealth* (Hoboken, NJ: John Wiley & Sons, 2013).

3. See, for example, Matt Krantz, "26 U.S. companies with no long-term debt," http://americasmarkets.usatoday.com/2014/05/29/debt-free-26-u-s-compa-nies-shun-debt, which states that as of May 2014, there were 26 nonfinancial companies in the Standard & Poor's 500 Index that had zero long-term debt. If you count leases for retail space and equipment, and short-term loans to be paid off within a year, that number goes way down.

4. See the concepts of weighted average cost of capital and the Modigliani-Miller Theorem: F. Modigliani and M. Miller, "The Cost of Capital, Corporation Finance, and the Theory of Investment," *American Economic Review* 48, no. 3 (1958); F. Modigliani and M. Miller, "Corporate Income Taxes and the Cost of Capital: A Correction," *American Economic Review* 53, no. 3 (1963); and S. A. Ross, R. W. Westerfield, and J. Jaffe, *Corporate Finance*, 10th ed. (New York: McGraw-Hill, 2013).

5. Those three companies are Johnson & Johnson, Exxon-Mobil, and Microsoft. Matt Krantz, "Downgrade! Only 3 U.S. companies now rated AAA," http://americasmarkets.usatoday.com/2014/04/11/downgrade-only-3-u-s-companies-now-rated-aaa.

6. For those interested in a fascinating anthropological study on the roots of debt, and how it relates to both social obligation and money, *Debt: The First 5,000 Years*, by David Graeber (Brooklyn: Melville House, 2011) is well worth the read—not because I necessarily agree with all of the author's suppositions and conclusions, but because the book opens up the historical landscape and encourages each of us to more broadly think about how we hold and relate to debt.

7. A discussion of risks and nuances of these facilities can be found in Appendix F.

8. Case studies are for educational and illustrative purposes only. They assume eligible assets and that funds are available on the facility. All client situations are unique, and all loans are subject to eligibility and approval by the lender. A lender may deny an advance on an ABLF, preventing the scenarios. Pledging assets reduces and may eliminate liquidity. A market correction could impact market values and/or security eligibility, which could impact the facility size and/or trigger a margin call and/or forced liquidations of assets. See complete disclosures and risks to using an ABLF in Appendix F.

9. Author's Note: The information in this chapter is to be considered in a holistic way as a part of the book and not to be considered on a stand-alone basis. This includes, but is not limited to, the discussion of risks of each of these ideas as well as all of the disclaimers throughout the book. The material is presented with a goal of encouraging thoughtful conversation and rigorous debate on the risks and potential benefits of the concepts between you and your advisors based on your unique situation, risk tolerance, and goals.

Chapter 2

Debt in Retirement

Conventional Wisdom, Right and Wrong

Doubt the conventional wisdom unless you can verify it with reason and experiment.

—Steven Albini

Thousands of well-meaning books have been written about retirement. Economists, financial advisors, accounting professionals, psychologists, successful businesspeople, and self-help gurus have given us their take on this crucial subject. A Google search for "retirement planning" yields 25 million suggestions. You can find everything from programs suggesting we all really yearn for a much simpler life and way of interacting with money[1] to down-and-dirty sites about investing, spending, health care, taxes, insurance, Social Security, and so on.

What makes this book different? Before we dive into the ideas of how it is possible to increase return, reduce taxes, and reduce your risk, it will be helpful to get an understanding of the current landscape of advice that is generally given to people as they approach retirement.

What Some Popular Retirement Books Get Right—and Wrong—about Debt

Never accept ultimatums, conventional wisdom, or absolutes.
                                        —Christopher Reeve

Nearly every popular book on retirement, brand new or decades old, warns about the dangers of runaway debt. The problem comes when *these books overdramatize and overfocus on the dangers of debt without mentioning the potential positives or upsides of better debt.* Let's take a brief look at a few of these books, which are well-written and have much to offer aside from their discussion of debt.

We reviewed books that fall into one of three camps.

1 **The "Good" versus "Bad" Debt Camp:** These focus on the distinction between "good debt" and "bad debt" (or some other contrast such as "smart versus dumb" debt).
2 **The Irresolutely "Against Debt" Camp:** Right from the start, these books declare that adopting a "no debt ever" perspective is imperative.
3 **The "Sometimes It's Okay to Have Debt" Camp:** These recognize that a certain amount of debt is healthy and necessary but never mention most or all of the available strategic options for better debt.

With one notable partial exception, almost all of the books start out with the "debt is always evil" mantra. With that primary assumption firmly in place, they leverage off of it with anecdotes and stories that prove they were right all along. They never consider the tremendous opportunities that might be available to people who are psychologically and financially predisposed to consciously embrace strategic debt. They want you to *not even think about* what's in this book—even if I show you how it all makes sense mathematically, derives from and is in accord with Nobel Prize–winning ideas, and is already being used to great advantage by many people in everyday circumstances.

You should decide what you are and aren't allowed to consider, especially if the information you've been denied could be the most powerful—and sometimes the only realistic means available—to help you achieve the retirement you want.

The "Good versus Bad" Debt Camp

The idea of "good" versus "bad" debt is probably familiar to you. In *The Value of Debt,* I ask readers to stop automatically employing the term "good" or "bad" to situations and circumstances involving debt. Whether you're considering paying off your mortgage or not paying off your mortgage, having debt in retirement or perhaps taking on even *more* debt in retirement, you must evaluate the likely impacts and effects of your actions. Debt is not good or bad. The central premise of my first book is that debt runs along a spectrum that includes different types and levels.

It is my belief that too many people are either way too highly leveraged or are completely debt adverse. I think that there is an optimal middle ground. My research indicates that too few people happen to be in that optimal zone. What is of more interest is that by and large, those that happen to be in what I define as the optimal range are there by luck and chance rather than because of a strategic choice. Imagine being on the conference call of a major company when the CFO comes on the line and says, "Hey, what do you think about our debt structure? I took a guess at it!" Companies proactively choose an optimal debt structure, and I would suggest that people can do the same.

In *The Charles Schwab Guide to Finances after Fifty* (New York: Crown Business, 2014), Carrie Schwab-Pomerantz presents the standard general distinction found in most retirement books. Ideally, she states, none of us would have debt even though debt can actually work for you. Pragmatic real-world understanding conflicts with utopian notions of a debt-free reality, somehow coming to the baseline conclusion that debt is inherently bad. *"In an ideal world,"* she writes, *"none of us would have any debt—ever."*[2] How do readers interpret the conflicting information? How much should they have at different points and why?

Well-known personal finances personality Suze Orman is a torchbearer for this message. "Ultimately," she says, "the goal of retirement is to *become as debt-free as possible*. For most of us, though, the first step will be to make sure the debts that we do have are intelligent ones."[3] Swapping the "good" versus "bad" debt distinction for the notion of "intelligent debt," she seems open to some types of debt being all right—at least for the time being. The goal of retirement, Orman preaches, is to become as debt-free as possible. Here again the notion seems to be that good debt might be okay, as long as you are rushing in to pay it off.

Bach Where We Started: The Irresolutely "Against Debt" Camp

Some books make it very clear—right from their titles—that they are in the "debt is purely evil" camp. David Bach's bestselling *Debt Free for Life* (New York: Crown Business/Random House, 2010) states that being debt free for the entirety of one's life is the highest priority. Bach reveals *"The best investment you can make over the next five years is going to be paying off your debts. So my advice is to pay off what you owe as fast as you can.* The faster you pay off your debt, the faster you will achieve financial freedom"[4] (emphasis added).

Jerrold Mundis's *How To Get Out of Debt, Stay Out of Debt, and Live Prosperously* (New York: Bantam Books, revised edition 2012) says that getting out and staying out of debt is directly equivalent to living prosperously. Mundis prefaces his book with these words: "This is a book about debt and about freeing yourself from debt—forever."[5] He promises to teach readers how to liberate themselves from debt, stay free of it forever, and live a life of prosperity and abundance.[6] He has no tolerance for debt of any kind. "But debt is debt," he writes, "no matter how much we earn or how much we owe, and sooner or later it can, and frequently does, poison our lives."[7]

In *Total Money Makeover* (Nashville: Thomas Nelson, Classic Edition, 2013), Dave Ramsey says that "tens of thousands of ordinary people have used the system in this book to get out of debt, regain control, and build wealth."[8] Throughout the book he touts "getting out of debt" and "being debt free" as necessary for building wealth. In Chapter 3, "Debt Myths: Debt Is (Not) a Tool," Ramsey lays out his central premise:

Myth: Debt is a tool and should be used to create prosperity.
Truth: Debt adds considerable risk, most often doesn't bring prosperity, and isn't used by wealthy people nearly as much as we are led to believe.[9]

Ramsey writes: "My contention is that debt brings on enough risk to offset any advantage that could be gained through leverage of debt. Given time, a lifetime, risk will destroy the perceived returns purported by the mythsayers."[10]

Mythsayers? To me, the real myth is the gross exaggeration that all debt is bad. I fully agree with Ramsey that people who don't have the psychological disposition to handle the responsibility associated with debt shouldn't use it. I'm certain he and Orman's advice has been helpful to many people. I just think it's time we had a broader, more intelligent conversation on this topic.

The (Very Small) "Sometimes It's Okay to Have Debt" Camp

A national debt, if it is not excessive, will be to us a national blessing.
—Alexander Hamilton

Our one and only exemplar from the "sometimes it's okay" camp is Jon Hanson's *Good Debt, Bad Debt—Knowing the Difference Can Save Your Financial Life* (New York: Portfolio/Penguin, 2005). "Debt is like cholesterol," the dust jacket says. "Too much of the wrong kind can kill you. But too little of the right kind can be a problem too."

Good debt, Hanson writes, earns its keep, increases your net worth or cash flow, secures a discount that can be converted to cash or net worth, and creates a leveraged position with a strong margin of safety such as debt for real estate at a safely leveraged level, debt for education that can be applied for a return of capital, or debt for a business you are competent to operate.[11] Bad debt, he writes, is typically for consumption, decreases your net worth or cash flow, and absorbs future earnings such as car loans that rob your retirement fund and continuous credit card debt.

This starts a great dialogue, but, ironically, Hanson goes on to recommend against having a mortgage. Hanson's book gets us on the road to a more neutral and conscious evaluation of strategic debt's value, but it doesn't go far enough. *The Value of Debt in Retirement* takes these ideas to the next level using tools that high net-worth individuals and companies have used for years.

Everyday Example #2: A Bridge Loan over Troubled Quarters

Increased Flexibility and Increased Liquidity can make a huge difference in a family's situation. In the following example, having access to better debt makes a huge difference in a couple's retired life.

EVERYDAY EXAMPLE #2: A BRIDGE LOAN OVER TROUBLED QUARTERS

Oliver and Rosemary, retired and both in their late seventies, own a home worth about $300,000 outright, consciously watch that their expenditures don't overtake their available cash flow, and have a $700,000 taxable investment portfolio.

As so often happens, life takes unexpected twists and turns. After some troubling incidents, Rosemary is diagnosed with rapidly worsening Alzheimer's disease. It becomes clear that they need $250,000 immediately to move into a nearby care facility that's perfect for them. They don't want to disrupt their investment portfolio, and they will need several months to get the best price for their home. On top of that, they would like the convenience of moving into the care facility, getting settled, and then selling their existing home.

Where can they get $250,000? They can't get a mortgage on a home they're selling, but they could borrow the money at around 3 percent interest by taking out a loan against their investment portfolio.

With no amortization as part of the loan, they can "cap and roll"—make no payments at all—until they sell their home.

If they sell their home six months later, and the total cost of the interest on the $250,000 is just $3,750 ($250,000 × 3% = $7,500 interest in a year, so one-half a year is $3,750), they can repay the full $253,750.

Oliver and Rosemary were able to act right away without having to sell their home first or disrupt their existing investments.

Of the thousands of books available on retirement planning, none address a balanced approach to debt nor do they provide a glide path for individuals to consider. Instead the consensus opinion is to encourage all people—regardless of net worth, age, or responsibility—to pay off all of their debt and generally avoid new debt for virtually any reason at any time. This doesn't make sense to me. I think that regardless of whether you choose to embrace debt from time to time (as the everyday examples illustrate) or continuously as a strategic choice, it can be a powerful tool to help you throughout your retirement.

AHAs! ADVISOR HIGHLIGHT ANSWERS

Question #1: What do I say to a client who wants to understand why the vast majority of books, articles, online websites, financial gurus, television pundits, syndicated radio show hosts, and so on, all seem to state that all debt is bad and that no matter what, I should begin to find a way to retire debt free?

Answer #1: This mainstream advice is generally geared to people that have a low net worth and/or lack the responsibility to handle debt. In a survey conducted by the Russell Sage Foundation, it was found that the American median household net worth, in 2013, was $56,335.[12] If your net worth is under $100,000, it's possible that you have access only to debt at high interest rates and with bad terms. This is what I call oppressive debt. If this is the case, then paying it off may not be all that bad an idea.

However, as your net worth grows (and assuming you are responsible), then it may make sense to consider the possibilities of liquidity, flexibility, leverage, and survivability that a strategic debt philosophy can create.[13]

Notice that consistently telling people to rush in and pay off their debt creates a different type of debt trap. You never get to break through to where you have enough assets to access lower cost debt. You never have liquidity nor do you ever have the flexibility. The next book in this series will address strategies to enable people to break through this trap.[14]

Notes

1. See, for example, the work of the New Roadmap Foundation at www.financialintegrity.org.
2. Carrie Schwab-Pomerantz, *The Charles Schwab Guide to Finances after Fifty* (New York: Crown Business, 2014), 127.
3. Suze Orman, *You've Earned It, Don't Lose It: Mistakes You Can't Afford to Make When You Retire* (New York: Newmarket Press, 1998), 163 (emphasis added).
4. David Bach, *Debt Free for Life* (New York: Crown Business/Random House, 2012), 1–2.
5. Jerrold Mundis, *How to Get Out of Debt, Stay Out of Debt, and Live Prosperously* (New York: Bantam Books, 2012), xv.
6. Ibid.
7. Ibid., xvii. Despite the overly broad statements imbedded in their books' titles, Mundis and Bach both admit that some kinds of debt in some kind of circumstances are all right before they reassert the notion that everyone's ultimate goal should still be to become and stay debt free.
8. Dave Ramsay, *The Total Money Makeover,* classic ed. (Nashville: Thomas Nelson, Classic 2013), 4
9. Ibid.,19.
10. Ibid., 20.
11. Jon Hanson, *Good Debt, Bad Debt: Knowing the Difference Can Save Your Financial Life* (New York: Portfolio Penguin, 2005), xx.
12. Fabian T. Pfeffer, Sheldon Danziger, and Robert F. Schoen, "Wealth Levels, Wealth Inequality, and the Great Recession," June 2014, www.russellsage.org.
13. Case studies are for educational and illustrative purposes only. They assume eligible assets and that funds are available on the facility. All client situations are unique, and all loans are subject to eligibility and approval by the lender. A lender may deny an advance on an ABLF, preventing the scenarios. Pledging

assets reduces and may eliminate liquidity. A market correction could impact market values and/or security eligibility, which could impact the facility size and/or trigger a margin call and/or forced liquidations of assets. See complete disclosures and risks to using an ABLF in Appendix F.

14. Author's Note: The information in this chapter is to be considered in a holistic way as a part of the book and not to be considered on a stand-alone basis. This includes, but is not limited to, the discussion of risks of each of these ideas as well as all of the disclaimers throughout the book. The material is presented with a goal of encouraging thoughtful conversation and rigorous debate on the risks and potential benefits of the concepts between you and your advisors based on your unique situation, risk tolerance, and goals.

Chapter 3

Why and Whether to Adopt a Holistic Debt-Inclusive Approach in Retirement

It's not how old you are; it's how you are old.

—**Jules Renard**

An ultra-abbreviated rendition of the ideas presented by other authors described in the last chapter might read something like this:

All debt is always bad, and retiring debt-free is of paramount importance no matter what anybody else says or might be able to show you. . . . No, some debt is good, some of the time. . . . No, all debt will eventually ruin you, especially if you haven't gotten rid of it before you retire. . . . No, while some debt will eventually ruin you, other debt might actually be good for you. . . .

And so it goes, this way and that, with resolutely antidebt financial gurus and pundits sometimes offering contradictory advice even within the same book. Very, very few popular financial gurus and authors are open to (or aware of) the slightest possibility that strategic debt philosophy and practice, when fully understood and used consciously, can actually make a big difference in the lives of both wealthy and ordinary people looking for a way to make their retirements work.

A First Look at the Three Main Types of Debt: Oppressive, Working, and Enriching

How could it possibly be that so many smart and well-intending individuals could be missing the boat entirely on something this fundamental and important? As we consider the three major types of debt—oppressive debt, working debt, and enriching debt—things will rapidly sort themselves out. These three types of debt are set out in Table 3.1.

Oppressive debt, as the name indicates, oppresses those who have taken it on. With high interest rates, strict deadlines and amortization schedules, no tax deductibility, and other unforgiving terms, this kind of debt should be avoided at all costs and is often associated with those

Table 3.1 Three Types of Debt

Type	Examples	Impact
Oppressive debt	Some payday loans, credit card balances	Oppresses debt holders and potentially makes them continually poorer
Working debt	Mortgage, small-business loan, student loan	Has a real cost but enables further life advances and gives access to indebted strengths
Enriching debt	Line of credit against your investment account	May increase returns, may reduce taxes, may reduce risk, and can potentially lead to full access to indebted strengths

in society who have the fewest resources. The archetypal examples of oppressive debt are high-cost credit card debt and payday loans, or in extreme cases, debt to a loan shark—with or without connections to organized crime. If you have oppressive debt, you will no doubt feel oppressed, probably sooner than later.

Virtually everything that the vast majority of popular financial writers have to say about debt applies *only to oppressive debt!*

When it comes to oppressive debt, I couldn't agree more with David Bach, Suze Orman, Dave Ramsey, and the rest that *this kind of debt is truly bad in almost all cases and should be avoided or paid off as quickly as possible.* If you have a lot of low-quality oppressive debt, then by all means follow Dave Ramsey's "Total Money Makeover" and adopt his "Debt Snowball"[1] process to get rid of it as soon as you can. Oppressive debt makes you poorer in real time, and you don't want it in your life.

Better than oppressive debt is what we call working debt. Working debt has a cost, naturally, but enables you to do what you want and need to do at a reasonable price. Good examples of working debt include a mortgage to buy a home or a small business loan to start a business. This kind of debt may afford you the opportunity to do something that you could not do otherwise.

Finally, there is enriching debt,[2] which can be defined as debt that you could pay off tomorrow but choose not to. You have the money in the bank but are making a proactive, strategic choice to have the debt. Choosing to have debt? This is where we are headed with our case studies and what the majority of companies do every day.

Why? Well, if done the right way it may give you all of the following: Increased Liquidity, Increased Flexibility, Increased Leverage, and Increased Survivability. Part II of this book will demonstrate that by having more total assets and total liquidity in your personal financial ecosystem, you may be in a better position to simultaneously take less risk and increase your rate of return. With enriching debt you may also be able to produce super-tax-efficient income in retirement with a hybrid sell and borrow strategy. Considering that there are different types of debt is an essential first step to moving forward with these ideas. Before we can dive into the case studies we have to lay a bit more of the foundation with respect to some ground rules, the possibility of a longer life, and the importance of a holistic approach.

Seven Rules for Being a Better Debtor

> No tendency is quite so strong in human nature as the desire to lay down rules of conduct for other people.
>
> **—William Howard Taft**

Let's consider a set of seven rules—think of them as rules of thumb rather than hard-and-fast laws—that can help you become a better debtor generally. Some of these rules align with some of the popular retirement books discussed earlier.

1. **Honestly Assess Whether You Can Handle Any Debt at All, Including Better Debt.** Do not take on any (or any additional) debt of any kind if you are not psychologically predisposed to successfully using debt. If you (or your spouse) have a previous history of runaway or unjustified debt, seriously examine why you think this situation would be any different. Having access to debt can go bad quickly if you're irresponsible. If you are susceptible to misusing any debt you take on, then . . . just . . . don't. Seriously. Just don't.

2. **Never Overextend Yourself, Even for Better Debt.** Do not take on any debt, even good debt, if you cannot afford to pay it back if things do not go as planned. *Financial shocks, such as 2008, need to be in your base plan.* I believe you will see at least one 50 percent correction in stock prices during your retirement—and I have math and history on my side. In fact a 70 percent correction needs to be in your base case. It is my base position that weird stuff will happen over the next 30 to 50 years. If you do take on debt, you must regularly monitor your asset allocation strategies and approach it as an interconnected, complementary process. You have to be prepared for big shocks. You should proactively stress against shocks and proactively monitor your accounts against various risks. Firms that can do this for you are offering a very valuable service. Understanding the risks of big market downturns and how to be prepared for them is essential!

3. **Make Sure Any New Debt You Take On Actually Is High-Quality (Better) Debt.** Only take on debt that qualifies as "high-quality" debt. High-quality debt will likely have a low rate, flexible terms, and perhaps some tax advantages.

4. **Only Take On Better Debt in the Context of a Thoughtful, Holistic, Professionally Vetted Plan.** Make sure you have a long-term comprehensive plan that looks at both sides of your balance sheet. Make sure your plan treats both parts—assets and debts—as dynamic contributors to your long-term financial outcome.

5. **Get Rid of All Low-Quality and Oppressive Debt as Soon as It's Feasible to Do So.** As soon as it's feasible, get rid of debt that is high interest, requires a regular monthly payment, and generally falls into the category of oppressive debt. Your rate of return on paying down debt is exactly equal to your after-tax cost of that debt. If you have debt at an interest rate of more than 10 percent, you should consider paying it off as fast as you can. One way to do this may be to refinance it. You may be able to follow Everyday Example #1 and borrow against your portfolio at 3 percent to pay off credit card debt that was at 6 percent. In the current environment, preference is that debt between 5 and 10 percent be paid off, but you need to overlay the values of flexibility, liquidity, and survivability. While low-quality or oppressive debt may, in some sense, provide you with more flexibility, that flexibility is very expensive. Make getting rid of it as soon as it is feasible to do so a high priority.[3]

6. **Don't Necessarily Rush to Pay Off Existing Debt.** If you already have some good debt, you don't necessarily need or want to pay it off just so that you have no debt. For example, many people pay off their mortgages early so that they own their house free and clear, not realizing that by doing so they may not have the ability to implement some of the strategies I will explain shortly. *In some cases, people who rush to pay off their home may actually mathematically guarantee that they will not be on track for retirement.*

7. **If You Do Take on Debt, Be Conservative and Scientific.** Taking on debt, even better debt, is inherently risky, so make sure you are following well-understood scientific principles of investing. Don't take unnecessary chances, and play it smart generally.

In the Company of Longer Life Spans

Learning is an ornament in prosperity, a refuge in adversity, and a provision in old age.

—Often attributed to Aristotle

Some people suggest that while a holistic, inclusive, and strategic debt philosophy may make nearly universal sense for companies, in many ways individuals and families are *not* like companies. Therefore, they conclude, strategic debt ideas do not apply to them. Critics point out that while companies can theoretically live forever,[4] people obviously do not, suggesting that the kind of long-term perspective and strategic thinking that is called for when managing a company's finances is not required for individuals and families.

One ready response to this criticism is that the genetic and financial legacy of an individual or family can and often does continue past death, so acting holistically to effectively plan for the long term makes sense even if individuals and families don't require the same kind of long-term planning that companies require. (Actually, very few companies make it past 100 years, so the entire premise of the critics here may be questionable.) At least as important, however, is the simple fact that many people—especially those with adequate resources to begin with—are indeed living far longer and having much longer retirements. Consider this introductory paragraph from the website of the National Institute of Aging[5]:

> ...And living to 100 is becoming increasingly commonplace. In 1950, there were approximately 3,000 American centenarians. By 2050, there could be nearly 1 million.

As Jamie Hopkins explained in *Forbes* magazine, the longer you live, the longer your life expectancy.[6]

For a married couple in which both spouses are 70 years old today, there is a 48 percent chance that at least one spouse will live to 90 and even a 5 percent chance that one will live to 100.[7] This is based on today's technology—but what if things change?[8] Think about the possibility that things may not simply continue the way they are; instead, dramatic scientific breakthroughs *may radically expand life spans* and therefore the duration of average retirements, *including yours.*

Recently I had the opportunity to present at a Barron's conference for top financial advisors. While there, I was fortunate to hear a presentation from Ric Edelman, a top independent advisor and industry thought leader. The point of his presentation was that incredible advances are taking place as a result of technology.[9] Some say that if you live to see 2035 you could see the year 2100. The logic that Edelman laid out was compelling: It's possible that boomers' life expectancy will be very different from that of their parents. This possibility has to be factored into any financial plan. You need to be sure that you can make your money last longer!

Like the fish in the fishbowl that is unaware of the water it swims in, most of us have become somewhat or greatly inured to living in a time of unprecedented technological acceleration. Already, it's becoming more and more common to solve many different types of medical difficulties that would have killed folks just a generation ago. Well, if you're going to live for a very long time, then you better start thinking about how to stretch your assets so that you don't run out of money!

Imagine if you or your spouse did run out of money at age 95. What do you do? Will government assistance programs be there? Do you want to depend on them? Will your children care for you? How old will they be at that time? Will they be on track for their own retirements? You need a plan that lasts a long time. To me this means you better be open to looking at the ideas that the vast majority of companies have already been incorporating into their financial planning for many years. Even if it turns out that in your particular case retirement was *not the lengthy affair you'd hoped for*, then your spouse, family, heirs, and favorite charities will all have potentially significantly benefitted.

Winging Your Way to a Successful Retirement: The "Whole Chicken" Approach

I credit my grandmother for teaching me to love and respect food. She taught me how to waste nothing, to make sure I used every bit of the chicken and boil the bones till no flavor could be extracted from them.

—Marcus Samuelsson

With longevity at the forefront of our minds, let's briefly consider what it means when we call our ideas "holistic" in nature. One common usage of holistic is in the phrase "holistic health and wellness," which refers to a natural approach that works with not just the physical but also the emotional and even spiritual health of the whole person.

But aside from this more specific meaning, holistic also has a larger, more inclusive meaning, which the Merriam-Webster dictionary defines as

> . . . relating to or concerned with wholes or with complete systems rather than with the analysis of, treatment of, or dissection into parts.[10]

From the 50,000-foot viewpoint, then, this book is about *holistic financial planning philosophy and action*, and by that I mean an approach that from the outset directly considers *both* one's assets *and* one's debts. To better understand the importance of a holistic perspective I want to share one of my favorite stories from business school at the University of Chicago.

Imagine it's 50 years ago, and you own a chicken processing plant. You roast, boil, can, freeze, and otherwise provide healthy chickens for sale to the public. For many years you have been chopping off and carting away the wings and selling just the breasts and legs because that's what people had always wanted. Then one day a new plant manager comes to work for you and says, "Hey, boss. I have an idea. Let's fry the wings, put some sauce on them, and see if we can sell them."

Despite your initial skepticism, you agree to give it a try and quickly find out that—son-of-a-drumstick!—there is a darn big business in chicken wings! You're very happy because of how profitable your overall combined business is now that you have turned what was essentially a breast/leg business into a breast/leg *and* wing business. Before your plant manager came to you, you thought it was fine to *just* be in the breast and leg business. You didn't even mind paying to have all the wings carted away. But now you know that by looking at and making use of the whole chicken rather than just the pieces you are already familiar with, you can do a lot better.[11]

Think, then, about conventional wisdom and the financial industry in general. Nearly all of the advice and guidance—the TV shows, magazines, industry publications, books, and advice from advisors—is about the asset side of your balance sheet. This is the equivalent of using only the chicken breasts and legs while unknowingly, repeatedly, and often with great vigor tossing out the other side of your balance sheet: your liabilities, that is, your debts. It is quite possible that this approach is throwing out the very wings that might enable you to financially fly longer, straighter, and truer into and throughout your retirement.

This book aims to provide you with the full range of ingredients and recipes that will enable you to take advantage of the whole financial chicken. I can't stress enough that you have to look at the whole chicken. The chicken can't fly with its wings alone, nor can it fly without its wings. It all works together; it's all interconnected. So while many critics will tell you that debt is bad and you shouldn't even ever consider taking on more of it, I am naturally hoping that you will "chicken in" rather than "chicken out" and be willing to consider how a holistic approach to your financial future—one that includes a conscious and strategic optimization of your debts (which almost no one does) as well as your assets (which almost everyone tries to do)—may benefit you tremendously in the long run in a variety of ways. Synergies and nearly magical outcomes can come from planning for and making intelligent use of both your debts as well as your assets.

"But wait," you might be saying. "Chickens don't fly very well, if they fly at all." Let's talk about that statement. The fact is, many chickens can fly. Granted, typically they don't fly far nor do they fly very well. But that isn't the point. The point is that I want you to come up with a proactive, integrated strategy that will last you your whole life, no matter how long that turns out to be. So, relax. Chickens fly, and they certainly fly better with their wings than without. There is no question the devil is in the details, and I invite any and all chicken metaphor critics to join me in the endnotes, appendices, and online debate and discussion at www .valueofdebtinretirement.com or www.vodr.com.

Everyday Example #3: A Holistic Business Recipe for Success

Everyday Example #3 shows how better debt can enable a businessperson to cook up a much better way of paying for a restaurant business. Have an open mind when applying it to your life—whether you are investing in a restaurant (or any other business) that you want to actively be a part of or perhaps as a minority partner in a business your son or daughter is starting.

EVERYDAY EXAMPLE #3: A HOLISTIC RECIPE FOR SUCCESS

The Johnsons have always been "foodies," and they want to invest in a new restaurant in their community. They determine that they need $300,000 to make the business a go.

The Johnsons spoke to a couple of banks and were offered a $300,000 "restaurant loan" at an 8 percent interest rate that amortizes over 10 years and has a five-year term (the interest rate is locked for five years). The Johnsons' monthly payment will be $3,640 per month, every month, for five years.

Fortunately, the Johnsons have a $1 million portfolio that is eligible for a securities based loan. They are willing to pledge these assets, which qualifies them for a $300,000 loan at a 3 percent rate. Their monthly payment is 300,000 × 3% = $9,000/12 = $750 per month!

Better yet, the loan does not amortize, so there are no required monthly payments. The Johnsons' interest savings is $15,000 per year, but their cash flow savings is about $35,000! They can better ride out the bad times and can pay off any amount of the loan at any time they want.

For someone starting a restaurant (or any other business), there are few things more important than having flexibility when it comes to cash outlays. If business goes well, they can pay down any amount any time that they want to. The Johnsons are in control—not the bank and not a goofy amortization schedule.[12]

A strategic debt philosophy and practice makes sense for many people who are in or approaching retirement. The claim that corporate strategic debt philosophy and practice makes no sense for individuals and families because they can't and don't live forever has been considerably weakened by the fact that people are, in fact, living longer and having much longer retirements. Even though some people are retiring later in life, there is no doubt—especially given the inexorable progress of modern biomedical science and the approaching technological "singularity"—that the overall trend is toward longer life and longer retirements. A holistic retirement planning philosophy—one that addresses both the debt side as well as the asset side of the balance sheet—is necessary to address these longer retirements.

AHAs! ADVISOR HIGHLIGHT ANSWERS

Question #1: How long a life expectancy should I use in my financial plans?

Answer #1: It is impossible to know. Many people in their 50s and early 60s are using a strategy that has a high probability of running out of money in their 80s or 90s. This may be a dangerous assumption. Too many people are looking backward. Technological advancements suggest we should use a different framework looking forward.

A proper plan should account for the possibility of at least one member of a couple living beyond the standard life expectancy tables; ideally you should assume one member could live to 100 and even beyond. People in their late 80s and 90s have few alternative sources of income, so it is clearly better to be safe than sorry.[13]

Notes

1. Dave Ramsey, *The Total Money Makeover*, classic ed. (Nashville: Thomas Nelson, 2013), Chapter 7, "The Debt Snowball: Lose Weight Fast, Really," 104–123.

2. An important note on the term *enriching*: The *Merriam-Webster Dictionary* defines the verb "enrich" as "to make (someone) rich or richer; to improve the quality of (something); to make (something) better; to improve the usefulness or quality of (something) by adding something to it." (See www.merriam-webster .com/dictionary/enrich.) I want to be clear, by embracing these concepts and considering adding a strategic debt component to your finances, your life, there are no guarantees. There are absolutely risks involved, so please, do not mistake the term "enriching" as a guarantee of success. Don't forget the important key point: This is debt you have the money to pay off. You've made an educated, conscious decision to take on this debt.

3. A feasibility analysis includes whether the amount of additional liquidity and flexibility that you are receiving from the low-quality debt you have is more important to you, in the very short run, than the fact that you are actually

losing money. As soon as you are not in a desperate need with regard to liquidity and flexibility, the low-quality debt should be paid off. Additionally, I believe debt over LIBOR plus five percent may be better off being paid down.

4. In fact, while U.S. companies can in theory exist in perpetuity, depending on their corporate charter and their state of incorporation, very few companies survive longer than 100 years.

5. See "Living Long & Well in the 21st Century: Strategic Directions for Research on Aging," www.nia.nih.gov/about/living-long-well-21st-century-strategic-directions-research-aging.

6. Jamie Hopkins, "Planning for an Uncertain Life Expectancy in Retirement," *Forbes* (2014), available at www.forbes.com/sites/jamiehopkins/2014/02/03/planning-for-an-uncertain-life-expectancy-in-retirement/.

   The face of aging in the United States is changing dramatically. People are living longer, achieving higher levels of education, living in poverty less often, and experiencing increasingly lower rates of disability. Life expectancy nearly doubled during the 20th century with a 10-fold increase in the number of Americans age 65 and older. Today, there are approximately 35 million Americans who are age 65 or older, and this number is expected to double in the next 25 years. The oldest old—people age 85 and older—constitute the fastest growing segment of the U.S. population. Currently about 4 million people, this population could top 19 million by 2050.

   To help identify the average life expectancy for a stated age and gender, the Social Security Administration provides a life expectancy calculator. The calculator indicates that a 60-year-old male born in 1953 has an average life expectancy of 83.4 years. If that same person lives to age 66, life expectancy extends to 84.6. Furthermore, if he lives to age 70, his life expectancy extends to age 86. This demonstrates a critical point about life expectancy—*the longer you live, the longer your life expectancy.* This means that as people age they need to alter their expectations about the length of their life and retirement.

7. See https://personal.vanguard.com/us/insights/retirement/plan-for-a-long-retirement-tool.

8. Go ahead and take a look at the Social Security Administration's Life Expectancy Calculator at www.socialsecurity.gov/oact/population/longevity.html and see how long you are expected to live given nothing but statistical averages. You can also look at one of the "long life" online calculators that will look at your health, habits, and other information to give you an estimate as to just how long you (and, if you are married, your spouse) are likely to live.

9. Ric Edelman, Barron's Top Advisor Conference February 2014.

10. See www.merriam-webster.com/medical/holistic.

11. This example was inspired by a lecture in my Managerial Accounting class at the University of Chicago in 2004, given by Professor Scott Keating.

12. Case studies are for educational and illustrative purposes only. They assume eligible assets and that funds are available on the facility. All client situations

are unique, and all loans are subject to eligibility and approval by the lender. A lender may deny an advance on an ABLF, preventing the scenarios. Pledging assets reduces and may eliminate liquidity. A market correction could impact market values and/or security eligibility, which could impact the facility size and/or trigger a margin call and/or forced liquidations of assets. See complete disclosures and risks to using an ABLF in Appendix F.

13. Author's Note: The information in this chapter is to be considered in a holistic way as a part of the book and not to be considered on a stand-alone basis. This includes, but is not limited to, the discussion of risks of each of these ideas as well as all of the disclaimers throughout the book. The material is presented with a goal of encouraging thoughtful conversation and rigorous debate on the risks and potential benefits of the concepts between you and your advisors based on your unique situation, risk tolerance, and goals.

Part II

THE POWER OF DEBT™ IN REDUCING TAXES, INCREASING RETURN, AND REDUCING RISK

Do not wait; the time will never be "just right." Start where
you stand, and work with whatever tools you may have at your
command, and better tools will be found as you go along.
                                        —**George Herbert**

Chapter 4

Returning to the Return You Need

How many millionaires do you know who have become wealthy by investing in savings accounts? I rest my case.

—Robert G. Allen

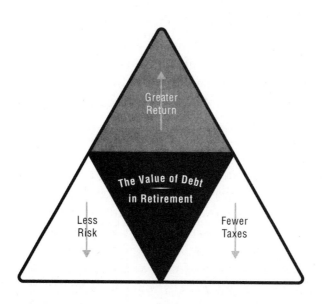

This should grab your attention: Many Americans may not be able to retire successfully without taking advantage of the ideas in this chapter. I'm about to show you how you could potentially increase your rate of return by 50 percent and/or get the rate of return you need to retire comfortably with less risk. We will do some simple math to prove why.

Suppose you are a boomer heading toward retirement. You have been paying attention to retirement articles and books for quite some time, and you already know that at the end of the day, what matters is whether you have enough after-tax cash in your account to pay for the things you need. You've calculated that to maintain your lifestyle you will need a certain average rate of return on the money you already have invested. Let's consider three cases:

1. You need an average return of less than 3 percent.
2. You need an average return of between 3 and 6 percent.
3. You need an average return of higher than 6 percent.

A few examples of the first situation, where you need a 3 percent return:

- You have $500,000 and need less than $15,000 per year.
- You have $1 million and need less than $30,000 per year.
- You have $5 million and need less than $150,000 per year.

If this is you, congratulations! In all likelihood, you won't *need* to incorporate a strategic debt philosophy into your financial life. You have a lot of resources relative to your needs. The ideas in this chapter may still be beneficial and you may still *want* to take advantage of them, but you likely do not *need* this chapter.

If you're in the second situation, needing an average return of between 3 and 6 percent, things become a little less clear. For example, you have $1 million and want $50,000 of annual income in retirement. You may *need* to take advantage of strategic debt, especially if the amount you need is closer to the 6 percent figure. As your required rate of return moves higher, you have to take risk. There is risk in having debt and there is risk in reaching for return. But with the tools I will give you to compare and contrast these risks, you will be able to choose which path you believe is the least risky—and you may be surprised by your conclusions!

If you're in the third category—*needing* an average return of higher than 6 percent—then you may be in a problematic situation. I think it will be very difficult for investors to generate a rate of return higher than 6 percent these days. As I will discuss (and mathematically prove) in Chapter 7, it's highly probable that a portfolio of U.S. stocks and bonds will average less than 5 percent for the next several years. Worse, 5 percent is likely the upper end of the range. A portfolio of U.S. stocks and bonds could average close to zero—or even negative returns over the next few years! So, you may not *want* to take advantage of strategic debt, but if you don't, the type of retirement you've always envisioned may rapidly turn into an unachievable dream rather than the promised destination you've been aiming at for many years. I will show you how to increase the size of your portfolio, thereby potentially *decreasing* the necessary return that you must aim for in order to have the retirement you want.

Cash Flow and Incoming Money: The Ultimate Key to Resource Management

> The greatest achievement of the human spirit is to live up to one's opportunities and make the most of one's resources.
>
> **—Luc de Clapiers**

Ultimately, the key to managing your resources is to get a handle on cash flow, or incoming money. The term "replacement ratio" is often used to describe the ratio between your current working income and the income you will need in retirement. Consider the words of bestselling author and life coach Ernie J. Zelinski:

> No doubt the people with the best opportunity to fulfill their dreams in retirement will be the ones with the biggest nest eggs. . . . Individuals looking forward to retirement must determine what sort of lifestyle will make them happy and how much money they will need to support it. . . . Most financial planners today believe that retirees need to "replace" at least 80 percent of the income they made in their working years. Some financial planners even say that retirees need a higher income than they made in their careers. . . . They may need to replace 105 percent of their working income if they hope to maintain their living

standards. It shouldn't take a genius to figure out that a rigid retirement replacement ratio—whether it's 80 percent or 105 percent—is irresponsible and misleading. . . . There is no formula that will fit everyone.[1]

While no formula fits everyone, a good deal of legwork and preparation can be done ahead of time to assess both your needs and your resources. Consider making a projected yearly budget for retirement. Of course, you may leave things out when making your projections, and things will change through the years and decades. Nonetheless, you should come up with a reasonable figure that should encompass everything you need to live, from housing to transportation to food to entertainment to medical and insurance costs, and so on.

Once you have the amount you will need in mind, you should assess your resources. With all of your existing, known, likely, and additional potential resources listed, you can calculate the level of outgoing cash flow that you will need as a percentage of your resources.

You Have to Get Your Numbers Right!

I have seen over and over that people make two fundamental mistakes when they are calculating how much money they will need in retirement. First, they start with the wrong number. Second, they forecast future expenses and inflation the wrong way.

Let's start with the first point—getting to the correct number. I have run retirement plans and forecasts for almost 20 years. For years I asked people how much money they needed in retirement. At first I accepted peoples' estimates at face value. After all, I figured, who could know how much money somebody needs more than the person I am asking? It took me years to realize that most people start with the wrong estimates. For example, many people assume that if they make $100,000 a year, they need $100,000 a year in retirement. Occasionally they adjust it by old rules of thumb and come up with 80 percent or $80,000. Only after working in the industry for years did I learn that the question is better asked a different way: How much incoming money do you need, after taxes, on a monthly basis, to cover all of your expenses?

Most people take a "top-down" approach. I recommend a "bottom-up" approach. When we make money, we pay into payroll taxes (Social Security and Medicare), federal income taxes, state taxes (in most states), and savings that go into a tax-deferred program such as a 401(k). Most people typically have other savings that they are building up to stay on track for retirement. The essential point is that your taxes are likely to be vastly different in retirement than they were when you were working. Further, *you are not trying to replace the saving component, just the spending component.*

> How much incoming money do you need, after taxes, on a monthly basis, to cover all of your expenses? Remember, you are not trying to replace the savings component, and your taxes may be vastly different than you anticipate.

The full impact of this will depend on your income and savings rate before retirement. If you are making less than $100,000, in all likelihood something around 80 percent (and potentially more than 100 percent) may be a reasonable number. The "traditional rules of thumb" may indeed be quite accurate. However as your income grows, these figures may change significantly. I know a successful attorney who was making $300,000 but realized that his family needed only $150,000 or $12,500 per month after taxes in retirement. This was because so much of the family's money was going to taxes, savings, and the kids' college expenses. A need of $150,000 is 50 percent of $300,000, and I assure you this makes a big difference in running their plan!

This phenomenon gets even more extreme with very large incomes. I know specialty physicians (think neurosurgeons) who refer to "the rule of thirds," in which about one third of income goes to taxes, one third to savings, and one third to lifestyle. A specialty physician making $750,000 may in fact need to replace only $250,000 of income or approximately $20,000 per month after taxes in retirement. At very extreme levels where individuals have incomes of, say, $2 million, it may turn out that the monthly need is in fact closer to $40,000 per month (especially when you take out the expense of kids). In this case, they only need to replace 25 percent of their income.

The bottom line is that the percentage doesn't matter; determining the right number for *you* does! Once you get to the right number, you need to subtract your other sources of income to determine how much you need to generate from your portfolio. For example, if you need $5,000 per month but have a pension of $1,500 and Social Security of $2,000, then you need $1,500 per month, or $18,000 per year, from your portfolio.

For reasons I discuss in the next chapter, I like to focus on your after-tax need. If you're properly positioned, you may be able to run at levels that are much more tax-efficient than most people estimate.

SOCIAL SECURITY STRATEGIES

Social Security is complicated. It is not something you should guess about, and there are many great books, websites, and calculators that I encourage you to use. There are strategies with respect to spousal rights and second marriages that will blow you away. This book can't cover all of these, but trust me; in addition to working with professional advisors who have masterful understanding, it is 100 percent worth spending a minimum of 20 hours understanding the system. Regardless of your net worth, I'll bet those could be the highest paid and most financially impactful 20 hours of your life. (You should also consider testing your advisors by asking them to give you two or three examples of killer Social Security strategies that they have seen and one example of failure.)

The *Wall Street Journal* did an excellent review of tools for analyzing your Social Security options, and we also love the online tools offered by BlackRock, T. Rowe Price, and AARP.

Generally speaking, you can approach Social Security two ways: conservatively or aggressively.[2] The conservative way is to take as much as you can as early as you can, knowing that it might not be there in the future. The aggressive way is to let it continue to grow and take out a higher amount later. It's impossible to know what strategy is right; after all, it depends not only on things like your risk tolerance, goals, and objectives, but also on your life expectancy and future politics.

I'm "bullish" on believing that unless you have a health issue, you will live longer than you think. Boomers vote, and I do not think they will vote to change their own benefits. Changes such as "means testing" may come in to the equation, but that implies building a 10-foot wall, and I generally believe the industry can build an 11-foot ladder. Therefore, I believe far too many people opt for the "take as much as I can as early as I can" approach, which I'm not sure is the right strategy. My strong personal preference is to encourage you to consider strategies that not only delay but also are focused on maximizing spousal benefits (the collective pot).

I am of the "aggressive" camp, meaning that if your net worth is less than $10 million and your health is strong, absent extraordinary circumstances, when I sit at your kitchen table I'll generally vote to delay and be sure spousal benefits are maximized.

Feel free to join the debate at www.valueofdebtinretirement .com or www.vodr.com.

Regardless of Your Net Worth, Distributions Are Rarely Constant over Time in Retirement

The second thing that people get wrong is assuming that distribution rates will be constant over time and that the distribution rate will grow by inflation. Although this could be true, my many years of experience have proven that it is simply not the case in 90 percent of the situations I've seen. To understand why, take a quick trip with me to visit my grandmother.

Grandma Kay Kay is 88 years old and lives in an eldercare facility in her hometown. It's the type of place that not only offers independent living but also an option to move into assisted living when she needs it. Grandma had to put money down to move into the facility (see Everyday Example #2 in Chapter 2), and she pays a monthly fee to be there. She lives on the independent living side, but her physical condition is weakening and the family thinks assisted living is not too far off.

Imagine that you give Grandma $50,000 in cash. You tell her that she cannot invest it or give it away. What would she do with it? She has a car, and buying a new one is off the table. She has all of her favorite art and furniture. Her place is much smaller than her old house, and nothing more could possibly fit into her apartment. She has all the clothes she could ever need. Her health has deteriorated so she can't travel; family comes to see her. The eldercare facility covers her meals. She has a pension that covers her modest monthly living expenses. There really is almost nothing for her to buy. She would probably just stuff the money under the mattress.

Make no mistake; I know that Grandma's in a fortunate situation. She has enough money to live in a great facility. The bigger-picture point is how much expenses converge later in life.

You tend to have one type of a life in your 60s. You may travel extensively, have a number of hobbies, and perhaps choose to have two (or more) homes. Regardless of net worth, these expenses generally start to change in your mid-70s. You slow down a little, start taking different trips and not as many of them. (The trips that you do take are often to visit friends and family.) Fast forward to your mid-80s. Typically you have one residence. If you have two residences, one tends to be a relatively low-key, easy-maintenance apartment or "crash pad." Very few individuals in their 90s maintain multiple homes or travel extensively.

Let's look at another example from my family. My grandfather was in an Alzheimer's care unit before he passed away a few years ago. He primarily worked with the federal government, had a wonderful life, and was what many would consider middle-class. In the room next to him was the matriarch of a family that owned a publicly traded company with a net worth that public records estimated in excess of $50 million. My grandfather's net worth was in line with that of a conservative middle-class family, yet they were in the same place at the same time with virtually the exact same expenses. It's amazing how much expenses tend to converge late in life!

You can test this yourself. You may know a decent number of people in their 60s who have two homes, perhaps are members of two country clubs, and perhaps travel extensively. Apply that same framework to older people you know. How many people can you identify who are older than 80, own two freestanding houses, and are members of two country clubs? *Outside of healthcare*—which is an important topic we will cover later in the guides—how many people over 85 do you know who spend more than $10,000 per month, after taxes? I'm not saying it isn't possible, nor am I saying that you can't come up with examples. I'm just saying it is unusual. If you remove healthcare and housing—two very big expenses that of course we must cover—and charitable and family gifts (which are discretionary expenses), I'm suggesting that the number for the rest of your expenses falls significantly faster and much lower than you think.

This is an essential point to consider because many traditional retirement plans start by assuming that if you spend $10,000 per month, those expenses will continue inflation adjusting upward for the rest of your life. This implies that at a 3 percent inflation rate you would be spending more than $240,000 per year in 25 years, which I consider very unlikely. Yes, more medical expenses come in, but many other expenses start going out.

The total impact of these phenomena depends largely on your needs and net worth. If your net worth is less than $1 million and your expenses are less than $60,000, then your expenses may in fact continue to increase at a rate of inflation and potentially higher as medical and care-facility costs could be longer than anticipated. If your net worth is between $1 million and $3 million, your expenses may ease off a bit or may increase; the degree of change will be based upon lifestyle decisions you make in later decades. I believe that if your net worth is more than $3 million, you want to consider the possibility that you will have different expenses over different decades in your lifetime and the likelihood that your expenses in the later decades may be much lower.

Getting a good handle on whether your expenses will rise considerably, level off, or fall considerably will significantly impact your retirement plan and your ability to be on track.

How Much Can You Safely Take Out?

If you have ever done a financial plan, most software programs and financial advisors assume that you can safely take out between 4 percent and 6 percent as distribution rates in retirement. These numbers come from both back of the envelope guesses and from a study. Let's review both and the potential problems with each of them.

Back of the envelope typically works like this. People assume that stocks have averaged around 10 percent over the long run. Perhaps they are more conservative with their future assumptions so they assume stocks will average say 8 percent going forward. They then assume that bonds have averaged around four percent. The logic goes that if you have a 50/50 portfolio then you should average about 6 percent. I could digress for a long time to analyze all of the problems with this approach. One obvious one is that it does not factor in inflation. It also doesn't factor in the sequence of returns, the central topic of Chapter 6. Perhaps there is something a little better. . . .

Fortunately what is called the "Trinity Study"[3] does some math for us. They looked at every 30-year period between 1926 and 1997 and found 43 overlapping data sets that they studied. Here is the summary of the results of a 50 percent stock and 50 percent bond portfolio:

- A 3 percent inflation adjusted distribution rate tested with 100 percent confidence. Interesting enough, it tested at 100 percent confidence regardless of your asset allocation between stocks and bonds over every 30-year period. This means that if you needed 3 percent or less your asset allocation didn't matter—really, nothing mattered. You were on track to not run out of money.
- If you took out inflation-adjusted withdrawals of 4 percent, then you ran out of money 5 percent of the time. Ninety-five percent of the time you didn't run out of money! Therefore 4 percent is generally considered a safe distribution rate.
- If you took out a 6 percent distribution, you made it 51 percent of the time. This means that you ran out of money 49 percent of the time. This is equivalent to the chances of a coin toss.
- If you took a 7 percent distribution, your chances of success fell to 19 percent. This means that you ran out of money 81 percent of the time before your 30-year period was up. Ouch!

Table 4.1 shows a summary of the results.

Table 4.1 Trinity Study Summary: Portfolio Success Rate with Inflation Adjusted Monthly Withdrawals : 1926–1997 (30 Years Only)

Payout Period	Annualized Withdrawal Rate as a Percentage of Initial Portfolio Value									
	3%	4%	5%	6%	7%	8%	9%	10%	11%	12%
75% stocks/25% bonds										
30 years	100	100	86	63	47	35	14	7	0	0
50% stocks/50% bonds										
30 years	100	95	70	51	19	9	0	0	0	0
25% stocks/75% bonds										
30 years	100	74	26	19	7	0	0	0	0	0

According to this study, the greater your need, the greater the benefit of having a meaningful equity allocation. Advisors use charts like this to convince clients that they need to keep a heavy allocation to stocks. As we will discuss in Chapter 7 this may or may not be the case looking forward, but for now let's work with this data as it is commonly used in the industry. It provides the framework for my earlier comments, and we can focus on the three different types of people: those who need less than 3 percent, those who need 3 to 6 percent, and those who need more than 6 percent.

Now remember your life is dynamic and changing. This table is a simple snapshot and I encourage you to keep the story about my grandmother in mind. Depending on your needs and net worth, you may not need to inflation adjust your distributions throughout time. For some people distribution rates may go down; for others they may in fact go up. Here are some things to consider:

• The greater your net worth the more you may feel comfortable running at a high distribution rate early in retirement. For example, if your net worth is $3 million and you run at a 6 percent distribution rate, you may be comfortable with the risk that your assets have a high chance they could gradually fall toward, say, $1 million as you get older. If they do, perhaps you could adjust your life and lifestyle at that time.

- The problem with this strategy of course is that 6 percent of $1 million is $60,000, so while you were spending $180,000 in the early years, you would need your expenses to fall considerably later in life.
- The older you are when you retire, then the more that you may be comfortable running at a higher distribution rate. For example, if you retire at 80 then you may not need your money to last as long.
- *But here is my central theme:* If you intend to retire before you are 70 years old, and your assets are under $3 million, and you need a distribution rate over 4 percent, then there is a chance you will run out of money. *Therefore, you need to consider all of the tools that are available to you so that you can increase the chances you make it!*

If you need a higher rate of return, you will need to do one of the following:

- Lower your projected retirement yearly budget.
- Do better with your financial investments over the long run (reach for a higher rate of return, which increases your risk).
- Find and access additional potential resources such as the wise use of strategic debt.

Of course, a combination of these may be most effective and the safest solution will always be to reduce your needs. But what if that isn't possible? If you need a higher rate of return, you have to take risk in some fashion.

Notice from the Trinity study that if you reach for return by increasing your allocation to equities it is only a partial solution. For example, if you need an 8 percent rate of return and you have a 75 percent stock portfolio, then you still ran out of money 65 percent of the time! Faced with risk, the question becomes, what is the least risky risk you can take?

How You May Be Able to Increase Your Rate of Return

Give me a place to stand and with a lever I will move the whole world.

—Archimedes

One way to amplify your wealth in retirement may be to use Enriching Debt to engage in what I call "capturing the spread." This definition is from *The Value of Debt*:

> Capturing the spread refers to targeting and then capturing a return on investment that is higher than the cost of the debt—after taking into account all tax implications and transactions cost—that you take on to make that investment.[4]

Capturing the spread is one of the major ways you can access the third Indebted Strength of Increased Leverage. It's simple, really: if you can make more money on the money you borrow than that money costs you, you may be able to increase your rate of return and amplify your wealth in the long run. Why especially in the long run? Because longer time horizons increase the possibility that your investments will have enough time to go through their ups and their downs, delivering the average return you were aiming at in the first place.

There are two ways to get to a 9 percent rate of return. The first is to invest in assets that pay 9 percent. Simple. But there is another way, and it involves buying assets that pay 6 percent and using some debt. Obviously, many more investments are likely to reliably return 6 percent than 9 percent. And in fact, investments targeting 9 percent will almost certainly be more dangerous, more risky, and more volatile overall.

This principle is completely consistent with what is known as Modern Portfolio Theory and the Capital Allocation Line, and it just makes sense.

This brings us to an important principle:

Everything else being equal, a lower-volatility portfolio with debt is better than a high-volatility portfolio with no debt. Similarly, a portfolio with no debt may actually be taking on more risk than a portfolio with debt yet achieve the same result.

If you need a certain income from your portfolio, attempting to obtain that income with high-risk investments is, well, risky. The volatility—the risk—associated with such investments means that things could go down, and go down a lot, and go down at exactly the wrong time for you. You might be better off bringing more money to the table through the strategic use of debt and then targeting a lower, less-risky return.

Is there risk to this strategy? Absolutely! But there also is risk in reaching for assets that have a 9 percent rate of return. There's always risk in taking on debt. Faced with different risks, the key is to understand your options and then choose the least risky path!

How Is This Possible? A Big-Picture Overview

Let's look at an example. Jane is renting a house, has no material assets, has just inherited $1 million, and is close to retirement. Jane decides she wants to buy a home worth $500,000 and have $45,000 of income per year in retirement.

There are two ways that Jane can have a return of $45,000 per year.

Jane could buy assets that pay her 9 percent.

- In a no-debt scenario, Jane has a $500,000 portfolio + $500,000 in her house, so $1 million in assets and no debt.
- Jane's net worth is $1 million, and her portfolio is worth $500,000.
  - ($1 million of assets − $0 debt = $1 million).
- To get a rate of return of $45,000 on her $500,000 portfolio, Jane would need to invest in assets that deliver a 9 percent rate of return.
  - ($500,000 × 9% = $45,000)

Jane could embrace the strategic use of debt.

- Jane could take out a $400,000 mortgage to purchase the same house.
- Assume that Jane's mortgage is at 3 percent and her CPA tells her that her after-tax cost of the mortgage is 2 percent.
- Jane's assets would be $1.4 million ($500,000 house + $900,000 portfolio) and her liability (her debt) is a $400,000 mortgage.
  - $1.4 million − $400,000 = a net worth of $1 million.
  - This is the exact same person with the exact same net worth, just making a different decision with respect to debt.

- If her investments return 6 percent, she would make *$46,000* per year.
  - $900,000 × 6% = $54,000 of income.
  - Less the interest expense of $400,000 × 2% = $8,000.
  - Equals: $54,000 income − $8,000 expenses = $46,000.

How can somebody with a 6 percent rate of return earn more than somebody who's getting a 9 percent rate of return? Let's look at Jane's second scenario again: 6 percent × $900,000 is $54,000. Jane has to pay for her debt, which may cost her 2 percent after taxes: 2 percent × $400,000 = $8,000. $54,000 − 8,000 = 46,000!

> There are two ways to get to a 9 percent rate of return. Way number one is to invest in assets that pay 9 percent. Way number two is to leverage investments that pay 6 percent.

I encourage you to turn to Appendix B to see this same material presented with tables, charts, and the math in more detail.

WHO ELSE DOES THIS? MR. WARREN BUFFETT

A recent research paper by Andrea Frazzini, David Kabiller, and Lasse Heje Pedersen estimated that Warren Buffett's leverage is about 1.6 to 1 (assets to equity) on average. "Buffett's returns appear to be neither luck nor magic," the authors state, "but, rather, reward for the use of leverage combined with a focus on cheap, safe, quality stocks."[5]

I recommend a leverage ratio around 1.5 to 1 (or 33 percent debt-to-asset ratio) and lower, a more conservative approach than the one outlined above. But Buffett's strategy is, in fact, almost the exact scenario outlined in this section.

Risks and Problems

Are there other risks? Potential problems? Important details that matter? Yep. What happens in a rising interest rate environment? What if your rate of return is under your cost of debt? Could Jane's cost of debt really be 2 percent after taxes? These questions (and more) are all essential to examine before undertaking a strategic debt philosophy. Make no mistake; this strategy is not a free lunch. But if the basic point is that *if* (and it is a big if) you can have a rate of return higher than your after-tax cost of debt, then the strategic use of debt will enhance your overall returns. At this point it's important that you understand the foundation. In Part III we will discuss implementation steps and risks.

Everyday Example #4: Retiring the "Loan" Survivor

Student loan debt, it turns out, is often the second-most significant form of debt that most people have throughout their lives. As recently reported in *Forbes*, "Over 16 percent of the $1.2 trillion in outstanding student loan debt belongs to individuals over 50 years old."[6] Student loan debt can be a significant barrier for people in saving for retirement—whether they're paying off their own student loans or loans they took out for their children. A reasonable solution to this potential problem is outlined in the following box.

EVERYDAY EXAMPLE #4: GETTING RID OF STUDENT LOANS ONCE AND FOR ALL

John, who decided to go to medical school and become a physician in his mid-30s, still has $100,000 in student debt at 5 percent. This isn't a terrible interest rate, but the money John has to pay monthly is preventing him from putting more funds into his other investments.

Fortunately, in addition to putting money into his IRA, John has a $250,000 taxable portfolio and finds a firm willing to give him a $100,000 loan at just 3 percent interest with no amortization if he pledges his taxable assets. John does so, and instead of having a $417 a month payment, he now has a $250 a month payment. More importantly, there is no required monthly payment, so he is able to much more effectively put away money in his various investment and retirement vehicles.[7]

In this chapter we discussed the importance of getting your numbers right. Focus on the bottom line, after-tax amount of income that you need to generate. From there, remember my grandmother and consider whether your distribution rates will change over time. The higher your net worth, the more they may actually fall over time. We then looked at distribution rates that you may want to conservatively consider. If you need a higher distribution rate, you either have to take risk by reaching for a higher return or consider a lower-risk portfolio with debt to potentially achieve the same result.

AHAs! ADVISOR HIGHLIGHT ANSWERS

Question #1: What rate of return should you target relative to your client's cost of debt?

Answer #1: A finance guy, a CFO, and I got together and debated this question (yes, I lead a fun and exotic life). I went first and said that I would want to capture a spread of 2 percent, meaning if I am taking risk I want to get paid for it. So if my cost of debt is 3 percent, I would like to shoot for a rate of return of at least 5 percent. The finance guy said that all things being equal, if you knew you had the exact same rate of return, you would take the liquidity all day. The CFO told us it was fun to watch us have this debate but that we were both idiots. He explained you would take a negative spread and that companies do it every day.

From his perspective, the value of liquidity, flexibility, and survivability are so valuable that you should of course be willing to pay for them. The goal is to narrow the spread, but his point was that if you are paying 2 to 3 percent after taxes on your debt and earning 0 to 2 percent, you might take that trade for up to $1 million or more versus having it tied up in an illiquid asset such as a house. $1 million liquid assets and $1 million in debt versus $1 million in a house is a completely different liquidity situation in a time of distress.

There isn't a right answer here but rather an important topic to debate. Customization is necessary for each individual. But I see now that my answer was wrong. The finance guy was closer than I was, and in my opinion the CFO was right. It's important that professionals stay open-minded and receptive to learning.

The concepts of liquidity, flexibility, survivability, perspective, and leverage are, frankly, boring for many clients—and who cares about this stuff in bull markets? Well, let me tell you, they matter considerably in bad times. As their professional advisor, it is essential that you consider each of these carefully with respect to each client's individual situation.[8]

Notes

1. Ernie J. Zelinski, *How to Retire Happy, Wild, and Free: Retirement Wisdom That You Won't Get from Your Financial Advisor* (Edmonton, Canada: Visions International Publishing, 2014), 28–29.
2. This topic was discussed at a conference, First Clearing Financial Advisor's Forum, hosted by First Clearing Correspondent Services, a division of First Clearing, LLC, in September 2014, in St. Louis, Missouri.
3. Trinity study, http://afcpe.org/assets/pdf/vol1014.pdf.
4. Thomas J. Anderson, *The Value of Debt: How to Manage Both Sides of a Balance Sheet to Maximize Wealth* (Hoboken, NJ: John Wiley & Sons, 2013), p. 77.
5. www.econ.yale.edu/~af227/pdf/Buffett's%20Alpha%20-%20Frazzini,%20 Kabiller%20and%20Pedersen.pdf.
6. See Robert Farrington, "Struggling with Student Loan Debt Over Age 50," www.forbes.com/sites/robertfarrington/2014/08/20/struggling-with-student-loan-debt-over-age-50/.
7. Case studies are for educational and illustrative purposes only. They assume eligible assets and that funds are available on the facility. All client situations are unique, and all loans are subject to eligibility and approval by the lender. A lender may deny an advance on an ABLF, preventing the scenarios. Pledging assets reduces and may eliminate liquidity. A market correction could impact market values and/or security eligibility, which could impact the facility size and/or trigger a margin call and/or forced liquidations of assets. See complete disclosures and risks to using an ABLF in Appendix F.
8. Author's Note: The information in this chapter is to be considered in a holistic way as a part of the book and not to be considered on a stand-alone basis. This includes, but is not limited to, the discussion of risks of each of these ideas as well as all of the disclaimers throughout the book. The material is presented with a goal of encouraging thoughtful conversation and rigorous debate on the risks and potential benefits of the concepts between you and your advisors based on your unique situation, risk tolerance, and goals.

Chapter 5

The Power of Debt™ Meets Our Ridiculous Tax Code

$5.5 Million Net Worth, $240,000 Income, and $4,000 in Taxes!

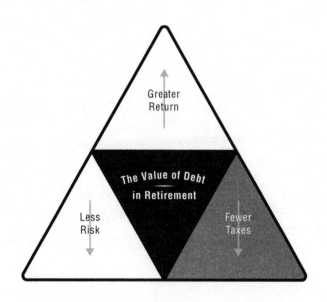

The world's largest cat weighs more than 900 pounds. Hercules is a "liger," a cross between a lion and a tiger. You can see a picture of him in Figure 5.1. This particular kitty's size is due to "hybrid vigor," defined as "increased vigor or other superior qualities arising from the crossbreeding of genetically different plants or animals."[1] This chapter will demonstrate some surprising, possibly shocking attributes of another kind of hybrid vigor, the kind that results from making use of a retirement strategy that involves both sides of your balance sheet.

During retirement, finding ways of bringing in money—cash flow—that comes from both your assets and your debts can produce a hybrid result that delivers a greater total amount of incoming cash, is more resilient and tax efficient, and pretty much better for you in many ways. Another way of thinking about this is in terms of "synergy," which is defined as "the benefit that results when two or more agents work together to achieve something either one couldn't have achieved on its own. It's the concept of the whole being greater than the sum of its parts."[2]

Figure 5.1   Hercules the "Liger"
Source:© Splash News/Corbis

Put differently, some things have "emergent properties" that you could not have predicted merely from the underlying ingredients. If you mix up flour, water, yeast, and heat, you get something completely different and not found within any one of those ingredients: bread. And if you create a proper mix of incoming cash flow both from selling down part of your portfolio, like your IRA or 401(k), and borrowing against another part of your portfolio through an asset-based portfolio loan, then an unexpected hybrid with synergistic and emergent properties results—one that yields a nice amount of a different kind of "bread."

A certain amount of math, figures, and tax calculations are a necessary part of this chapter. I will make things understandable by presenting you necessary information in multiple ways, including the use of words, diagrams, and spreadsheets that will further reinforce the central concepts. Ultimately, what really counts is your own situation, and to get a thorough handle on your situation you should work with your own advisor to see if the ideas and practices make sense for you.

Some Brief Preliminaries: Income versus Incoming Money

Don't let yourself fall into "empty." Keep cash in your house. Keep gas in your tank. Keep an extra roll of toilet paper squirreled away. Keep your phone charged.

—Gretchen Rubin

A few preliminary definitions are necessary here. The first concerns the definition of "incoming money." At the end of the day, when you are in retirement, the single most important resource—and a large determinant of your lifestyle—is the amount of money you will have available to you, month after month, in your banking or checking account. As certified financial planner Mark Singer puts it:

The most important step is understanding your cash flow needs. Cash flow is the number one driver of a successful retirement. You could be worth millions of dollars, but if you are not able to generate the income needed to live the lifestyle you desire, then you will not have a successful retirement.[3]

There is no question that incoming money—cash flow, if you will—is of paramount importance. The strategy demonstrated in this chapter involves creating incoming money in part by using a line of credit. Now, when you look at the IRS definition of "income," you will see that it includes a lot of things, including earned income as a wage, profits from stocks or real estate sales, stock dividends, lottery or gambling winnings, and even the cash value of bartered items. It does *not* include writing yourself a check from your portfolio line of credit. (The fact that this *isn't* income is great news, because that means it is not taxed as income.)

To make it perfectly clear, since money from a line of credit is *not* income and therefore *not* taxable, I will refer to it as "incoming money" instead of income. The term "incoming money" *does* include all the other types of income listed above, such as dividends, money from stock sales, earned wages, and so on. Our focus, then, is on incoming money or retirement cash flow, not on income per se.

The Websters: A Tale That Taxes the Imagination

The hardest thing to understand in the world is the income tax.
—Albert Einstein

In *The Value of Debt* we presented the example of Mr. and Mrs. Webster. Because a lot of the details were in footnotes, I go through the Websters' example a little more slowly when I go around the country giving presentations on strategic debt philosophy and strategy. What I find is that the audience members' jaws tend to drop as they grasp what I'm showing them and they wonder how it can really be possible.

Let's take another look at the Websters' scenario in a step-by-step fashion. As for how it could be possible, well, a lot of it is because of the U.S. Tax Code, which is more than 4 million words long and has thousands of changes made to it annually. The code is nearly incomprehensible and kind of crazy in many ways. But we're not here to question the wisdom of the U.S. Tax Code but rather to find a way to work with it so that you can have the best possible retirement.

STRATEGIES OF THE SUPER RICH

I am about to share with you the exact strategies of the super rich and use them as a basis that may frame opportunities in your personal life. To better understand it, let's look at a few articles from the recent press.

Edward McCaffery is a professor of law, economics, and political science at the University of Southern California. On September 25, 2012, he wrote an article for CNN called "Why Do the Romneys Pay So Little in Taxes?" He explained that the Romney's pay an effective tax rate of 14.1 percent. He then states, "This is a low tax rate, lower than the typical middle-class American worker pays, especially when one considers payroll taxes. . . ."

He goes on to say, "*The simple strategy of the super-rich is to buy and hold, and to borrow when needed to finance their lifestyles.*"[4] [emphasis added]

On April 9, 2013, McCaffery wrote another article for CNN about Mark Zuckerberg called "Zuk Never Has to Pay Taxes Again." In it he says, "The truly rich do not have to pay any tax once they have their fortunes in hand. They can follow the simple tax-planning advice to buy/borrow/die. Buy assets that appreciate in value without producing cash, borrow to finance lifestyle, and die to pass on a 'stepped up' basis to heirs wherein the tax gain miraculously disappears."[5]

Whether your net worth is much smaller or even higher than the Romneys or the Zuckerbergs, you will be as shocked as I was when I learned these secrets. I hope to create a path for you to use them as well.

Chances are very small that your life looks exactly like the Websters. But even if your situation is very different, you can glean some idea of what might be possible in your case. *If your net worth is higher or lower, we will see how we can keep your taxes around the same levels as this example.*

If you are the type of person who wants to dive into details and throw elbows, I encourage you to read this whole book cover to cover—including the details in Appendix C where I discuss this chapter's assumptions in detail. Ideally, I'd also love for you to read *The Value of Debt* and engage me in a public or private debate; I like nothing more than a good conversation. To facilitate this debate and discussion, please go to www.valueofdebtinretirement.com or www.vodr.com, where you are welcome to share your thoughts, ideas, and takeaways from these strategies.

I make some broad assumptions here, and it's impossible to give an example without doing so. It's most important that you understand the purpose of the exercise. I'm frankly trying to stir the pot and generate public debate and conversation on this important topic. The goal is to empower you and your advisor and to encourage you to think more holistically.

OK, then, here is the Websters' situation as found in Table 5.1. They are each 65 years old and retired—he was a business executive, and she was a schoolteacher—and they have done pretty well. They own their primary residence outright, and it is worth $1 million. They also own a vacation home worth $1 million, and they have a $500,000 mortgage on it. And they have a total investment portfolio worth $4 million, half in an IRA and the other half in an after-tax (meaning taxable) account. Their investments are in a globally diversified portfolio of stocks and bonds, mostly using mutual funds and index funds.

The Websters' assets are $1 million home + $1 million vacation home + $2 million portfolio + $2 million IRA = $6 million. Their only debt is a $500,000 mortgage. $6 million − $500,000 = $5.5 million net worth.

After working through their budget with their financial advisor, the Websters determine that to maintain their lifestyle at the level they want, they will need about $20,000 per month, or $240,000 per year, *after taxes* to cover all of their expenses. This excludes the fees they pay their financial advisors.

Table 5.1   The Websters' Balance Sheet

Assets		Liabilities
Home 1	$ 1,000,000	
Home 2	1,000,000	($500,000)
Taxable Account	2,000,000	
Retirement Account	2,000,000	
Total	$ 6,000,000	($500,000)
Net Worth	**$5,500,000**	**8% debt ratio**[*]

[*]Debt ratio = Liabilities/Assets ($500,000/6,000,000).

Table 5.2   Tax-Deductible Expenses: The Websters

Expenses	
Charitable Donations	($20,000)
Property Taxes	(20,000)
Mortgage Interest	(10,000)
Professional Fees	(30,000)
Total	**($80,000)**

Of course, the Websters also have some significant expenses. Some of these are tax-deductible and some are not. Tax-deductible expenses total up to $80,000 and include $20,000 in charitable donations, $20,000 in property taxes between their two homes, $10,000 in mortgage interest, and $30,000 in professional fees, which are mainly paid to their financial advisor who manages their portfolio on a fee-only basis. Their income need is $240,000 plus the $30,000 to their advisors, so $270,000 total. $270,000 minus $80,000 of tax-deductible expenses means that they are paying about $190,000 in living expenses. It doesn't really matter how this breaks down, but let's say it's about $12,500 per month for general living (taking care of the homes, food, medical, entertainment, etc.) $30,000 per year in travel, and $10,000 per year helping out family.

For tax purposes, we really care about their tax-deductible expenses. Table 5.2 shows what their tax-deductible expenses look like.

What about income? Let's start with the easy parts. The Websters don't have a pension (she didn't teach long enough to qualify) or a deferred compensation program. They have only $20,000 of Social Security.

What about their portfolio? In 2015, it's tough to get income. Almost half of government bonds around the world pay under 2 percent[6] and the S&P 500 dividend yield is just under 2 percent.[7] The Websters' taxable portfolio could be $1 million in the S&P 500, generating $20,000 of dividends. Their $1 million in bonds at 2 percent is paying them $20,000 in interest. Their portfolio manager triggered $20,000 of gains while rebalancing their portfolio. Fortunately, all of these were long-term gains.

Table 5.3   Taxable Income: The Websters

Income	
IRA Distribution	$ 80,000
Interest	20,000
Dividends	20,000
Social Security	20,000
Long-Term Capital Gains	20,000
Total Taxable Income[*]	**$157,000**

[*]Only a portion of a taxpayer's Social Security benefits may be taxable. Here, the Webster's received $20,000 in Social Security benefits but only $17,000 is considered taxable income. Please see IRS Publication 915 for details.

What about their IRA? That account, of course, is tax-deferred so the Websters don't pay tax on the interest, dividend, or capital gains. They pay taxes on only the money that they take out. Let's say that they take $80,000 from their IRA. This is a 4 percent distribution on a $2 million IRA. ($80,000/$2 million = 4%). See Table 5.3.

The multimillion-dollar question, then, is whether the Websters will ultimately have *enough* cash flowing, because they are afraid they might get socked with a significant income tax on the incoming money that they need to live on each year.

A quick recap: The Websters, who have a net worth of $5.5 million, have $160,000 of income. With memories of what it was like to be in the highest tax bracket while they were in their peak earning years, the Websters *are afraid that they might owe tens of thousands* in taxes. So, take a guess: How much do you think the Websters will pay in income tax given this scenario? Will it indeed be in the tens of thousands of dollars range? If so, will they need to sell off more of their IRA each year?[8]

Perhaps the Websters' tax rate will be as little as 20 percent, that is, in the $32,000 range or even less . . . maybe it will be 10 percent, or only $16,000 a year? Or could it, might it, possibly be even less than that because they are now retired, and some of their incoming money sources, like their IRA distribution, might receive favorable tax treatment?

To answer this question, let's turn to Intuit's TurboTax TaxCaster tool, generously provided for free online. I suggest that you do this online

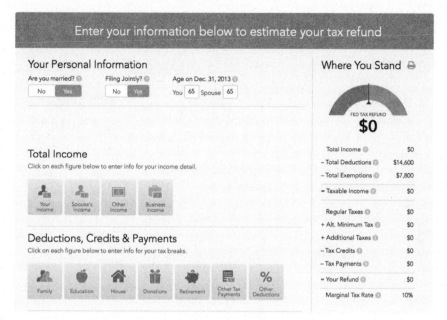

Figure 5.2   The Websters' Basic Personal Information

exercise for yourself, but I'll also provide you with a series of screenshots so that you can follow along as you see exactly what I did here, step-by-step. To start, go to www.TurboTax.com/tax-tools. There, you can access the TaxCaster tool by clicking on "Get Started" on the left hand side of the page. (They update this webpage frequently, so you may have to dig around a little to find the TaxCaster tool. A TaxCaster app is also available on iTunes and Android through Google Play.)

Once in TaxCaster, we can input the various facts and figures for the Websters (see Figure 5.2). We start by inputting their basic personal information, that is, married, filing jointly, and age on December 31, 2013 (65).

Because neither of the Websters are working any more, we can click on the box that says "Other Income" and fill in the figures from above, so that it looks like Figure 5.3.[9]

Now it's time to input the Websters' tax deductions as outlined earlier. After clicking "Continue," find "Deductions, Credits, and Payments" and click on "House." For mortgage interest payments, type in $10,000, and for real estate tax payments, insert $20,000. Click "continue," then click

Enter your information below to estimate your tax refund

Total Income
Click on each figure below to enter info for your income detail.

[Continue]

Your Income | Spouse's Income | Other Income | Business Income

Where You Stand 🖨

FED TAX REFUND

$-21,514

Other Income
If you have other kinds of income, such as investments or pensions, enter them below.

Interest	$20,000	IRA/Pension Distributions	$80,000
Qualified Dividends	$20,000	Social Security Benefits	$20,000
Gains/Losses (short-term)	$0	Miscellaneous Income	$0
Gains/Losses (long-term)	$20,000	Alimony Received	$0

Total Income	$157,000
− Total Deductions	$14,600
− Total Exemptions	$7,800
= Taxable Income	$134,600
Regular Taxes	$21,514
+ Alt. Minimum Tax	$0
+ Additional Taxes	$0
− Tax Credits	$0
− Tax Payments	$0
= Your Refund	$-21,514
Marginal Tax Rate	25%

Figure 5.3   Other Income: The Websters

on "Other Deductions," and under "Employee Business Expenses," type in the $30,000 professional fee the Websters pay their financial advisor. Finally, click on "Donations" and plug in the $20,000 that the Websters gave to charity (which, given their net worth, is really not all that much). See Figures 5.4, 5.5, 5.6, and 5.7.

Once we've input all relevant information, we come up with the Websters' 2013 income tax estimate *of just $3,956!* Less than $4,000! Think about it: These folks, worth $5.5 million with $160,000 of reported income, will pay *less than $4,000 of income tax a year!* (If you ask me how that is even possible, my response is that the tax code is basically nuts. That's just the way it is.)

By paying less than $4,000 in taxes (Figure 5.8), the Websters end up having about $156,000 of income each year (the $160,000 they put together, minus the $3,956 that they have to pay in tax).

But wait. The Websters need $240,000 of income, so $156,000 after taxes isn't enough. They need $84,000 more: $7,000 more per month!

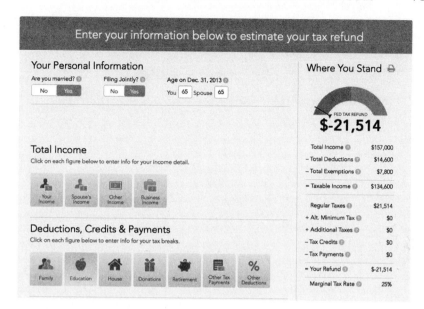

Figure 5.4   Total Taxable Income before Deductions: The Websters

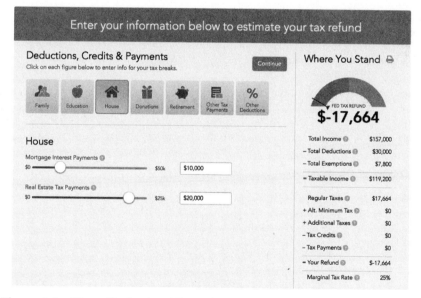

Figure 5.5   House Deductions: The Websters

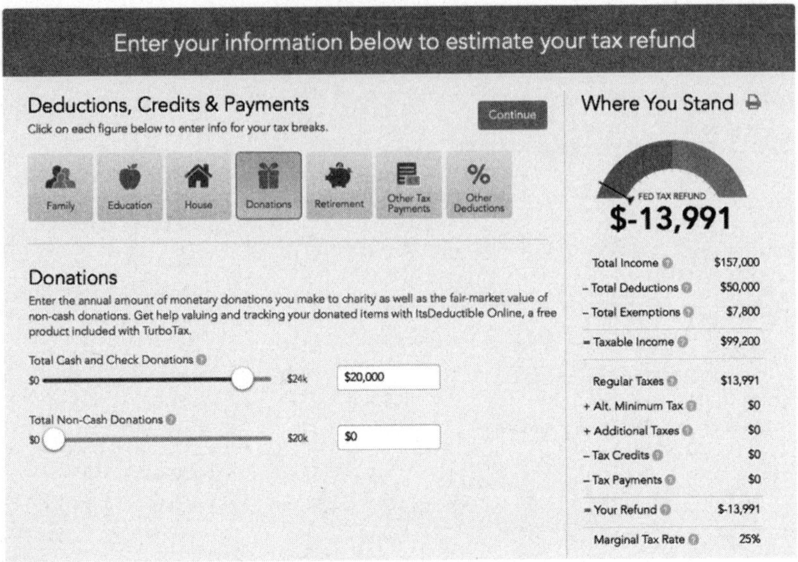

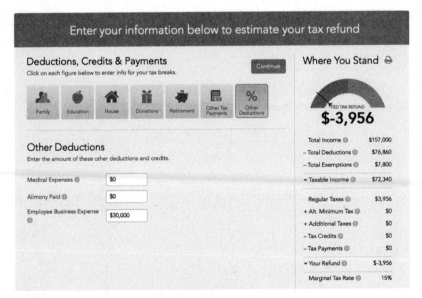

Figure 5.6   Donations: The Websters

Figure 5.7   Other Deductions: The Websters

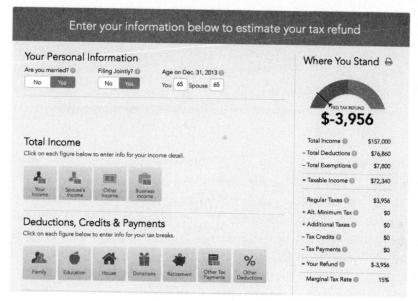

Figure 5.8 Final Estimated Taxes Due: The Websters

IT IS KIND OF A JOKE

I must admit I'm laughing as I write this. Sentences like "$160,000 after taxes isn't enough" sure seem ridiculous. I've taught these strategies for years and know that there are plenty of people who want more. People have paid me lots of money to give them ideas on how to get more income. Here comes some of my best stuff.

Some people will have negative feelings about ideas that minimize taxes. You could consider these ideas unpatriotic, but the bottom line is that it isn't my tax code. I didn't write it. When Congress creates something with 4 million words, it's easy to take advantage of the loopholes. Many companies and the super rich take advantage of it every day! It isn't fair for everyday Americans not to be aware of how the system can work for them too. My goal is simply to level the playing field. I believe that the fairest thing is to make everybody aware of these strategies so they're no longer secrets used only by ultra-high-net-worth individuals.

> Of course the tax code will change. These ideas are most bene-
> ficial in the current environment, but if somebody builds a 10-foot
> wall, people like me build 11-foot ladders. I can do this stuff all day
> long—and you can too!

The Websters might say to me, "Tom, we are thrilled that we're only
paying $4,000 in taxes, but we need more income—$84,000 to be precise.
What do we do?" How can the Websters generate that incoming money
and what will the tax impact be? After speaking with their caring, competent, open-minded financial advisor (who is making $30,000 a year
from the Websters, so let's hope the advice is good), the Websters decide
the simplest and best thing to do is to borrow that $84,000. They could
do this by writing a check from their portfolio line of credit. For example,
they could pay for their income taxes (approximately $4,000), their prop-
erty taxes ($20,000), their trips ($30,000), their charitable contributions
($20,000), and help their family members ($10,000) by writing a check
from their line of credit that is backed by their investment portfolio.

Now for the really crazy part: What are the tax consequences of doing
this? There are none. Zero. (There are also zero estate tax consequences
should the Websters die suddenly, at least under current law, as well as zero
capital gains consequences because they have not sold anything.)[10]

It gets even crazier. When the Websters die, the cost basis on the investments in their taxable account would step up. But for now, with $240,000
or $20,000 a month of incoming money, *the Websters are still paying income
taxes of just $3,956 per year and are unlikely to pay any other taxes, ever.*

That means, essentially, that the Websters are now paying about 1.65
percent income tax on their $240,000 of incoming money. Be mad.
Don't be mad. I'm just the messenger.

Wait! Are there risks? And won't the Websters have to pay interest on
the money they borrow? Yes, to both! This is a complex strategy; so let's
dive a little deeper. Of course the Websters will pay interest on money
that is borrowed. While their overall debt might be going up over time,
their overall net worth may go up at a faster rate—or it may not. In any
case, the Websters have made use of the hybrid vigor that comes from

borrowing from their portfolio line of credit and selling off a reasonable amount of their IRA, all to their great amazement and advantage.

And what about enjoying life more? What if the Websters decide they'd like to buy a $100,000 car for $250 per month? Well, they may be able to do that too!

Figure 5.9 shows a diagram that summarizes both of these scenarios. Is this crazy? Well, the tax code may or may not be crazy, but it *would be crazy* for the Websters not to take advantage of the hybrid borrow-and-sell model that we have outlined here. Importantly, if the Websters did *not* have a sizable taxable portfolio, they would not be able to take advantage of the hybrid model. The lesson there is that you might want to consider putting money *not* just in your tax-deferred accounts, such

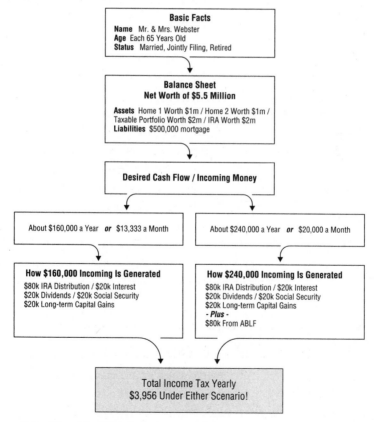

Figure 5.9   How The Websters Generate Sufficient Cash Flow in Retirement

as an IRA or 401(k), but also into a taxable account that can provide you with this highly efficient hybrid solution.

Your De Facto Tax Advisor

Your financial advisor, unless he or she also happens to be a CPA—which is relatively rare but not unheard of—will usually tell you that he or she is not qualified to give you tax advice. In my view, this is the wrong way to think about things.

You see, when you are retired, you don't have any control over your pension (if you're lucky enough to receive one), the amount of Social Security you receive, and the minimum distribution requirements for your 401(k) or IRA. *But guess what? You do have control over most everything else!* Assuming you have no or limited ordinary income, the amount you sell from your IRA or 401(k) and the amount you sell from your other taxable investment accounts—and the capital gains that result—are what controls your taxes. You also, of course, have control over the amount of charitable donations you can deduct and whether or not you have a mortgage or home equity line or loan.

The point is that you are constructing a "big picture" with your financial advisor that very much affects how much you will pay yearly in income taxes, as opposed to your CPA or other accountant who often comes in after the fact to tell you how much you owe. If nothing else, your financial advisor can use the TurboTax TaxCaster or a similar tool to help estimate what you can do to create the most tax-efficient big picture possible.

When your financial advisor says that he or she cannot give you tax advice, just say, "That's not so!" You should demand that they know tax facts! Make sure they are factoring in everything of significance before you make any major moves.

FUN FACT: YOU CAN GET CLOSE TO THIS SCENARIO WITHOUT DEBT

If the Websters were debt-averse, they could create a tax-efficient situation by selling from their taxable portfolio instead of borrowing against the portfolio. In this case they would only owe taxes, likely long-term gains, on the portion that they sell. Let's pretend their basis was 50 percent and they sold $80,000 instead of borrowing. Their long-term gains would be an additional $40,000 for a total tax bill near $16,000.[11] Not too shabby!

So, should the Websters borrow or should they sell? There are risks either way the Websters go. Selling means intentionally depleting their capital. It reduces their liquidity, and they know their future return on an asset they sell is zero. If they borrow, they still own the asset but have the offsetting liability. The question is, will the asset provide a rate of return higher than their after-tax cost of the debt? Are they better off depleting their assets or keeping them and having an offsetting liability (debt)?

The honest answer is, nobody knows. It depends on the Websters' investment decisions, but selling is by no means a free lunch nor is it a solution to their income problems. Selling intentionally depletes their assets.

An Inconvenient Truth

In my opinion, the majority of the financial services industry, and most people, guess with their money. You heard me right. Random guesses drive most people's financial life. For example, many people—either through their financial advisor or on their own—take out $30,000 from their IRA for a cash need one time and sell $30,000 from their taxable portfolio the next time they need money. You can almost hear the conversation, "Well, we took it from the IRA last time, so let's take it from the taxable account this time." Worse, I have seen people take 100 percent of their distributions from either their IRA or their taxable account based on a "guess" that it was better to let the other one keep cooking.

Guessing isn't scientific, and it can lead to disastrous results. Regardless of whether you choose to embrace a strategic debt strategy, there is a mathematical answer to your distribution strategy. An optimal amount of ordinary income can and should be generated for each individual that is unique to his or her personal situation. Think of it as a range more than a specific number—but there is an ideal range. The idea is to work with your financial advisor before you pay taxes to determine what is optimal for you. After that optimal amount of income is in place, an optimal amount of borrowing or selling can take place. And there are optimal combinations of all of these strategies. The key point is to make sure that either you are doing the math or you are working with somebody who will do the math for you.

How to Pay Almost No Taxes in Retirement: A Few More Examples

If you are paying taxes in retirement, it may be because of decisions you and your advisors have made in your life, not because of the government.

What do we mean by this? In Appendix C we go through the following scenarios:

- Individual with $1,250,000 in net worth who desires $50,000 in income and pays $0 in taxes
- Individual with $2,300,000 in net worth who desires $90,000 in income and pays $0 in taxes
- Individual with $4,500,000 in net worth who desires $180,000 in income and pays $0 in taxes

No scenario will be exactly like your situation, but they help illustrate the power of these ideas. Please also turn to Appendix C for a more in-depth discussion of this strategy and the assumptions made above.[12]

FROM $3,000 TO $10,000: THE MAGICAL AND FRUSTRATING RANGE, REGARDLESS OF YOUR NET WORTH

Jaramee Finn, CPA, CFP®, and a debt expert, came up with this example of how the strategic use of debt can work for the average person.

Joe, age 67 and single, has recently retired from XYZ Corporation after 40 years on the manufacturing line. Joe saved into his 401(k) over the years and has a balance of $500,000. He's paid off his $300,000 house, so he's debt free. He has $50,000 in his checking account but no other investable assets. Therefore, Joe's net worth is $850,000.

Joe is excited about retirement. He worked very hard and will earn $20,000 a year as a pension from XYZ and $20,000 a year in Social Security benefits. He's looking forward to a simple life of fishing and playing with his grandkids. He engages me as a financial advisor for his retirement. (This happens *all the time*! So many clients have come to me in retirement, and then it's almost too late! I would have loved to help Joe with cash and debt management in his working years.)

After talking to Joe, I recommend that he roll his 401(k) to me to be put in an IRA, which I would invest appropriately. There's not much else I could advise him on! If he took a 4 percent draw from his IRA ($500,000 × 4% = $20,000), this would give him a cash flow of $60,000 per year when you add his pension and Social Security.

Because Joe paid off his house, he doesn't have the mortgage interest deduction, which is what pushes most people over the threshold from standard deduction to itemized deduction and helps me control their taxes. Basically, I can manage Joe's $500,000 IRA but I cannot help him manage his taxes and cash flow.

Now let's talk about Dan. Dan is a personal friend, and I encouraged him to think more holistically about his finances over the years. I encouraged him not to be afraid of debt and to make sure he was building taxable investment accounts—not just his 401(k).

Dan is also age 67, single, and has recently retired from XYZ Corporation after many years on the manufacturing line. Dan saved into his 401(k) over the years and has a 401(k) balance of $300,000. He also lives in a $300,000 house but has a $240,000 mortgage on the property that is at 6 percent and is 15-year amortizing. He has $50,000 in his checking account and has saved $440,000 into a separate investment account. Dan's assets are $1,090,000, and his liabilities are $240,000, so his net worth is $850,000—the same as Joe's.

Dan is my dream client! I can do so much to help his cash flow and tax situation. First of all, I'll look at Dan's mortgage. His monthly payment is $2,025. I would recommend a 3 percent interest-only mortgage that would drop his payment to $600 per month. This move alone saves Dan more than $1,400 per month! That's a great increase in cash flow and a true value-added service from a holistic financial advisor!

Next we can do a tax analysis. We can assume Joe's and Dan's tax deductions are the same, except for Dan's mortgage-interest deduction that I have updated for the 3 percent interest-only loan I recommended.

Social Security and pension are the same for both men. Joe takes a 4 percent draw from his IRA ($20,000) for a total of $60,000 income. Dan takes a 4 percent draw from his IRA ($12,000) and a 4 percent draw from his portfolio ($17,600). Because I invested Dan's taxable investment portfolio in a tax-efficient index fund, he is only taxed at about a 2 percent dividend rate on that portfolio, not the actual amount he draws.

Using the strategy outlined Joe is paying annual taxes of $6,275, which is about 10 percent of his gross income. Dan, on the other hand, is paying annual taxes of $3,525, which is only 5 percent of his gross income. (You can find the detailed calculations on our website, www.valueofdebtinretirement.com or www.vodr.com.)

The difference in Dan's pocket every month that Joe is sending to Uncle Sam is $229. Even after Dan pays his mortgage interest his cash flow is greater than Joe's by $429 a month. That's a lot of money that many retired people would be happy to keep in their own pockets. For two men with the same net worth, same pension, and same Social Security, the monthly difference is $429—just by embracing the power of debt.

No matter how I ran the numbers for Joe, I could not get his taxes down. He's a very typical American in retirement: house paid for, pension, Social Security, a tax-deferred account and very little in a taxable savings account. On the other hand, Fred (another fellow on our team) can run scenarios with clients who have millions and pay less than 2 percent in taxes. Seems like something's wrong with the system, but we can't hate the players—we can only hate the game. Let's teach more regular people how to play the game.

Everyday Example #5: "Auto" You Not Be Sure You Are Getting the Best Loan?

When someone is approaching or already in retirement it becomes very clear that what makes him happy—what really turns him on—is his somewhat expensive hobby, which might be owning and racing sports cars, sailboats, or thoroughbred horses, or traveling extensively in a recreational vehicle. Everyday Example #5 considers the best way to pay for such rewarding, though admittedly expensive hobbies.

EVERYDAY EXAMPLE #5: "AUTO" YOU NOT BE SURE YOU ARE GETTING THE BEST LOAN?

Danny Driver, five or so years from retirement, is a fairly successful but not incredibly wealthy entrepreneur who has made good money in the software industry. He has always wanted to travel around the country in a recreational vehicle (RV).

Danny always scans the classifieds and has just spotted a RV that he has always wanted and can "steal" for only $100,000.

One option is for Danny to get a "car loan" from a bank that specializes in recreational vehicles. Danny is offered the loan at 6 percent. Of course, the loan will amortize—always requiring a monthly payment—with the entirety of the remaining principle due at the end of five years. Danny's monthly payment would be $1,933.

Danny realizes that the $600,000 of taxable investments he has with his brokerage firm gives him access to an assets-based loan at only 3 percent, that is, $3,000 a year of interest. Critically, the loan will *not* amortize, so if Danny has a slow month or two, he will not be required to make any payments. His monthly payment is $250 per month. His required payment is $0. Danny can do 100 percent financing and pay down any amount any time he wants to.

Bottom line: By eschewing the idea of a "specialty car loan," Danny can make use of both sides of his balance sheet and find a much better, low-cost, nonamortizable way of getting the RV he really wants.

"Auto" you look into similar financing for the things and hobbies that will make you happiest, whether before or after retirement? As you will see in Guide 2, these ideas apply to most any type of loan, whether for a car, boat, or horse.[13]

This chapter illustrated a beautiful and elegant combination of borrowing and selling that can, in retirement, produce incredibly tax-efficient streams of incoming money. It's hard for many people—especially professional financial advisors—to see and understand this combination, because most people have been indoctrinated by the "debt is always evil" mantra. I hope you are feeling a bit more empowered to have good conversations with your advisors about these strategies, and, most importantly, I hope I've encouraged everyone to Stop Guessing With Your Money™!

AHAs! ADVISOR HIGHLIGHT ANSWERS

Question #1: If I am reading this correctly, this has vast implications on Roth versus traditional IRAs and the impact of other sources of income in retirement. Is that true?

Answer #1: *Yes!* A detailed understanding of distribution strategies has vast implications on assumptions with respect to Roth and traditional IRAs as well as assumptions with respect to other sources of ordinary income such as proceeds from an annuity.

I would encourage you to start by recognizing that many of the traditional assumptions and "rules of thumb" that the industry uses regularly are in fact mathematically backward. Many advisors incorrectly assume that because their client is in a high tax bracket while working that they will be in a high tax bracket when they retire. As we saw with the Websters, that assumption simply isn't true. Their tax rate in retirement was much, much lower than it was when they were working.

I'd turn the question back to you. With the Websters' scenario in mind, who should contribute to a Roth and why? Knowing that the tax code can (and most likely will) change, under what scenario would a Roth be better than a traditional IRA?

Question # 2: I understand the general points that this chapter is making, and even the math, but isn't it true that numbers, tax calculators, and spreadsheets can be made to show anything you want them to?

Answer #2: While the saying "lies, damn lies, and statistics" is widely known, we believe the examples in this chapter are realistic with regard to what individuals and families can expect to experience based on whether they do, or do not, embrace strategic debt philosophy and practice. For example, all of the inputs, costs, and so on in the Websters' story are realistic and point to the incontrovertible assertion that a family worth millions of dollars and receiving up to $240,000 of incoming money a year, by taking advantage of the hybrid borrow-and-sell strategy outlined here, can pay less than $4,000 of income taxes a year. It may be a "made-up fact," but it is still a fact. Similarly, there is little doubt that using one's line of credit to retire high-priced debt for low-priced debt and paying for important purchases can add to the bottom lines of liquidity, flexibility, and net worth in the long run. To get more into the details I strongly encourage you to visit Appendix C.

Question #3: How did you figure this stuff out, and how do I learn more?

Answer #3: I think you could get away with being an average advisor even five years ago. Not anymore. Technology is catching up and getting better. Fees are falling. Clients want independent, low-cost advice. They want to pay for things that really add value and don't want to pay for commodity products that should be nearly free. I think if you want to add value, you have to master concepts like this and mastering a subject is never easy. It takes a lot—a whole lot—of time, energy, and effort. I suggest you start by running between 100 and 500 tax scenarios. Eventually it becomes like the movie *The Matrix*. You can almost "see" the code.[14]

Notes

1. *The American Heritage® Dictionary of the English Language,* 4th ed., © 2000 by Houghton Mifflin Company, updated 2009, published by Houghton Mifflin Company. All rights reserved.
2. See www.investinganswers.com/financial-dictionary/investing/synergy-1633.
3. Mark Singer, *The Six Secrets to a Happy Retirement: How to Master the Transition of a Lifetime* (Medford, MA: ATA Press, 2013), 15.
4. www.cnn.com/2012/09/24/opinion/mccaffery-romney-tax.
5. www.cnn.com/2013/04/09/opinion/mccaffery-zuckerberg-taxes.
6. www.bloomberg.com/news/print/2014-09-04/almost-half-of-government-bonds-yield-less-than-1-bofa-says.html.
7. http://online.wsj.com/mcd/public/page/2_3002-peyield.html.
8. As discussed in detail throughout the book, the standard "safe" figure for the percentage of a distribution is 4 percent. In the Webster's case, 4 percent of $2,000,000 is $80,000.
9. Note that although input of other income totals to $160,000, it only shows up here as $157,000 of total income because of some intricacies having to do with Social Security phase-outs.
10. See www.irs.gov.
11. Please see Appendix C for additional details.
12. Tax laws are complex and subject to change. Tax information contained in this presentation is general and not exhaustive by nature. It is not intended or written to be used, and cannot be used, by any taxpayer for the purpose of avoiding U.S. federal tax laws. This material was not intended or written to be used for the purpose of avoiding tax penalties that may be imposed on the taxpayer. Individuals are encouraged to consult their tax and legal advisors (a) before establishing a retirement plan or account, and (b) regarding any potential tax, ERISA, and related consequences of any investments made under such plan or account. These materials and any statement contained herein should not be construed as tax or legal advice. Tax advice must come from your tax advisor.

People argue with us all of the time that you should slam all of your money into a tax-deductible IRA versus a taxable investment account. And we completely agree with that fact that it takes $1,389 to invest $1,000 after tax (assuming 28 percent tax bracket) and dollar for dollar $1,389 will grow to be more than $1,000 all other things equal. But we also see all of the time people who have no liquidity and flexibility to weather hard times when all of their money is tied up in a tax-deferred account. We are suggesting a balanced and holistic approach. We also know it is impossible to know what your tax rates are going to be in retirement and many times they are significantly less than your taxes in the working years.

You will see that in our tax scenarios we generally assume the investment management fees are paid from the taxable account, and we deduct them. You should read this great article and notes about deducting IRA investment fees and discuss the various strategies with your financial advisor and CPA. See www.kitces.com/blog/irs-rules-for-paying-investment-fees-from-taxable-and-retirement-accounts/.

13. Case studies are for educational and illustrative purposes only. They assume eligible assets and that funds are available on the facility. All client situations are unique, and all loans are subject to eligibility and approval by the lender. A lender may deny an advance on an ABLF, preventing the scenarios. Pledging assets reduces and may eliminate liquidity. A market correction could impact market values and/or security eligibility, which could impact the facility size and/or trigger a margin call and/or forced liquidations of assets. See complete disclosures and risks to using an ABLF in Appendix F.

14. Author's Note: The information in this chapter is to be considered in a holistic way as a part of the book and not to be considered on a stand-alone basis. This includes, but is not limited to, the discussion of risks of each of these ideas as well as all of the disclaimers throughout the book. The material is presented with a goal of encouraging thoughtful conversation and rigorous debate on the risks and potential benefits of the concepts between you and your advisors based on your unique situation, risk tolerance, and goals.

Chapter 6

Risk Matters More Than Return

Wherever there is danger, there lurks opportunity; wherever there is opportunity, there lurks danger. The two are inseparable.

—Earl Nightingale

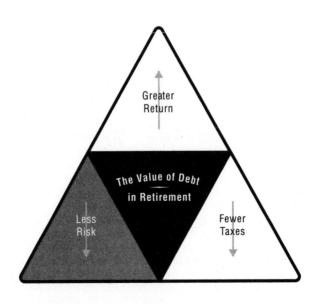

The relationship between risk and reward is extraordinarily pervasive—you find it not just in the financial arena but also everywhere from management philosophy to professional athletics to personal-growth seminars. You find it in the second-century Jewish ethics teaching book known as the *Pirkei Avot,* or *The Ethics of the Father:*

Rabbi Ben Hei says, "According to the pain is the gain."

You find it in the Robert Herrick's 1650 poem *Hesperides:*

If little labour, little are our gains; Man's fate is according to his pains.

And you find it being echoed by classic American figures, from founding father Benjamin Franklin ("there are no gains, without pains") to the founding father of Facebook, Mark Zuckerberg ("the biggest risk is not taking any risk").

That risk and reward are inextricably related cannot be doubted. What can be doubted and expanded upon is the best way of approaching risk, especially in the financial domain and certainly with regard to retirement. While more reward seems to necessitate more risk, *there is not always a lockstep relationship between the two*. It can take very little additional risk to get a great deal more reward, and in some cases you can get more reward with *less* risk.

As we've seen, the antidebt ideology that dominates most discourse on investing and retirement—that debt, any debt, is so innately highly risky and dangerous that no rewards could ever justify taking it on in the first place—prevents thoughtful conversation about risk and reward as seen through the eyes of strategic debt philosophy and practice.

This section will fundamentally change the way that you invest throughout retirement and for the rest of your life. We have to do a little math. I'll make it approachable. See Appendix D to dive in to the nitty-gritty.

Why Your Personal Risk Tolerance May Not Matter

In investing, what is comfortable is rarely profitable.

—Robert Arnot

You read that headline right. Your risk tolerance, as traditionally labeled in the financial services industry, may not matter. Let me explain. If you work with a financial advisor, you may have already been given a questionnaire to help determine your "risk tolerance," which in turn helps determine how risky to get with your investments. Risk tolerance is defined by Investopedia.com as:

> The degree of variability in investment returns that an individual is willing to withstand. Risk tolerance is an important component in investing. An individual should have a realistic understanding of his or her ability and willingness to stomach large swings in the value of his or her investments. Investors who take on too much risk may panic and sell at the wrong time.[1]

Most books on investing will tell you that risk tolerance is at the very heart of asset allocation. Consider the following passage from *The Winner's Circle: Asset Allocation Strategies from America's Best Financial Advisors*:

> Both mathematically and practically, risk tolerance and associated topics are at the heart of asset allocation and modern portfolio theory. The whole point of diversifying a portfolio (by including less than perfectly correlated assets) is to reduce risk, measured as volatility, without greatly diminishing return. Put differently, the whole point is for an investor to take on no more than an acceptable amount of risk while still maximizing return. Two questions arise: What is an acceptable amount of risk for an investor, and how can an advisor work with clients to help them understand and identify their true risk tolerance?[2]

The standard story is that some people can handle slight or large downturns in the worth of their portfolio while others who simply can't might panic and make terrible real-time decisions that will haunt them forever. These are the people who sold some or the bulk of their investments right after the steepest declines during the Great Recession, who are kicking themselves today as, sure enough, those investments have surpassed their previous highs. Now they're stuck wondering if they should buy back in. Or worse, they just dive right back in. I see people buy at 1,400 on the S&P, sell at 900, buy back in at 1,600. Buy and hold would have had a return of 15 percent. The "trader" had a return of negative 35 percent. This happens all the time!

I understand the value of this traditional take on risk tolerance and the great lengths that some advisors and clients take to figure out the clients' risk tolerance. But I think the industry is doing it backwards, focusing on risk and then needs. I propose focusing on your needs and letting your needs determine your risk.

> Focus on your needs and then focus on your risk.

If you know your goals, your budget, and how much income you will need during retirement, then you should structure your personal financial life in the least risky way to return that objective . . . regardless of your risk tolerance. Your risk tolerance is a function of your needs, not a function of your personality. Your needs should dictate your risk tolerance.

> Your portfolio should be allocated as a function of your needs, not as a function of your personality. Your needs dictate your risk tolerance.

When people are young and accumulating assets, this notion may or may not be as true. When you're closer to retirement, or already retired, it is surely most important to consider. If you need a 4 percent average return on your investment portfolio to make it through retirement comfortably, you should invest your money to return that 4 percent . . . regardless of your risk tolerance. The only other alternative is to change your needs and structure your life in the least risky way to achieve that objective. You need the money, so you pretty much have to take the risk. Put differently, *your goals, and what you need to do to achieve them, outweigh any conversation or considerations about your risk tolerance.*

This practice is common in medicine. If I walk into a doctor's office and complain about chest pain, the doctor doesn't start by asking me about my tolerance for pain. She determines the problem and prescribes a solution. I may need a pill, a moderately invasive procedure, or my chest cracked open. My tolerance for pain is not a factor in their diagnosis and prognosis. The financial services industry needs to start thinking the same way.

Of course, everyone would prefer to not take risk. But in life and in investing, it turns out that most of us have to take risk. In today's environment, cash pays you zero. So unless you have all the money, adjusted for inflation, that you will need for the rest of your life, you have to take risk. I always suggest that when facing two risks, you take the least risky path.

> If your needs go down, your risk can go down. If your needs rise, you may need to take more risk to achieve that objective.

A Simple Understanding of Risk

What exactly do we mean by risk? In the world of investing, risk is usually measured in terms of "standard deviation," which in turn is calculated as the square root of "variance." Investopedia.com explains standard deviation as:

> Standard deviation is a statistical measurement that sheds light on historical volatility. . . . A large dispersion tells us how much the return on the fund is deviating from the expected normal returns.[3]

To illustrate, let me ask you this: How long does it take to drive from Los Angeles to San Diego? I could give you a single-figure answer, but the correct answer will depend on traffic, time of day, weather, and so on. If I gave you a single number, you wouldn't be able to tell if I were being optimistic or pessimistic.

A better way to answer would be: It usually takes about two hours and 30 minutes with a standard deviation of 30 minutes, which means roughly two-thirds of the time it should take you between two and three hours. Approximately 95 percent of the time, the trip will take between an hour and 30 minutes and three hours and 30 minutes. If it takes you longer than three and a half hours, something went really wrong, and if it takes you less than an hour and a half, you were driving way too fast.

My wife often asks me what time I'll be home. It's a normal question, and I understand why she wants to know, but it's often hard to predict. If I say 6:00, and I'm there at 6:05, I'm late. At 6:10, she's getting disappointed (or mad!). But we all get curve balls on a regular basis. A better answer would be, "6:00 with a standard deviation of 10," which means I'm pretty sure 5:50 to 6:10. It could be 5:40, but not likely to be any earlier; could be 6:20 but unlikely to be later than that. Communicating in standard deviation terms may sound dorky, but the information is much more helpful for the recipient.

Fortunately for investors, computers and professionals use sophisticated tools to determine the risk of different investments. Many of these systems, however, have problems, including their historic perspective on risk. Risk in the past may or may not be a reflection of future risk.

For now, let's make the crazy assumption that you could know the future risk of an asset in which you're invested. How would you use—and more importantly how could you benefit from—this information? I'm about to prove that you would most certainly accept a lower rate of return in retirement if it came with a lower risk. "Lower" meaning compared to investments that typically have higher risk and higher returns, such as an all-equity portfolio. In fact, I will prove that risk is equally important to—if not more important than—return–in retirement.

All things being equal, you don't want to invest in anything that's very risky. But again, *you might not have that option,* depending on your goals and the average return you need from your portfolio. And you might not want to watch your investments go up and down over time, but they will, and therefore it's critically important for you to understand the "sequence of returns."

The Odds of a 6 Percent Rate of Return over the Next 30 Years Are Exactly Zero

Let's say the best average return you can hope for on your investments these days is 6 percent. It can be any number you think you can reasonably obtain, but for this example I'll use 6 percent. This leads to my favorite trick question, "What are the odds of an exact 6 percent return over the next 30 years?" The answer to the trick question is "0."

The odds of a 6 percent rate of return for the next 30 years are zero.

To understand this, think about flipping a quarter. If you flip a quarter once, the odds of heads are 50 percent. If you flip a quarter twice, the odds of heads are 25 percent. The odds of heads three times in a row are 12.5 percent. The odds of heads 25 times in a row are close to zero.

It's theoretically possible that a given stock or portfolio of investments will average 6.0 percent return exactly on a given date, but extraordinarily unlikely. Unlike quarter flipping, which can have only two outcomes, investments offer many, and each one brings the odds of an exact 6.000 percent rate of return quickly toward zero. There will be times when a portfolio is above 6 percent and times when it will be below it. The critical factor is the risk measured in terms of standard deviation—that is, how much above or below that 6 percent figure it's likely to go at any given point in time.

Even If You Know Your Average Rate of Return, It's Impossible to Know Your Future Net Worth

Here's the most important point: Even if you are fairly confident that over time your well-diversified investments will average a 6 percent return, you could run out of money if they go down before they go up. A portfolio designed to produce higher returns is inherently riskier (meaning it will have more variance and a higher standard deviation), and the problem with that is that low or negative returns on the front end could easily cause you to run out of money during retirement.

That brings us to one of the most important concepts in this book: understanding the importance of your sequence of returns.

While Risk Tolerance May Not Matter, the Sequence of Returns Does

Okay, so you're never going to get an exact 6 percent rate of return on your investments over time. But if I told you that you will average a 6.0 percent rate of return—we seemingly can now magically know the unknowable—what inflation-adjusted income stream can you take from that portfolio?

Inflation-rate thinking is important—and impossible to know. But let's keep up the make-believe and say that we know that it will be a straight 3.0 percent per year (which is of course virtually impossible). If your portfolio averages 6.0 percent and inflation is a straight 3.0 percent, what inflation-adjusted income stream can you take out of the portfolio and not run out of money before you die?

Although we want to think 3 percent (6 percent return − 3 percent inflation = 3 percent), it turns out that is not the right answer. We still cannot answer the question because we do not know the sequence of returns. We don't know how we got to the averages.

> No person or computer can answer the following simple question: If your portfolio averages 6.0 percent and inflation is exactly 3 percent per year forever, what income stream can you take from that portfolio and not run out of money before you die?

It's like a man who has his head in an oven and his feet in a bucket of ice water. His body temperature is exactly average, yet he's not in good shape. The sequence of returns—the order in which you receive your returns—is an equally if not more important factor in determining your ultimate net worth in retirement. If somebody says they don't care about risk during the accumulation phase, you can't argue with them, but *when distributions start from a portfolio, risk is equally important as return over time.* Let's see why.

> In retirement, risk is equally important to return!

For the two types of people—those who want to know what time it is and those who want to know how the watch works—I'll explain this two ways.

An Overview: "What Time Is It?"

Equations 6.1 and 6.2 demonstrate that any way that you multiply a series of numbers you get to the same ending number.

Equation 6.1	Equation 6.2
3	4
× 4	× 2
12	8
× 2	× 3
24	**24**

Some people use this to suggest that while you're saving, risk doesn't really matter. We could argue about this from a big-picture perspective (it is my fundamental belief that risk always matters), but conceptually the simple math is true: any way you multiply a series of numbers you get to the same end result.

This is not true when you introduce subtraction into your formula. Equations 6.3 and 6.4 demonstrate what happens if we insert "–2" into the series above.

Equation 6.3	Equation 6.4
3	4
× 4	× 2
12	8
× 2	–2
24	6
–2	× 3
22	**18**

If we change the order just a little, we get a very different result! This phenomenon is what is most important to you in retirement. Most people focus on return and say things like, "What is the rate of return on my portfolio?" There needs to be an equal—and perhaps greater—focus on risk.

Let's say you start retirement with $1 million and know that you will have an average return of 9.5 percent per year for 25 years—not too shabby!

But you're taking out $60,000 per year (a 6 percent distribution) and will need to increase that amount by 2.5 percent per year to adjust for inflation. Even knowing your exact average rate of return, exact number of inflation, and exact amount of distributions, it's still impossible to know what your final net worth would be because *we don't know your sequence of returns.*

> Knowing your exact average rate of return, exact rate of inflation, and exact amount of distributions, it's still impossible to know what your final net worth would be because we don't know your sequence of returns.

In the next section of this chapter, we show that on the one hand you could take out more than $2 million in income over 25 years and have a final net worth of more than $5 million. Or you could end up dead broke in just 18 years! Same person, same distributions, same average returns—just a different sequence of returns.

These figures are not the extremes either. You could have run out of money earlier or died with a far larger fortune; it's impossible to know because your portfolio's standard deviation—its risk—has a greater impact than virtually anything else.

Or let's say you start with $1 million and get an average return of 7.5 percent (much *lower* than your friend who brags about 10 percent). You too take out $60,000 per year and will need to increase it by 2.5 percent per year to adjust for inflation.

We will illustrate that in the lower risk portfolio, regardless if you had the the "good" or "bad" return series, you would take out more than $2 million in income and die with money passing on to your heirs. You don't run out of money! The difference is that your portfolio has much less risk!

The sequence of returns may, in fact, be the most important part of your financial life. But this does raise a question: What on earth does this concept have to do with debt? There are two answers to this: nothing and everything. For the nothing answer, *the importance of sequence of returns is true and is important with or without debt.* You can throw out all my ideas about debt, but I hope you'll remember this and target a portfolio with more consistent returns rather than a portfolio that targets large returns and large risk.

What about with respect to debt? Remember that Chapter 4 made two key points that are relevant here.

PRINCIPLE #1:

Everything else being equal, a lower-volatility portfolio with debt is better than a high-volatility portfolio with no debt.

Similarly, a portfolio with no debt may actually be taking on more risk than a portfolio with debt yet achieves the same result.

PRINCIPLE #2:

There are two ways to get to a 9 percent rate of return. Way number one is to invest in assets that pay 9 percent. Way number two is to leverage investments that pay 6 percent.

Mathematically it is possible that a lower-returning but lower-risk portfolio with debt can get better results than a higher-risk portfolio without debt—meaning there's a greater likelihood that you won't run out of money in retirement and have a greater legacy to pass on to your heirs.

In fact, it is mathematically possible that a strategic debt philosophy can increase the chances that you will not run out of money from 20 percent to 100 percent—and more!

The details are a bit complicated so if you don't like numbers, fast forward to page 105, "Proof That Debt Can Reduce Your Risk in Retirement." If you like numbers, I'll demonstrate some amazing things about risk, retirement, and the role debt may play.

A Detailed Understanding: "How the Watch Works"

I don't know the future. Nobody does. Now that you're expertly trained in statistics, you and I both know there's a *100 percent chance* that your life, no matter what you invest in, will not look like any of the scenarios we are about to go through. These figures do not represent any historic investment nor do they represent any future investment. I'm simply illustrating math.

So, let's look at the numbers. You start with $1 million and get a 9.55 percent average annualized rate of return and a standard deviation of 19.9. (Ironically, these figures happen to be close to long-term averages of risk and return for the S&P 500. Which is not to imply, predict, or project that past performance will repeat![4]) Table 6.1 shows the impact of accumulating assets at these hypothetical rates of return.

Table 6.1   Sequence of Returns in Accumulation

$1,000,000 Beginning Balance—No Distributions

Year	Return	Ending Balance
1	11.2%	$ 1,112,445
2	54.0%	1,713,164
3	35.2%	2,315,352
4	−1.4%	2,283,309
5	−28.3%	1,636,523
6	13.9%	1,863,448
7	16.9%	2,178,973
8	18.2%	2,575,460
9	40.3%	3,614,399
10	9.2%	3,946,314
11	13.9%	4,495,597
12	19.0%	5,350,854
13	29.2%	6,913,242
14	28.2%	8,863,786
15	−18.5%	7,223,396
16	34.8%	9,733,555
17	12.2%	10,924,413
18	0.4%	10,964,459
19	−11.1%	9,744,945
20	−4.0%	9,350,833
21	7.7%	10,066,432

Year	Return	Ending Balance
22	19.4%	12,017,361
23	−0.9%	11,906,373
24	−23.9%	9,064,434
25	7.8%	**$ 9,768,949**
Average Annual Return	**9.5%**	
Standard Deviation	**19.9**	

Not too shabby. One million dollars grew to $9.77 million. Table 6.2 shows the results if they had the series in reverse.

We get the same answer of $9.77 million! Why is this? Because as we previously discussed: 3 × 4 = 12 and 4 × 3 = 12. Simple math. We can interpret this to mean that on the surface it's hard to mathematically argue with anyone who says they don't care about risk during accumulation.

What about when we retire? Table 6.3 shows the results if you take $60,000 a year out of the portfolio and inflation adjust those distributions.

Here you look pretty good. You took out more than $2 million in income and still have over $5 million in your account. Table 6.4 shows what happens if you had the exact same return series, but in reverse.

Wait a second. Here we have exact same return, exact same risk, exact same distribution, but you ran out of money in year 18!! In fact, if your expenses continue to grow, the kids will have to support you with about $800,000. What happened?! When introducing a subtraction component—a withdrawal such as a distribution—risk becomes equally important as return in determining your ultimate net worth.

> When you introduce a subtraction component—a withdrawal such as a distribution—risk is equally as important as return in determining your ultimate net worth.

What could be an alternative? Table 6.5 shows us the results of a hypothetical portfolio that had a lower return and lower risk. Here we show a portfolio that averages 7.5 percent annually and has a standard deviation of 8.

Table 6.2   Sequence of Returns: Reverse Order

$1,000,000 Beginning Balance—No Distributions

Year	Return	Ending Balance
1	7.8%	$ 1,077,723
2	–23.9%	820,481
3	–0.9%	812,903
4	19.4%	970,448
5	7.7%	1,044,714
6	–4.0%	1,002,463
7	–11.1%	890,965
8	0.4%	894,231
9	12.2%	1,003,636
10	34.8%	1,352,404
11	–18.5%	1,102,119
12	28.2%	1,413,078
13	29.2%	1,825,680
14	19.0%	2,173,004
15	13.9%	2,475,462
16	9.2%	2,702,787
17	40.3%	3,793,090
18	18.2%	4,483,280
19	16.9%	5,242,405
20	13.9%	5,969,333
21	–28.3%	4,278,416
22	–1.4%	4,219,207
23	35.2%	5,702,285
24	54.0%	8,781,514
25	11.2%	**$9,768,949**
Average Annual Return	**9.5%**	
Standard Deviation	**19.9**	

Looking good with $2 million of income and $1.8 million left to heirs. Note that in the scenario shown on Table 6.3 you would have left $5 million to the kids and in the scenario on Table 6.5 you would leave $2 million to your heirs. A $3 million gap is significant, so perhaps you're feeling a little crabby about these ideas. But how do we know this is what your outcome would have been? Table 6.6 shows what would happen if you had *the same series,* in reverse.

You made it! It was close, but the point is that you made it all the way with both scenarios. Now it's only a question of how much you have left in the bank!

If I were a child (and aren't we all?), and my parents asked me to choose between these two scenarios, what do you think I would choose?

Table 6.3 Sequence of Returns: With Distributions

$1,000,000 Beginning Balance

Year	Return	Withdrawal	Ending Balance
1	11.2%	(60,000)	$1,052,445
2	54.0%	(61,500)	1,559,264
3	35.2%	(63,038)	2,044,318
4	−1.4%	(64,613)	1,951,413
5	−28.3%	(66,229)	1,332,413
6	13.9%	(67,884)	1,449,284
7	16.9%	(69,582)	1,625,101
8	18.2%	(71,321)	1,849,483
9	40.3%	(73,104)	2,522,460
10	9.2%	(74,932)	2,679,169
11	13.9%	(76,805)	2,975,274
12	19.0%	(78,725)	3,462,574
13	29.2%	(80,693)	4,392,914
14	28.2%	(82,711)	5,549,646
15	−18.5%	(84,778)	4,437,814
16	34.8%	(86,898)	5,893,074
17	12.2%	(89,070)	6,524,996
18	0.4%	(91,297)	6,457,618
19	−11.1%	(93,580)	5,645,795
20	−4.0%	(95,919)	5,321,544
21	7.7%	(98,317)	5,630,473
22	19.4%	(100,775)	6,620,915
23	−0.9%	(103,294)	6,456,472
24	−23.9%	(105,877)	4,809,496
25	7.8%	(108,524)	**$5,074,781**
Average Annual Return	**9.5%**	**Ending Value**	**$5,074,781**
Standard Deviation	**19.9**	**Total Income**	**$2,049,466**

- In scenario number one I could have inherited $5 million or had to help them by paying out $1,298,000.
- In scenario number two I receive between $2 million and $100,000.

Is this a trick question? I hope my parents are reading because I would choose the second scenario every time!

Table 6.4   Sequence of Returns: Withdrawal Reverse Order

$1,000,000 Beginning Balance

Year	Return	Withdrawal	Ending Balance
1	7.8%	(60,000)	$ 1,017,723
2	−23.9%	(61,500)	713,302
3	−0.9%	(63,038)	643,677
4	19.4%	(64,613)	703,811
5	7.7%	(66,229)	691,444
6	−4.0%	(67,884)	595,595
7	−11.1%	(69,582)	459,769
8	0.4%	(71,321)	390,133
9	12.2%	(73,104)	364,760
10	34.8%	(74,932)	416,584
11	−18.5%	(76,805)	262,683
12	28.2%	(78,725)	258,073
13	29.2%	(80,693)	252,734
14	19.0%	(82,711)	218,105
15	13.9%	(84,778)	163,684
16	9.2%	(86,898)	91,817
17	40.3%	(89,070)	39,786
18	18.2%	(91,297)	0
19	16.9%	(93,580)	0
20	13.9%	(95,919)	0
21	−28.3%	(98,317)	0
22	−1.4%	(100,775)	0
23	35.2%	(103,294)	0
24	54.0%	(105,877)	0
25	11.2%	(108,524)	$ 0
Average Annual Return	**9.5%**	**Ending Value**	$ 0
Standard Deviation	**19.9**	**Total Income**	**$1,291,669**

Table 6.5 Lower Volatility Portfolio with No Debt

$1,000,000 Beginning Balance

Year	Return	Withdrawal	Ending Balance
1	13.9%	(60,000)	$ 1,078,739
2	11.7%	(61,500)	1,142,986
3	12.9%	(63,038)	1,227,528
4	22.1%	(64,613)	1,434,689
5	0.6%	(66,229)	1,376,785
6	14.0%	(67,884)	1,501,926
7	−5.3%	(69,582)	1,352,291
8	14.5%	(71,321)	1,476,782
9	17.1%	(73,104)	1,655,678
10	7.8%	(74,932)	1,709,227
11	−1.1%	(76,805)	1,614,304
12	9.7%	(78,725)	1,692,428
13	7.7%	(80,693)	1,742,390
14	11.0%	(82,711)	1,850,820
15	−3.5%	(84,778)	1,702,188
16	6.8%	(86,898)	1,730,699
17	11.5%	(89,070)	1,841,307
18	14.3%	(91,297)	2,012,450
19	6.3%	(93,580)	2,044,969
20	9.9%	(95,919)	2,151,706
21	−16.1%	(98,317)	1,706,964
22	7.3%	(100,775)	1,730,943
23	6.7%	(103,294)	1,743,103
24	9.7%	(105,877)	1,805,471
25	5.5%	(108,524)	**$1,795,526**
Average Annual Return	**7.5%**	**Ending Value**	**$1,795,526**
Standard Deviation	**8.0**	**Total Income**	**$2,049,466**

Table 6.6   Lower Volatility with No Debt in Reverse

$1,000,000 Beginning Balance

Year	Return	Withdrawal	Ending Balance
1	5.5%	(60,000)	$ 994,600
2	9.7%	(61,500)	1,029,099
3	6.7%	(63,038)	1,034,703
4	7.3%	(64,613)	1,045,710
5	−16.1%	(66,229)	811,122
6	9.9%	(67,884)	823,620
7	6.3%	(69,582)	805,645
8	14.3%	(71,321)	849,153
9	11.5%	(73,104)	874,019
10	6.8%	(74,932)	858,346
11	−3.5%	(76,805)	751,928
12	11.0%	(78,725)	755,689
13	7.7%	(80,693)	731,335
14	9.7%	(82,711)	721,876
15	−1.1%	(84,778)	629,446
16	7.8%	(86,898)	591,393
17	17.1%	(89,070)	603,239
18	14.5%	(91,297)	599,291
19	−5.3%	(93,580)	473,769
20	14.0%	(95,919)	444,273
21	0.6%	(98,317)	348,534
22	22.1%	(100,775)	324,924
23	12.9%	(103,294)	263,583
24	11.7%	(105,877)	188,432
25	13.9%	(108,524)	$ 106,051
Average Annual Return	**7.5%**	**Ending Value**	**$ 106,051**
Standard Deviation	**8.0**	**Total Income**	**$2,049,466**

	High Return/High Risk		Lower Return/Lower Risk	
	Lucky Series	Unlucky	Lucky Series	Unlucky
Income	$2,049,466	$1,291,669	$2,049,466	$2,049,466
Ending Assets	$5,074,781	**RAN OUT!**	$1,795,526	$ 106,051

NOTE TO ENGINEERS AND STATISTICIANS

You could argue that statistically my selection above is suboptimal. It's possible that my expected return in the first scenario is higher but since nobody knows the real odds, it is impossible to know.

If your kids have an extra $1 million in the bank that they can't wait to use to support you in your old age, then perhaps you should play the odds. Maybe they fall in your favor and perhaps this stuff doesn't matter.

For most of the people I know, the thought of running out of money is a big deal. If you are in that camp then, you can clearly see that risk matters more than return in determining your ulti-mate net worth!

Proof That Debt Can Reduce Your Risk in Retirement

What about debt? Remember our key principal:

Everything else being equal, a lower-volatility portfolio with debt is better than a high-volatility portfolio with no debt.

We know from Chapter 4 that it is a mathematical fact that if you earn a constant rate of return higher than your after-tax cost of debt, you will earn a higher rate of return overall. In Appendix D we run multiple sce-narios and illustrate the Power of Debt and the Value of Debt®. We present the details there for those who like to see them, but here is the overview: You will see that applying a debt ratio of 33 percent (less than Warren Buffett!), you may considerably increase your likelihood of success.

Let's revisit the Trinity table, this time using debt (see Table 6.7) and also updated numbers through the end of 2013.[5] See Appendix D for our study results in greater detail and look at several different portfolio allocations.

Notice the mathematical proof that the greater your need, the greater your probability of success using debt. Notice as well that a 50/50 stock and bond portfolio with debt tests significantly higher than a 75 percent stock/25 percent bond portfolio without debt. In fact, if you need a rate of return over 5 percent, the strategic use of debt has a high probability of increasing the chances that you will not run out of money.

Whew—we can all rest easy now. Apparently an updated version of the Trinity study makes this debt thing a slam-dunk and a piece of cake!

Caution! If you have a bad sequence of returns, debt can absolutely increase your risk. In fact, even in a low-risk portfolio,[6] if you had most of the bad numbers first, such as the 1946 retiree, you would in fact run

Table 6.7   Our Updated Version of the Trinity Study Summary Table: Probability of Success of Different Distribution Rates over a 30-Year Period, with and without Debt: 1946–2013

Annualized Withdrawal Rate as a % of Initial Portfolio Value									
Payout Period	**3%**	**4%**	**5%**	**6%**	**7%**	**8%**	**9%**	**10%**	**11%**	**12%**
75% stocks/25% bonds										
Without debt	100	95	69	54	46	41	28	18	3	0
With debt	100	100	87	72	59	54	51	44	41	38
50% stocks/50% bonds										
Without debt	100	87	56	46	33	15	13	3	3	0
With debt	100	95	77	59	51	46	38	28	23	18
25% stocks/75% bonds										
Without debt	100	72	31	18	15	13	8	3	0	0
With debt	100	79	54	36	21	15	13	13	10	10

Note: This is not the Trinity Study's exact numbers, but our version of their methodology and updated through 2013.

out of money in year 23 with debt and run of money in year 29 without debt. In this case, debt destroyed value. It made you run out of money faster!

Wait a second. Isn't this supposed to be about the value of debt? Remember that debt is never good or bad; all that debt does is magnify your decisions. If you make bad decisions then they will be much worse with debt. If you make good decisions, then they will look better. The takeaway then has nothing to do with the risk of debt. The takeaway should be that—with or without debt—you cannot afford the risk of a major decline in value or a long period of flat returns early in your retirement. This creates a great segue to the risks of these strategies.

Everyday Example #6: A Lot to Think About? Not Really

EVERYDAY EXAMPLE #6: TAKING BIG ADVANTAGE OF A HOUSING OPPORTUNITY

Peter and Penny are approaching retirement and want to both downsize and build their dream retirement home in three years. They found the perfect lot for $100,000.

Fortunately, Peter and Penny have a $500,000 portfolio that was already set up as collateral, establishing a securities-based line of credit. They can use their line to act instantly without disrupting their investment portfolio, selling their investments, or accruing any tax consequences.

Peter and Penny are thrilled, because it will cost them only $250 per month ($100,000 x 3% = $3,000; $3,000/12 = $250/month) to pay for the lot. When they sell their current house, they anticipate they will have enough equity and plenty of money to pay off the line of credit, build their dream home, and perhaps have extra for their portfolio.

Their biggest decision will be whether to get a mortgage on their new house or pay cash.[7]

"What is my return?" Financial advisors hear this question again and again because that's what people have been trained to watch. Regardless of your debt philosophy, I think we just proved that "what is my return?" might not be the most important question in determining whether you're on track for a successful retirement. It may be possible to create a lower risk—a more certain outcome—by using a combination of debt and a lower-volatility portfolio.

AHAs! ADVISOR HIGHLIGHT ANSWERS

Question #1: What is the right trade-off between risk and return, and what is the right leverage ratio to have the best outcome?

Answer #1: This is a very important question. It is perhaps the most important question. I generally outline a range of 15 percent to 35 percent adjusted up and down for your risk tolerance and cost of distress. This is a nice guideline, and we can make it better. What you really want to consider is the debt ratio relative to the standard deviation of the portfolio. What I mean by this is that you may want to consider having more debt if the portfolio has a lower standard deviation and less debt if the portfolio has a higher standard deviation.

It is of course impossible to know future risk—future standard deviations—just as it is impossible to know future returns. My macro theme is that when you are in retirement, you would take a 20 percent reduction in return for a 50 percent reduction in risk all day long.

My other theme is that if it were possible—and I am not saying that it is—to have a portfolio with a standard deviation of 8 with an expected return of 8, then a portfolio with those characteristics is much better suited to support a debt ratio up to 35 percent than a portfolio that has an expected return of 10 and a standard deviation of 20.

The key theme is that according to Modern Portfolio Theory, Figure 6.1, the trade-off in risk for the trade-off in return is not a linear relationship of 1:1. This is an essential point in developing your overall debt strategy![8]

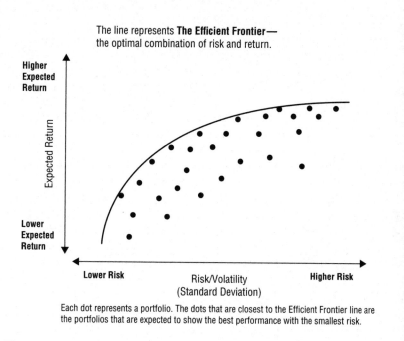

The line represents **The Efficient Frontier—** the optimal combination of risk and return.

Higher
Expected
Return

Expected Return

Lower
Expected
Return

Lower Risk

Risk/Volatility
(Standard Deviation)

Higher Risk

Each dot represents a portfolio. The dots that are closest to the Efficient Frontier line are the portfolios that are expected to show the best performance with the smallest risk.

Figure 6.1 Modern Portfolio Theory, the Efficient Frontier

Notes

1. http://investopedia.com/terms/r/risktolerance.asp.
2. An excellent review of Modern Portfolio Theory, asset allocation, and diversification strategies can be found in R. J. Shook's *The Winner's Circle: Asset Allocation Strategies from America's Best Financial Advisors* (Hammond, IN: Horizon Publishers Group, 2006).
3. http://investopedia.com/terms/s/standarddeviation.asp.
4. According to NYU's Stern School of Business, the geometric average is 9.55 percent for 1928 to 2013 and the arithmetic average is 11.50 percent over the same period. The difference between the two is not the point of this discussion but, for those who are curious, see http://pages.stern.nyu.edu/~adamodar/ New_Home_Page/datafile/histretSP.html.
5. The Trinity Study used the monthly returns of the Salomon Brothers Long-Term High-Grade Corporate Bond Index, as well as the Standard & Poor's monthly high-grade corporate composite yield date. For my table, I have chosen to use the 10-year U.S. Treasury Bond historic returns. See Appendix D for details.

6. One hundred percent bond portfolio tested at a 3 percent distribution rate to represent the low-risk portfolio.

7. Case studies are for educational and illustrative purposes only. They assume eligible assets and that funds are available on the facility. All client situations are unique, and all loans are subject to eligibility and approval by the lender. A lender may deny an advance on an ABLF, preventing the scenarios. Pledging assets reduces and may eliminate liquidity. A market correction could impact market values and/or security eligibility, which could impact the facility size and/or trigger a margin call and/or forced liquidations of assets. See complete disclosures and risks to using an ABLF in Appendix F.

8. Author's Note: The information in this chapter is to be considered in a holistic way as a part of the book and not to be considered on a stand-alone basis. This includes, but is not limited to, the discussion of risks of each of these ideas as well as all of the disclaimers throughout the book. The material is presented with a goal of encouraging thoughtful conversation and rigorous debate on the risks and potential benefits of the concepts between you and your advisors based on your unique situation, risk tolerance, and goals.

Part III

HOW TO GET THERE: A GLIDE PATH

Preparation for old age should not begin later than one's teens. A life which is empty of purpose until 65 will not suddenly become filled on retirement.

—Dwight L. Moody

Chapter 7

The World Is Full of Risk—Especially Now

Trying to predict the future is like trying to drive down a country road at night with no lights while looking out the back window.

—Peter Drucker

I n Appendix C of *The Value of Debt*, I wrote:

We live in a radically indeterminate world. Not only do we not know what will happen next, in principle—according to modern physics—we cannot know what will happen next. *This is true whether we are walking down the street or investing our hard-earned money for retirement.*[1]

Many of us feel uncertain about the future of our investments and our economic situation, and that makes perfect sense. We live in a world of both "endogenous risks" that come from the inside, that we already know about and have factored in and "exogenous risks" that occur outside of our assumptions and that we couldn't have possibly factored in.

Anyone who tells you that they know what is coming down the road, whether it involves the direction of a particular stock or sector of the stock market,[2] a national economy (whether our own or another country's), or a breakthrough technology company that will be the next Google/Apple/Facebook, is pretty much lying to you. They don't know and can't know, and you don't know and can't know. That's just the way it is. With that basic understanding, you can begin to make rational decisions with the understanding that ultimately, economic matters (as well as everything else, including matters of personal and family health) are indeed unknowable and any and every action you take can end up proving to be anywhere from slightly risky to incredibly risky.

This chapter is divided into two sections: the risk of not having debt and the risks of asset allocation and particular assets.

Not Your Usual Serious Caution

Danger, Will Robinson! Danger!
> **—From the TV show *Lost in Space***

Here's an unusual warning that you're unlikely to read elsewhere:

> Given the unusual times that we're in, failing to consider your strategic debt options and failure to take on better debt when it's accessible and feasible to do so may be among the worst mistakes you can make as you head into retirement.

Learning from What Companies Do—Value Liquidity!

I recently spoke on a panel with representation from the Federal Reserve, academia, and me there as an expert on individual debt strategies. The conversation took an interesting turn to a discussion of how individuals and companies responded to the 2008 financial crisis in nearly opposite ways.

Companies: Generally chose to reduce their reliance on the banking system. They have done this by *increasing* the amount of cash they had on hand *and increasing* the amount of debt they had. They issued longer-term debt and increased their access to credit. In short, their perspective changed and they placed a greater value on *liquidity, flexibility, leverage, and most important, survivability.*

People: Generally decided that debt was the evil that created the crisis and therefore they rushed in to pay off all of their debt. Ironically, it may turn out that by paying down their debt they actually reduced their liquidity and flexibility should another crisis occur.

I believe that 2008 was as much (if not more) a liquidity crisis than a "debt-driven" crisis. Let's imagine that, like many Americans, you have a mortgage, your money is mostly in retirement accounts, you have some (but not much) credit card debt and some (but not much) money in your checking and savings accounts. You miraculously win a $100,000 lottery ticket in late 2007. You follow conventional wisdom, pay off the credit card debt, and pay down your mortgage.

When 2008 rolls around, you lose your job. Your monthly expenses keep coming in. But wait, you can't access that $100,000! Even though your home equity is higher, you can't refinance because you don't have a job. Your reserves are eaten up in a few months. If you access your retirement accounts you may have to pay taxes and penalties, and you are likely selling assets at the exact time that you should have been buying (at the low!). Your credit card debt starts to skyrocket, you stop making mortgage payments, destroy your credit, and almost (and possibly do) go bankrupt. Mortgage rates go down in 2013 and your equity recovers, but you can't refinance because your credit was crushed.

Here is what I would have done in the same situation: Keep the $100,000 in a very conservative, liquid account so that if a shock came I would have many, many months of reserves. I would have liquidity, flexibility, and survivability—and better perspective. I could take advantage of increased leverage, ride out the storm, and refinance my house when rates fall.

Never, ever underestimate the power of having $100,000 (and more) in a very conservative account versus paying down on an asset. Forget rates of return. Yes, if your money is earning $0 in the bank and your debt costs 4 percent, this strategy costs you $4,000 a year. But it affords you incredible opportunity and survivability in times of distress. Think of it as a type of self-insurance policy. Who else does this? Companies do this, and after 2008 they are now doing it at extreme levels.

In fact, I would suggest that until you have enough built up to completely pay off your house, *you should consider if you should pay off any of your house.* The only benefit in paying down principal is that you will effectively be receiving a guaranteed rate of return equal to the after-tax cost of your mortgage. The cost that it comes with is a significant reduction in your liquidity and flexibility. For most mortgages your payment doesn't change and in most cases it is hard (and perhaps impossible) for you to access that money again if you need it for any reason along the way. Never underestimate the value of liquidity in increasing your flexibility and survivability!

Conventional wisdom has people so excited to get out of debt that they can threaten their own survivability! Liquidity is what you should value most. It makes you a flexible force. If you are liquid, you always can pay off your debt. If you do not have liquidity you can get into a liquidity trap.

ONE OF THE WORST FINANCIAL DECISIONS I SAW SOMEBODY MAKE . . .

This story from *The Value of Debt* is one of the most important lessons I know. Perhaps one of the worst financial decisions I saw an individual make was to purchase a vacation home on a 15-year amortizing loan. I wasn't shocked at the purchase price, but I was stunned when I heard she chose an amortizing loan.

She was an advertising executive, seven years from retiring, with a high income and a seemingly unassailable career. Well, wouldn't you know it, about two weeks after she bought the vacation home, she lost her job in a corporate reorganization. Suddenly she had to come up with the money to pay for both her main home and the vacation home.

This person had to liquidate many of her assets to make the sky-high payments for the second home, experiencing an intensified level of financial distress including higher direct and indirect costs. Of course, this forced liquidation was happening during a rotten time in the market (2008!).

Far too often people with big incomes take on second cars, second homes, or other expensive items through financing that includes amortization, and more often than you might guess, they end up greatly regretting this.

What could they do instead? Guide 2, at the end of this book, offers strategies for buying the things you want that could actually increase your flexibility.[3]

What about Interest Rate Risk? Fixed versus Floating Rate Debt

The most common question I receive is about the risk of rising interest rates and the potential impact on these strategies. This is a significant potential risk and needs to be carefully understood and properly managed. Recognizing that nobody knows, it is possible that rates could stay lower longer than most people think, and it is my opinion that they then could do crazier things than most people think—go to levels that were traditionally unheard of. You need to be prepared for both environments.

To protect against this risk you may want to consider using fixed-rate loans. *Loans with fixed interest rates represent a form of insurance.* Like all insurance you need to quantify the cost of the insurance versus the potential benefits and your ability to self-insure. A fixed rate is similar to an insurance policy against the risk of rising rates in the future. Clearly there are many advantages to fixed-rate debt, especially in a rapidly rising interest-rate environment. Depending on your personal circumstances, your economic view of the world, or the current interest rate environment, buying such insurance might not be a bad thing—in fact it might be the smartest thing to do!

That said, you should always consider the extra cost of that insurance versus your ability to self-insure against the risk of rising interest rates, especially because in most (but not all) economic times, loans with floating (i.e., nonfixed) rates tend to embody the lowest cost of capital at any given moment.

MAKING THE WRONG CHOICES

So often what I find is that individuals who can afford the risk of floating-rate debt are set on having fixed-rate debt, and individuals that should have fixed-rate debt choose floating-rate debt.

Those who can afford to self-insure don't choose floating-rate loans, and those who can't afford to self-insure do choose floating-rate loans.

If you choose floating-rate debt based on the rate, then be sure that you have your floating risk managed in some way. One of the best ways to protect against the risk is to have a greater amount invested in liquid assets that may do well in a rising rate environment. You could then choose to pay down the debt at any time.

Make no mistake: Not properly managed, floating-rate debt can easily increase your risk and cost of financial distress.

Like so many things that have been discussed here, more often than not people choose the exact opposite of what would be optimal for their situation.[4]

WHAT DO COMPANIES DO?

Like the other ideas we have discussed, the goal is to eliminate the terms *good* or *bad* with respect to fixed- and floating-rate debt. Both have their advantages and disadvantages. Like everything in this book the relative merits of each should be considered based on your individual situation. Companies recognize this and often use a combination of both fixed- and floating-rate debt. You may be able to do the same![5]

Investment Risks: It Isn't the Debt That Matters, It Is the Quality of Your Investment Decisions!

History and math are mean, very mean. Cruel. So are overvalued markets. Be prepared, and be cautious! Borrowing money to invest in assets that do poorly is a dumb idea.

Through borrowing it is possible to express a view with respect to inflation and/or devaluation. As an example, take a look at the hyperinflation in Germany and the Weimer Republic after World War I. Imagine an oversimplified example of two Germans, one who borrowed with a debt-to-asset ratio of 35 percent and invested in a 60/40 (or 40/60) Weimer Republic stock and bond portfolio and one who borrowed in the local currency and invested in a world-neutral portfolio (which would have resulted in an investment of less than 10 percent of assets in their home country). Person number one may have gone bankrupt, while person number two may have made incredible returns when they repaid the debt at pennies on the dollar.

My point is that debt isn't good or bad. *All debt does is act like a magnifying glass on the asset-allocation decisions you make.* Good decisions will look better, and bad decisions will look worse. But the debt is not the determining factor in the return—the portfolio is!

All debt does is act like a magnifying glass on the asset-allocation decisions you make. Good decisions will look better, and bad decisions will look worse. But the debt is not the determining factor in the return—the portfolio is!

Asset Allocation and Investment Considerations

We have no working crystal balls, in life or in investing. Instead we try to use common sense and logic from the information around us. We can only do our best by taking into account what we know about the nature of risk and reward—and by taking advantage of some of the wisdom imparted to us by the Nobel Prize–winning ideas and advancements in the studies of finance and investing.

Based on my studies, I've arrived at a common sense investing philosophy consisting of six steps. Of course, my approach to diversified investing is only one possible approach, and you should work with your financial advisor before implementing any of these specific ideas. My goal is not to step on the toes of any advisor nor present any of the following as absolutes. Rather, I suggest that you consider the following as a part of an integrated conversation with your different advisors to understand their opinions on each of these topics.

A Six-Step Approach to Diversified Investing in Retirement

Let every man divide his money into three parts, and invest a third in land, a third in business, and a third let him keep in reserve.

—The Talmud

As you invest during retirement, consider the following six steps:

1. Use a goal-based approach to your asset allocation.
2. Adopt a world-neutral view to your asset allocation.
3. Stress test your portfolio for a range of outcomes.
4. Play offense and defense. For your defense, as in American football, make sure you have a safety playing deep so that you are protected if things go really wrong.
5. Be familiar with valuations and how they impact expected returns.
6. Study economic history—passionately.

I believe that nearly everyone should *adopt a goals-based asset-allocation strategy* that starts with what you will need in retirement and work backwards from there. In a world without crystal balls and that can suddenly be full of risks, if you don't know what your long-term goals are and work backwards from them, it's very difficult to fully prepare for your future. This means, among other things, determining what you (and your spouse) hope to accomplish throughout the length of your retirement, keeping in mind the possibility of a longer life expectancy, the need to get your replacement number right (focus on replacing the spending portion), and the possibility that your needs may increase or decrease throughout retirement (distribution rates are rarely constant). All of this will generate a number that you need. I then suggest that you position your life in the least risky way to accomplish this need.

Second, you should consider adopting a world-neutral view that does not overemphasize investments in your home country, presumably the United States for most readers. The United States, at this point, makes up only around 27 percent of the world's total economy.[6] Many opportunities can be found throughout the world. Plus, basic principles of prudence—back to the notion of diversification and not putting all your eggs in one basket—dictate that you should not be overconcentrated in any one country's securities, including those of the United States. This notion is particularly important when looking at basic lessons that we can learn from math and economic history.

Third, have your portfolio stress tested for a broad range of outcomes, taking into account both the endogenous risks that you are now aware of as well as exogenous risks that you know will be out there eventually, even if you have no idea what they are. If it's been 5 or 10 years since the last huge financial crisis, you can expect another one to come down the pike sometime in the not-too-distant future. A financial crisis needs to be in your base case scenario.

Along these lines, you might want to consider playing both offense and defense by taking out a kind of *insurance against disastrous economic downturns*. Investing a small percentage of your total holdings so that they would profit if things turned really bad really fast may accomplish this goal. (You may want to review the use of options or other strategies with your financial advisor. This is called "hedging" in the financial services industry.)

Finally, the passionate study of valuations, math, and history may help us better understand their potential influence on expected returns. The insight gained through this diligent study may be as close as we can get to having looked into a crystal ball.

Lessons from Math and History Suggest Caution

In *The Value of Debt,* I explained the risks we could face with respect to interest rates and the economy. In my opinion, the next 30 years cannot look like the past 30 years.[7] Over the past 30 years interest rates went from high to low. Inflation went from high to low. United States government debt went from relatively low to high. None of these macro trends are likely to repeat (and in fact they may be the opposite!). While most people look at the most recent history to base their investment decisions, I believe we need to start with a different framework with respect to our beliefs about asset classes and their expected returns.

High levels of absolute and relative debt pose risks to economies. *We could have a world of rising interest rates (and therefore falling bond prices), falling stock prices, rising taxes, rising unemployment, falling real estate values, and a falling value of the dollar.* You read that correctly—virtually all of the traditional major asset classes could fall in value at the same time. So if you had seven different scenarios that you stress tested and you called this situation "Tuesday," I would call it Tuesday, Wednesday, and Thursday.

In my opinion, it is essential that investors are familiar with basic math, history valuation, and their impact on expected returns. Part of this is relevant to the current market environment, but the framework should be used to transcend time in all markets and all economies throughout the world.

A Federal Reserve study[8] shows that in the history of more than 50 events in more than 10 countries, significant busts have tended to follow significant booms throughout the past 100 years. In all of these scenarios, investors could have had vastly different outcomes within one return series, depending on when they were buying and when they were selling. It's perhaps most important to recognize that 50 percent corrections happen with much more frequency than you would anticipate, as do 65 percent–plus corrections. I suggest that you either review the data yourself or take my advice that the odds are strongly in favor of you seeing at least one if not two corrections of at least 50 percent on equities during your retirement.

In today's world, it is important that we apply a framework of simple math facts and history to the current landscape and valuation of U.S. stocks and bonds because, frankly, that's where a lot of U.S. investors tend to have a lot of their money.

First, a quick lesson in how bonds work. A bond provides a fixed return per year based on the interest rate and term at which you purchased it, assuming it does not default. If you buy a 10-year bond at 3 percent, it would provide a return of 3 percent per year for 10 years. Accordingly, the best predictor of bonds' future returns is current yield to maturity.

In today's landscape, five-year bonds are yielding around 1.2 percent for AAA municipal bonds to 2.1 percent for riskier A-rated corporate bonds.[9] Applying basic math to the current landscape, investors would predict a return on bonds in the 1.2 percent to 2.1 percent range for the next five years. But for purposes of our discussion, let's assume an expected return of 2 percent, *excluding taxes, fees, and inflation.*

Now let's look at the history of the U.S. stock market. The average bull market in the United States has lasted 31 months with a median price increase of 73.53 percent. The bear markets that follow have been 10 months long and 35.43 percent deep on average.[10] The size of the upswing in a bull market has not predicted the result of the subsequent correction.

The recent bull market started in March 2009, which makes it the sixth longest since 1929. Its roughly 200 percent price increase ranks as the fourth-biggest percentage movement in that period. The "experts" think the rally is likely to continue. Let's assume they are right. What happens?

If the S&P advances another 50 percent to 3,000 by January 2019, it would be the second longest and second biggest bull market since 1929. If an average bear market follows the rally over the next 12 months, the S&P's ending value in 2019 would be equal to where it is today. In this scenario, the five-year expected return for U.S. equities is roughly zero.

Our discussion so far gives us a five-year return on U.S. stocks of 0 percent and a five-year return on bonds of 2 percent. The good news is that nothing—including asset allocation and fund selection—really mattered all that much. The bad news is that any way you average it, your returns are 0 to 2 percent.

Thankfully, the exercise was just math and not based on anything like valuation or where things are trading. A prudent person would overlay the math with valuation in coming up with expected returns. So let's do that next.

The Shiller price earnings multiple is currently trading at 26.87 (www.multpl.com/shiller-pe/), a 62 percent premium to its historic value. Every bull market in which gains have been more than 100 percent since 1929, including this one, began where the starting point was below average from a valuation perspective. At the same time, most bear markets started when the index was trading more than 20 percent above its long-term average.

In fact, looking backward, when the starting Shiller PE ratio has been over 25, the subsequent five-year returns have averaged 0.4 percent.

Armed with this information, how do we move forward? You have to be prepared for the risk of a dramatic drop in the value of assets that have gone up significantly. Borrowing from the ideas in the last chapter, a major movement down early in your retirement is one of the worst things you can go through. It has one of the greatest impacts on your long-term net worth and on your ability to survive and not run out of money!

Lessons from math, history, and valuation suggest that investors need to be prepared for the possibility of a prolonged period of returns under 2 percent in a U.S. stock and U.S. bond portfolio, virtually regardless of your asset allocation.

Additionally, investors need to be prepared for the risk of a considerable drop in the value of these assets.

Finally, regardless of your beliefs with respect to debt, investors need to know that mathematically, a significant decline in the value of your portfolio early in your retirement can be devastating to the chances that you will make it long term.

Be Careful What You Watch!

TV, newspapers, and stock strategists rarely get it right. The simple truth is that they don't know either. In fact, if you ask economists to guess the direction of interest rates—not the level but just the direction (up or down)—they get it wrong 65 percent of the time.[11] Here is one of many examples: in 2012 Adam Parker, the Chief Equity Strategist for Morgan Stanley gave the "three reasons stocks are going down in 2012." Stocks went up 13.4 percent. Now that is a head-scratcher. Parker anticipated stocks would go down, and instead they went up. So coming into 2013 he adjusted his forecasts and predicted a flat year. He did have an upside scenario of 1,733 but had an equal probability on his bear case of 1,135, or a decline of about 20 percent. The year finished up 29.6 percent, which was not only a miss, but also meaningfully exceeded his upside scenario. Up 30 percent is not flat. Well, since he guessed down and was wrong, then guessed flat and was wrong, he came into 2014 not only guessing up but saying that the S&P 500 was likely to go up 50 percent over the next few years.[12]

I can't make this up! You are welcome to think whatever you want, but here is my take: Listening to these predictions can be very expensive. As I said before, nobody knows, and if they tell you they do, they are either lying to you or lying to themselves—or both.

THE YELLOW RIVER OF RISK

The Mississippi River is known for its high silt content. You may be familiar with the deltas that build up where the Mississippi hits the Gulf of Mexico.

The Yellow River in China also has a very high silt content, estimated to be 10 times the silt content of the Mississippi. In ancient China, people wanted to live near the river, but it would often flood. They managed this risk by building levees. The problem is that as the river flowed by, the silt would build up and the river would flood over the levy. Residents responded by building higher levees. As the silt built up higher, the residents built the levees higher, and so on—the process continued.

Then one day the levee broke.

The site of this awful tragedy is sometimes called the Chinese Pompeii, a terrible disaster that killed an estimated 9.5 million people.[13] When T. R. Kidder, the well-known anthropologist from Washington University, told me this story, it resonated with me as a fabulous metaphor for what is taking place in the financial world today. Instead of addressing our problems (high country-specific debt levels!), we keep turning to easy solutions and building bigger and bigger levees.

I believe the levee will break someday. Whether you implement a debt philosophy or not, my sincere hope is that you are at least prepared for the possibility.

My Opinions on Asset Allocation

My goal for this book is to present math facts for you to consider in order to make better decisions throughout your retirement. My personal opinions are different and a bit controversial but a significant number of readers of the last book and early copies of this book wanted more specific asset allocation thoughts—my opinions. This is pretty easy because if there is one thing I know for sure, it is that I *know* that I don't know the future. That said, I'll try to highlight some things for you to consider.

If you are overweight in U.S. assets (and most U.S.-based investors are), consider making a change. Our exercises have demonstrated a high possibility of returns of less than 2 percent for the next five years in U.S.-centric portfolios. History has been cruel to investors who have over-weighted their home country at times of high levels of government debt and record prices in their stock and bond markets. Global diversification and a world-neutral asset allocation model may help you be prepared for a range of outcomes.

Change your perspective. If you were talking to a friend in Spain, would you suggest that she invest all of her money in a Spanish stock and bond portfolio, denominated in euros? If you were talking to somebody from Japan, would you suggest that he invest all of his money in a Japanese stock and bond portfolio, denominated in yen? It sounds kind of foolish, doesn't it? The prudent place to begin is with a world-neutral weighting and then perhaps adjusting up and down, accounting for where things are from a *valuation* perspective. Consider using equity market capitalization for your equity weightings and GDP weightings for your bond weightings to determine a neutral position and then adjust from there.

Try to have yin and yang in your portfolio. Ideally you want to have a portfolio that is comprised of assets that move differently or independently of each other so that everything isn't going the same direction at the same time—especially down. How assets move relative to each other is called correlation in the financial industry. I think that you should consider having no less than seven different low-correlated asset classes with a minimum weighting of 5 percent in each for a "well-diversified" portfolio. These include things like U.S. stocks, developed international stocks, emerging-market stocks, U.S. bonds, developed international bonds, emerging-market bonds, gold, commodities, and real estate.

I'LL MAKE YOU A BET

I'll bet that the last three paragraphs didn't sound that interesting or controversial and I'll bet that it probably sounded like something you are already doing. My bet is that those suggestions would actually represent a significant change to your overall asset allocation.

My experience is that most investors think that they are doing something like this but the reality is that 70 to 90 percent of their assets are typically in stocks and bonds of the United States (or their home country if you are outside the United States). Typically I find that 80 percent (and more!) of investors' assets are typically exposed to two assets, stocks and bonds, in a single country and in a single currency.

It is my opinion that most U.S. investors dramatically underweight gold. Table 7.1 is a twist on the Trinity study that influences me. At the top are the original numbers from the original study using success rates for traditional allocations. The bottom row is a portfolio of 60 percent stocks and 40 percent gold with a 33 percent leverage ratio entering retirement.

Table 7.1 Trinity Study Comparison: The "Traditional Way" versus an Alternative Allocation, with Gold and Debt: 1946–2013

Annualized Withdrawal Rate as a % of Initial Portfolio Value										
Payout Period	**3%**	**4%**	**5%**	**6%**	**7%**	**8%**	**9%**	**10%**	**11%**	**12%**
75% stocks/25% bonds										
Without debt	100	95	69	54	46	41	28	18	3	0
50% stocks/50% bonds										
Without debt	100	87	56	46	33	15	13	3	3	0
60% stocks/40% gold										
With debt	100	100	100	97	97	90	67	44	31	26

Note: These are not the Trinity Study's exact numbers, but our version of their methodology and updated through 2013.

A 97 percent confidence of taking a 7 percent, inflation-adjusted distribution is stunning. In fact this suggests that you can take out 7 to 8 percent inflation adjusted, from a 60 percent stock, 40 percent gold portfolio with debt, with approximately the same level of confidence as a 75 percent stock/25 percent bond portfolio—twice the income, same level of risk.

To be clear, I am not implying that this should be your asset allocation because as indicated, I think a portfolio should have at least seven different asset classes. However, it is my opinion that most U.S. investors dramatically underweight gold and that gold may have diversification benefits due to its low correlation. It also is my opinion that there is no point in owning a 5 percent or less position in gold, as the diversification benefits are nominal. Accordingly I recommend considering a 10 to 20 percent weighting as a starting place for testing and conversations, which, from my experience, is much higher than the typical holdings of most investors.

It also is my opinion that most U.S., European, and Japanese investors are dramatically underweight emerging market bonds and emerging market stocks, especially if you use GDP weightings (not market capitalization!) to determine a starting place for a world neutral perspective. I would suggest that Europe, the United States, and Japan may all be facing the same structural challenges and that there may not be as much diversification between those markets as many investors think. It is also my opinion that there is a tremendous amount of risk in municipal, corporate, and high-yield bonds when they are trading near generational lows in their yields. Investors should carefully evaluate the potential risks and benefits of these investments.

History shows that over-indebted nations (Japan, Europe, the United States today) solve their problems by one of four measures: they default, grow their way out of it, inflate their way out of it, or devalue their way out of it—or some combination of these four "solutions." If you are not getting the growth that you need or expect, smart money may want to shift its bet toward the possibility of inflation and/or the possibility of devaluation. Through borrowing it is possible to express a view with respect to inflation and or devaluation and it is possible to magnify the impact of your investment decisions—for better or for worse.

Table 7.2 provides a broad asset allocation framework to consider where I combine the information above: GDP, market capitalization,

Table 7.2   One Opinion on an Asset Allocation Framework to Consider

Asset Class	Weighting	Valuation in Early 2015 Might Suggest
U.S. stocks	10–20%	Underweight
Developed international stocks	5–15%	Equal weight
Emerging market stocks	10–20%	Overweight
U.S. bonds	10–20%	Underweight
Developed international bonds	5–15%	Underweight
Emerging market bonds	5–15%	Overweight
Gold	10–20%	Overweight
Commodities	5–15%	Overweight
Real estate	5–15%	Equal weight

valuation, correlation, and lessons from math and history across multiple asset classes. None of this is intended to be a forecast but rather a framework to encourage thoughtful debate and discussion with your advisors. For those with considerable assets, "alternative assets" such as private equity and hedge funds may serve as additional diversification tools to consider.

For those who are passionate on this topic I would encourage you to study economic history in more detail and the potential impact throughout time of borrowing in a relatively strong currency, when their debt to GDP ratio is high yet they are trading near generational lows in interest rates. I would suggest this represents the United States, Europe, and Japan in 2015. I suggest you compare investing in a globally diversified portfolio versus a static 60/40 stock and bond allocation in that home country. You will find examples from the United States, Japan, France, England, Greece, Argentina—among many others. The evidence in favor of the global portfolio is compelling to me, but I encourage you to draw your own conclusions.

From these lessons we can draw some conclusions that may stand the test of time:

- It is better to buy low and sell high.
- Sometimes the tortoise beats the hare.
- You have to avoid a major decline in value early in your retirement.

- Big shocks and "unexpected" events are to be expected—plan that at least one happens during your retirement.
- Missing out on short-term gains in a certain asset class is okay and to be expected—it is part of a disciplined, diversified process.
- Assets that have gone way up or down may have different risk and return characteristics looking forward.
- Study economic history passionately. Recognize that our past 30 years cannot be like our next 30 years as virtually everything is at a different starting place. We need to look at other times in other economies that had similarities to where markets are today.
- Mathematically, lower-risk portfolios with debt can be much better than high-risk portfolios without debt.

This section has just been my opinion and as I said before, the one thing I know for sure is that I know that I don't know what the future will bring. My advice: be prepared, and be cautious. Be open-minded and be studious. And certainly be prepared for a wide range of outcomes![14]

AHAs! ADVISOR HIGHLIGHT ANSWERS

Question #1: Are you really serious about the risks you are discussing? A return under 2 percent on a U.S. stock and bond portfolio seems unreasonable.

   Answer #1: Nothing I am saying is intended to be a prediction but rather the identification of potential risks. My greatest fear is that people will use the ideas in this book irresponsibility. They will run up their debt and not save (as much as they ought) and will invest in a portfolio that isn't well diversified and is made up of overvalued assets.[15]

Notes

1. Thomas J. Anderson, *The Value of Debt: How to Manage Both Sides of a Balance Sheet to Maximize Wealth* (Hoboken, NJ: John Wiley & Sons, 2013), 186. For more details on this chapter and the risks we could face, I encourage you to see the citations and references on pages 204 to 207 of *The Value of Debt*. The

notion that the past 30 years can not be like the next 30 years is inspired by a presentation given by Jeffrey Rosenberg, Chief Investment Strategist for Fixed Income, Blackrock at the Barron's Top 100 conference, fall 2012. Lectures from David Wessel, Luigi Zingales, Ed Lazear, Martin Feldstein, Paul Krugman, Gary Becker, and Naill Ferguson in 2012 and 2013 all inspired some of the views expressed in this section. Readers looking for additional detail should familiarize themselves with their work.

2. Burton Malkiel's *A Random Walk down Wall Street,* 9th ed. (New York: W.W. Norton & Co., 2007) is the classic investing book for understanding why no one—no one—knows what the price of any given stock will do the next day.

3. Anderson, *The Value of Debt*, 104.

4. Ibid., 105.

5. Ibid., 107.

6. See http://tradingeconomics.com/united-states/gdp.

7. Anderson, *The Value of Debt*, 94–96.

8. Federal Reserve Bank of St. Louis—Working Paper 2006-051A. See http://search.stlouisfed.org/search?&client=Research-new&proxystylesheet=Research-new&site=working-papers&output=xml_no_dtd&num=30&filter=0&getfields=%2A&q=2006-051A.

9. According to www.bondsonline.com at the time of publication.

10. Stephen Suttmeier, Jue Xiong, "A Closer Look at the Best Bull Markets in Excess of 20%," Merrill Lynch Global Research, August 13, 2013. Additionally, the following is a great research piece on the long run as well: www.merrilledge.com/Publish/Content/application/pdf/GWMOL/GlobalStrategyApictureguidetofinancialmarketssince1800.pdf.

11. Davis Advisors, "2014 Portfolio Review and Outlook Presentation," updated 12-2013 (#3910)[1], see page 5.

12. See http://online.barrons.com/articles/s-p-3-000-morgan-stanley-bullish-on-rest-of-decade-1412076606?tesla=y.

13. Rachel Nuwer, "Humans Have Been Messing with China's Yellow River for 3,000 Years. When Humans Try to Tame Nature Things Rarely Go According to Plan," *Smithsonian Magazine,* June 20, 2014. See www.smithsonianmag.com/smart-news/3000-years-humans-alterations-chinas-yellow-river-created-catastrophic-situation-exists-today-180951815/?no-ist.

14. Case studies are for educational and illustrative purposes only. They assume eligible assets and that funds are available on the facility. All client situations are unique, and all loans are subject to eligibility and approval by the lender. A lender may deny an advance on an ABLF, preventing the scenarios. Pledging assets reduces and may eliminate liquidity. A market correction could impact market values and/or security eligibility, which could impact the facility size and/or trigger a margin call and/or forced liquidations of assets. See complete disclosures and risks to using an ABLF in Appendix F.

15. Author's Note: The information in this chapter is to be considered in a holistic way as a part of the book and not to be considered on a stand-alone basis. This includes, but is not limited to, the discussion of risks of each of these ideas as well as all of the disclaimers throughout the book. The material is presented with a goal of encouraging thoughtful conversation and rigorous debate on the risks and potential benefits of the concepts between you and your advisors based on your unique situation, risk tolerance, and goals.

Chapter 8

The Sooner the Better

Moving from Oppressive to Working to Enriching Debt

Wisdom and penetration are the fruit of experience, not the lessons of retirement and leisure. Great necessities call out great virtues.

—Abigail Adams

This section uses a series of sequential illustrations to help you understand the three types of debt—oppressive debt, working debt, and enriching debt—and how and why you might want to consider moving from the first of these to the last as soon as you can. It's appropriate not just for people approaching retirement, but for everyone who is both psychologically and financially qualified to make use of better debt, including forward-thinking professionals and younger people who

Table 8.1   The Different Types of Debt

Type	Examples	Impact
Oppressive debt	Payday loans, credit card balances	Oppresses the debt holder, and makes them continually poorer
Working debt	Mortgage, small-business loan, student loans	Has a real cost, but enables further life advances and gives access to Indebted Strengths
Enriching Debt	Debt you strategically choose to have but can pay down whenever you want. Line of credit against your investment portfolio	May increase returns, may reduce taxes, may reduce risk, and can potentially lead to full access to Indebted Strengths

already have some significant assets at their disposal. (Share these ideas with your kids!) We'll lay out a glide path based on debt-to-asset ratios and another kind of glide path that can help you understand the various types of debt and move more rapidly from the lowest to the highest quality.

To help transcend the not-so-helpful use of simplistic contrasts like "good" versus "bad" debt, I describe the differences between the three types of debt—oppressive, working, and enriching—in Table 8.1.

Based on the descriptions in Figure 8.1, for the majority of people, it's in their best interests to move from oppressive to working to enriching debt over time. Your cost of debt falls and, perhaps most important, by definition you have the ability to pay off all of your debt at any time. Your entire personal financial ecosystem becomes maximally productive as you move from oppressive to working to enriching debt.

THE CONTINUUM OF DIFFERENT TYPES OF DEBT

EFFICIENT USE OF DEBT

OPPRESSIVE   WORKING   ENRICHING

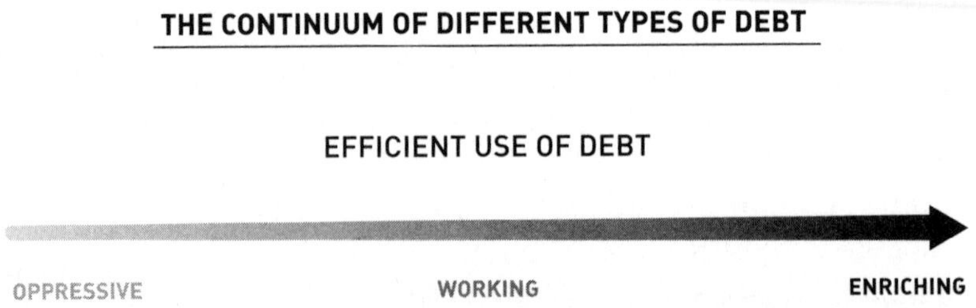

Figure 8.1   The Continuum of Different Types of Debt

Oppressive debt is difficult to unload, and people with the most oppressive debt tend to have the least assets. The relationship between the amount of one's assets and where one is on the oppressive-to-working-to-enriching glide path can generally be characterized as looking something like Figure 8.2.

How does this play out in real life? Figure 8.3 shows, when people are younger, let's say just out of college, they tend to have few assets but quite a lot of debt: credit cards, student loans, car loans, and so on. The line at the top, then, shows that many people have a good deal of oppressive debt until they can pay most or all of it off in 10 to 20 years and begin to access working debt such as a mortgage. Then, eventually, people pay off that working debt. What I've seen repeatedly, however, is that this is also the time for these same people to be building up taxable assets so that enriching debt will become available to them.

In an ideal world, a lucky few (and many of the super rich) will then begin to make use of the enriching debt now available to them if they're psychologically/emotionally and financially qualified to do so. They'll use enriching debt to capture the spread and amplify their wealth. Making use of maximal available enriching debt may enable them to amplify their wealth without exposing them to too much risk.

**AMOUNT OF ASSETS HELD BY THOSE
THAT HAVE DIFFERENT TYPES OF DEBT**

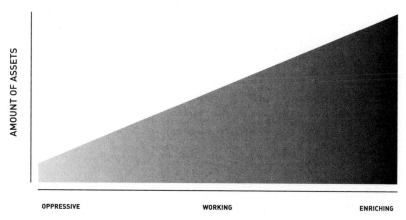

Figure 8.2   Amount of Assets Held by Those That Have Different Types of Debt

DEBT EVOLUTIONS OVER TIME

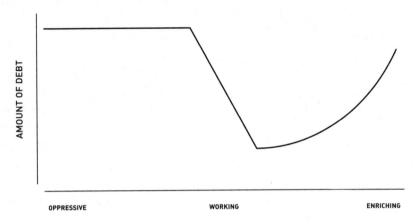

Figure 8.3 Debt Evolutions over Time

Ultimately, then, as Figure 8.4 shows, while you may indeed take on more total debt as you move through time, enriching debt goes hand-in-hand with, and helps in part to generate, a much greater amount of total assets and net worth over time. People who are knowledgeable about the value of debt may, at a certain point, want to ramp up their debt—especially their high-quality debt—as part of ramping up their overall assets base and net worth. This would be especially true if the organization providing

ASSETS AND DEBT OVERLAY

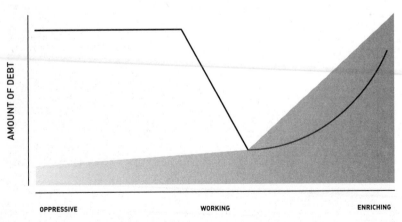

Figure 8.4 Assets and Debt Overlay

them with the enriching debt loan would provide them with a system of notifications, warnings, and live telephone help so that they're entirely aware of their coverage ratios and the amount of risk they've taken on, which diminishes any danger of being forced into a margin call or having some of their assets sold willy-nilly to maintain the needed coverage ratio.

This illustration demonstrates the opportunity available to those who psychologically and financially qualify for better debt over time. Once again, the trajectory goes from having a good deal of oppressive debt to paying that debt off and moving into the working debt zone. Following traditional antidebt advice, people who get on the downward sloping line and begin to pay off debt often continue to pay off that debt until they have absolutely no debt left. Some will begin to "head up" the line and begin taking on enriching debt, by turning that curve upwards. This isn't a bad way to go, but there is an even bigger opportunity demonstrated in Figure 8.5.

Those who didn't wait until their working debt bottomed out (the point at which the curve turns at the bottom of the pie shape) and instead began taking on and making use of enriching debt earlier in their lives, heading onto the up-sloping straight line that constitutes the top of the pie. The golden (bar) opportunity comes from making the decision earlier on to make conscious and wise use of enriching debt. It's a worthwhile risk. Handled intelligently and patiently, it can generate a great deal of additional wealth in the long run.

THE OPPORTUNITY TO CHANGE COURSE

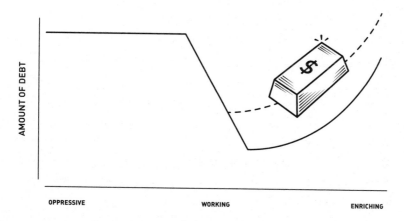

Figure 8.5 The Opportunity to Change Course

Understanding the Implications of These Ideas for Your Life Plans

It may not make sense to rush in and pay down your working debt. The traditional goal of "retiring mortgage-free" may not be a good strategy for you. Of course, being mortgage-free may be a great strategy if you're on track to accumulate sufficient assets that can conservatively generate the return you need. If you've undersaved for retirement, however, it's possible that rushing in to pay off your mortgage may in fact mathematically guarantee that you will not be able to have the retirement you have envisioned without taking on risk in reaching for return.

Getting a Handle on Whether You Should Adopt a Strategic Debt Approach

The following tools will help you assess where you stand with regard to having an optimal debt ratio both now and in the future. Your debt-to-asset-ratio will be the basis for showing you how the right "glide path" to retirement can bring you better long-term results and a great deal of comfort. Finding out that you're *not* on a sustainable path isn't necessarily a bad thing, either, because it can spur you to make changes now, before it is too late, while you can still do something meaningful about your situation.

These tools will help you get a handle on whether you and your family should seriously consider the holistic debt philosophy and practices set out in this book. So far, we've presented two sets of questions for determining (in consultation with your financial advisor) whether strategic debt philosophy and practice are appropriate for you.

- **The "Four Questions" from Chapter 1:** Do you possess adequate resources, the correct psychological disposition, open-mindedness, and the ability to find and work closely with the right kind of financial advisor?
- **The *Seven Rules for Being a Better Debtor*:** These are presented near the end of Chapter 3; ask yourself again, can I really follow *all* of these rules?

Building on those questions, I have two new tools:

- **The Need-Want-Have Matrix:** Wanting or not wanting better debt needs to be separated from having or not having it already and from having or not having access to it. Once you see the different possibilities, where you stand vis-à-vis better debt should become much clearer for you.
- **Calculating and Using Your Ideal Debt-to-Asset Ratio to Create a Glide Path**: Following up on framework from *The Value of Debt*, I'll present a visual metaphor—a glide path—that can help you determine if you're on course.

The Need-Want-Have Matrix

One of the first steps in deciding whether the ideas, practices, strategies, or possibilities in this book make sense for you is to get very clear about where you stand about taking on working debt or enriching debt. Figure 8.6 illustrates four different inquiries—in vector form—that taken together will help visually make clear your overall need, want, current possession of, and access to better debt.

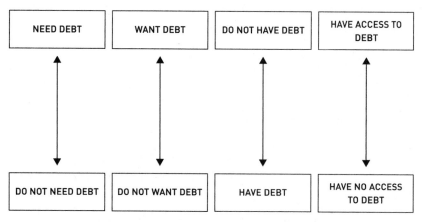

Figure 8.6   Need–Want–Have Access Chart

The questions are whether you:

- Need debt
- Want debt
- Have debt
- Have access to working debt or enriching debt

You will fall somewhere between being all or most of the way to one side of the vertical line that connects the two opposite poles. Sometimes you will be all the way at the top or the bottom; in more uncertain times you'll want to think through the alternatives very carefully to determine your best path.

Let's start with the first question: *Do you need debt?* I've been stressing that your need is a function of your desired return, and debt may be the *only* way to create a financially desirable scenario for retirement. Let's do the math. First determine how much money you think you will have saved up on your retirement date. From our earlier discussion on statistics, we of course know that this won't be an exact number so let's use a conservative estimate. Then look at your needs. If your needs divided by your anticipated assets indicate you are likely to need over 4 percent, you may need debt!

For example, you determine that you're going to retire in five years with liquid investable assets of approximately $1 million. In addition to your other sources of income, you estimate you will need about $60,000 per year from your portfolio. This represents a 6 percent distribution rate. Anything over 6 percent is a high indication that you likely will need debt. Achieving a distribution rate between 4 and 6 percent will depend on your asset allocation, and for anything under 3 percent you may not necessarily need debt.

Notice an important and powerful tool comes into play with this calculation. If you retire and discover that you have plenty of assets and a conservative need of under 3 percent, guess what you can do—you can pay off your debt! But if you do not have the debt, and you discover that your need is high, you may discover that you are between a rock and a hard place.

I want to be even more clear on this very important point. If you can determine that your future need is greater than a 6 percent annual distribution rate, you will want to very carefully consider the implications and consequences of paying down any working debt at a rate less than your required rate of return. Let's say you also have a $200,000 mortgage at 3 percent. Getting to a return over 4 percent might be hard if you take your excess assets and direct them to something that is at 3 percent. *Your rate of return on paying down debt is exactly equal to your after-tax cost of that debt.* The more you rush in to pay down debt that is at a rate lower than your required rate of return, the harder it may be for you to accomplish your objective.

Of course paying off your mortgage removes the payment, but you lose all the liquidity you had. Once you retire, it's much more difficult to get working debt. It's hard to get a mortgage without a job. You may find that it's very difficult to access the equity in your home without selling your house. This liquidity is incredibly valuable. The higher your required rate of return, the greater your need for liquidity and flexibility. Having a larger portfolio working for you may reduce the required return on your assets to achieve your goals.

Equally important, if you're looking at making a major purchase such as a car, home improvement, or second home, you may not want to pay cash or sell assets from your investment account to buy it. The guides at the end of this book offer advice on each of these topics.

The next question is simple but a bit unusual: *Do you want debt?* Many people don't want debt under *any circumstances*…because they don't want *any* kind of debt under any circumstances. They're either afraid of debt (potentially from a bad experience with oppressive debt early in life) or they are afraid of themselves (fearful they can't handle the responsibility associated with debt) or they believe the antidebt ideology that rules the day. Regardless, your receptivity to these ideas is essential to their success.

The next question is simple: Do you already have debt? If you have debt, how much and what type (oppressive, working, or enriching) matters. If you are above a 35 percent debt ratio, your situation is complicated. If you have oppressive debt, you'll likely want to pay it down as quickly as possible. Remember that Rule #5 in Chapter 3's Seven Rules for Being a Better Debtor states that you need to pay off that debt as soon as it's feasible. Having low-quality debt in the picture makes your need for better debt greater. It's a situation you want to avoid or minimize, as quickly as possible.

If it's working debt such as a mortgage, you'll want to overlay a conservative projection of your future debt ratio. Your debt ratio will fall if you pay down your debt or build up your savings; this is just the way math works. The question of what will put you on the best path to your retirement goals will take some sophisticated analysis by you or your advisor. If you do not have debt, you may be in a stronger position to gradually and strategically bring debt into your financial picture over time to put you on the proper glide path.

WHAT IF I KNOW I'M NOT ON TRACK?

What if you are not on track? What if your current debt ratio is high, you only have oppressive debt, and you anticipate your required need is over 8 percent? First, I want to give you sincere congratulations for recognizing that you are not on track. Many people are ostriches, hiding from the reality that faces them.

Here are some things to consider:

- Consider reducing your expenses and trying to increase your savings.
- Consider delaying retirement.
  (I know the first two are obvious, but they do make a big difference.)
- Consider some form of income in retirement to reduce your required need—any income is powerful even at a fraction of what you were earning before.
- Consider refinancing as much of your debt as you can against your house and perhaps locking the rate for as long of a time period as you can.
- Consider refinancing other debt on a line of credit against your portfolio.
- Consider a payment plan process to eliminate all debt over 10 percent.
- Carefully consider if you should pay off any debt that is at a rate under the required rate of return that you need in retirement.

For example, if you need a 6 percent return, I'm not sure I would rush in to pay off any debt under 5 percent. You need the liquidity, flexibility, leverage—all of which are invaluable for increased survivability.

- Look at your taxes carefully and be sure you are making the right assumptions with 401(k)s, IRAs, and Roth IRAs. You likely want to minimize taxes and maximize savings!
- Are you taking full advantage of any matches in your retirement plan that your employer may offer?
- Look carefully at how much you are paying for insurance and why—is that your top priority at this point in your life? Are there any alternatives?
- Focus on principal protection—be very careful that you are not chasing the hot dot and reaching for return by buying risky assets. A severe correction would be devastating if you are already in a fragile place.
- Look carefully at the distribution tables and probability analysis to have a debt ratio and asset allocation that you want to strive toward.
- Are there any products with guarantees that may help you?
- Carefully consider the creditor protection status of your retirement savings assets and DO NOT use retirement funds under 60 for any reason. It is very hard for me to think of any single reason why I would want you to take money out of a retirement plan if you are under 65 if you are not already on track. It will mathematically be very hard for you to make it.

The final question is empirical: *Do you currently have, or can you create access to, better debt?* This depends on whether you have liquid taxable assets you can pledge and borrow against with your existing brokerage firm or another financial entity that enables securities-based lending and whether you're in a position to take out a home equity line of credit or refinance your mortgage.

There's a strong case to be made that this individual could move forward with one or more better debt solutions. But before doing anything at all, she should consider the equally important question of optimal debt ratio ranges—what they are, and how they can help guide her smoothly into retirement and beyond when the time comes.

Watch Those Ratios! A First Glide Path into Retirement

The term "optimal debt ratio" is foreign to most people—naturally enough, as they've been trained to see it as a contradiction. In fact, however, both experience and theory have shown that there is indeed an optimal debt ratio—more properly, an optimal debt-to-assets ratio, that you should shoot for at any given point of time. Not surprisingly, many individuals and families are either too highly leveraged and have taken on way too much debt or have not taken advantage of their Indebted Strengths out of debt aversion. Like companies, individuals and families should aim for that middle ground, the not-too-much and not-too-little Goldilocks solution that will benefit them the greatest over the long run.

The basic formula used to calculate your current debt ratio is easy:

Debt-to-asset-ratio = total debt/total assets

Suppose your current debt ratio is 20 percent. Is that good? Bad? And how does that relate to the journey into and through retirement? Overall, a debt ratio of 15 to 35 percent is optimal for many people. Some commentators believe this is too conservative and that it should be between 25 and 45 percent, while others believe it's too aggressive and the ratio should be more like 5 to 25 percent. How does knowing that you're at 20 percent and have five years until you and your spouse retire help you?

Imagine an aircraft getting ready to descend at night. The pilot sees one row of lights shining on his left and another row shining on his right and a sweet-spot path—the glide path—guiding him to where he needs to land the plane. A good pilot will follow the illuminated glide path—not venturing too far to the left (too little debt) nor too far to the right (too much debt)—to bring the plane and its occupants to a

**Optimal Asset-to Debt Ratio Range
Glide Path Into Retirement & Beyond**

15%	retirement and after retirement	35%
15%	1 year before retirement	35%
15%	3 years before retirement	35%
15%	5 years before retirement	35%
15%	10 years before retirement	35%
15%	15 years before retirement	35%
15%	20 years before retirement	35%
15%	25 years before retirement	40%
20%	30 years before retirement	50%
25%		60%

Figure 8.7 Optimal Debt Ratio Glide Path over Time
Source: © Tom Anderson, 2014.

safe, smooth landing. Figure 8.7 shows what this glide path could look like over time.

The term "glide path" is also used in a different way by the brokerage and investment industry, which may cause some confusion. Investopedia.com explains that a "glide path"…

> …refers to a formula that defines the asset allocation mix of a target date fund, based on the number of years to the target date. The glide path creates an asset allocation that becomes more conservative (i.e., includes more fixed-income assets and fewer equities) the closer a fund gets to the target date. …Target date funds have become very popular among those who are saving for retirement. They are based on the simple premise that the younger the investor, the longer the time horizon he or she has and the greater the risk he or she can take to potentially increase returns.[1]

For our purposes, this specific notion of "glide path" is potentially misleading in a couple of ways. First, by continually replacing equities with fixed income investments, it suggests an inevitable narrowing of the "safe down the Goldilocks middle" glide path over time—to a point when it will be just a straight line, not a path with easy-to-see left and right borders ("glide-lines") guiding you to a safe, smooth landing. What was a path becomes narrowed to a line, incorrectly suggesting that such precision is both possible and as useful as a wide illuminated Goldilocks path.

Second, and more importantly, while it's true that investing assets more conservatively may make sense for some people over time, it's not at all clear that having less debt or a lower debt ratio over time also makes most sense. Strategically increasing your better debt—and consciously and wisely taking advantage of the Increased Liquidity, Increased Flexibility, Increased Leverage, Increased Survivability, and Increased Perspective that come with taking on such better debt—may be the *more conservative* move by nearly any definition of "conservative."

It's important to consider the volatility of your asset portfolio when analyzing your debt-to-asset ratio. Inherently, the more volatile your portfolio, the lower in the range your debt ratio should be. Conversely, the less volatile your portfolio, the higher your debt ratio can be. For example, if your investment portfolio is 100 percent in U.S. stocks (think S&P 500) and your debt ratio is on the high side, around 35 percent, your portfolio might fall quite quickly in a major market correction similar to 2008. Depending on how your debt is structured you might be exposed to a margin call, potentially forcing you to sell at the exact wrong time (at the low!). If, on the other hand, your portfolio is mostly conservatively allocated among global government bonds, you can likely have a debt ratio toward the high side with very limited odds of your portfolio falling to a level that would trigger a capital call.

It's important that you understand your own situation, including what you *need* and what you *want*, apply what you've learned, and assess it against where you fall in the general optimal debt ratio glide path (which we continue to posit is, on average, between 15 percent and 35 percent). Assuming you've transcended (or never had) any problems with oppressive debt, if you see yourself moving too far to the left—to a debt ratio that is below 15 percent—as you approach retirement, you'll probably want to make a course correction unless something in your Need-Want-Have Matrix, general circumstances, or psychological makeup indicates it makes sense to go lower than 15 percent. Similarly, if you find your debt ratio moving out of the glide path and substantially over the 35 percent level, you may want to rein it back in to the middle, or change your asset allocation, unless you have other information or advice that indicates it's all right for you to be that high.

What If You Are Not Optimal Today?

I am against people making sudden and dramatic changes unless the full consequences are very well thought out and understood. I understand that mathematically moving to an optimal ratio can happen at any point in time, but it's easier psychologically if you move along a glide path—with gradual nudges that improve your overall outcomes rather than drastic changes. For example, if your debt ratio is not optimal I am generally against a cash-out refinance against your house and reinvesting the difference. In many cases this is restricted—or outright prohibited. More important, I worry that people will be tempted to do it at the exact wrong time. People will tend to take on more debt in good times and tend to pay off debt in bad times. It is my general belief that this practice is backwards. People should consider paying down debt when things are looking really good (or reallocating to other assets), and they may want to consider letting their debt ratio drift up a little higher if things are looking pretty bad.

How do you determine when are good and bad times? Unfortunately there is no easy way. It is my experience that if you think the world is falling apart and three random people tell you that "the market" stinks, you may want to consider letting your debt ratio drift higher. If stocks are hitting new highs, or if three random people comment on how excited they are about "the market," and especially if the media is excited, you may want to consider lowering your debt ratio.

Dying with Debt?

Yes, this glide path implies the controversial idea that you could end up dying with debt. Here are two scenarios to choose from. In scenario one, you pass along $2 million of assets and no debt to your kids. In scenario two, you pass along $4 million of assets and $1 million of debt to your kids. Which scenario do you think your kids would choose?

Scenario number two? Why on earth would they choose to inherit $1 million of debt? Because everybody knows that $4 million–$1 million = $3 million, and everybody knows that $3 million is more than $2 million. It isn't the debt that matters; it is the total amount of assets that matters. Are the assets greater than the debts? If they are, then passing along debt will always be okay. Make no mistake, if the debts are greater than the assets, then there are all sorts of problems and you need a different type of book.

This is exactly what most companies do, though the debt ratios that I'm suggesting are much more conservative than the debt ratios of most American companies.[2] Companies tend to increase the amount of debt that they have over time while people tend to pay theirs down. Companies tend to keep their debt ratios relatively constant, just like the glide path above. In 1993 Coca-Cola had $12 billion in assets and $2.8 billion in debt. In 2013 Coca-Cola had a whopping $90 billion in assets and $36 billion in debt.[3]

Now imagine that you get a phone call and somebody tells you something crazy happened and you just inherited Coca-Cola. You own the company. You just inherited billions in assets but, guess what else you inherited—all that debt. If you do not want that phone call, send it on over to me. I would take it in a heartbeat—and be one of the wealthiest people in the world as a result.

Final Mortgage Considerations

Many times mortgages offer the best ability for you to have a low-cost fixed or floating rate debt. In most instances mortgage debt may offer the borrower significant tax benefits. Further, mortgage debt is permanent debt. What this means is that once you close on a mortgage, the bank cannot take the money back (rescind the loan) as long as you are current on your payments. This is not true with many other forms of debt, including a line of credit versus your portfolio. That line can be called in the event of a market downturn. Accordingly, there are tremendous benefits to attempting to achieve your optimal debt ratio through mortgage debt rather than by using a line of credit versus your portfolio.

One of the best ways to do this is to consider not paying down your mortgage and using that additional money to build up more liquidity and therefore flexibility.

You now have the Indebted Strengths of Increased Liquidity, Increased Flexibility, Increased Leverage, and Increased Survivability. You have the "Four Questions" in Chapter 1, The Seven Rules for Being a Better Debtor in Chapter 3, The Need-Want-Have Matrix in this chapter, and a glide path to consider throughout time. We have discussed that oppressive debt is generally bad and typically should be repaid as fast as possible while pointing out that rushing in to pay off your working debt may not always make sense. We've suggested carefully weighing your alternatives before making major purchases and the likelihood that you could stay on track for the retirement you desire using better debt.

These tools should be combined with the ideas for increased return, reduced taxes, and reduced risk from Part II and the guides at the end of this book—and always wrapped up with the risk discussion in the next chapter—for a framework that you can implement in your personal life![4]

AHAs! ADVISOR HIGHLIGHT ANSWERS

Question #1: How early should you start the glide path to an optimal debt ratio?

Answer #1: Early—as early as possible and the earlier the better. If somebody is retired then there are few things you can do to get him or her to an optimal debt ratio. I am generally opposed to doing a cash-out refinance against a house to get somebody to an optimal position. Mathematically it is the same but psychologically it is not, and there can be some complex restrictions to the process (see my book *The Value of Debt*, Chapter 5, for a detailed discussion). I would much, much rather see a glide path to an optimal ratio.

If somebody's debt ratio is low then you can get there a number of ways: Stop paying down the mortgage. Put the next tax bill or expensive trip on the line of credit and SAVE what you would have spent (the savings part is the key part to success here). Here, too, a full discussion of optimal debt ratios can be found in *The Value of Debt*, Chapter 5.

Always be mindful of the risks—the greatest one being the psychological risks that positioned the wrong way this can seem like a free lunch and people can ramp up their debt ratios way too fast with nothing to show for it. All that would end up being is a gradual destruction of their wealth—so be careful![5]

Notes

1. www.investopedia.com/terms/g/glide-path.asp.
2. Thomas J. Anderson, *The Value of Debt: How to Manage Both Sides of a Balance Sheet to Maximize Wealth* (New York: John Wiley & Sons, 2013), "Second Tenent: Explore Thinking and Acting Like a Company," 6–10.
3. http://financials.morningstar.com/balance-sheet/bs.html?t=KO&region=usa &culture=en-US.
4. Case studies are for educational and illustrative purposes only. They assume eligible assets and that funds are available on the facility. All client situations are unique, and all loans are subject to eligibility and approval by the lender. A lender may deny an advance on an ABLF, preventing the scenarios. Pledging assets reduces and may eliminate liquidity. A market correction could impact market values and/or security eligibility, which could impact the facility size and/or trigger a margin call and/or forced liquidations of assets. See complete disclosures and risks to using an ABLF in Appendix F.
5. Author's Note: The information in this chapter is to be considered in a holistic way as a part of the book and not to be considered on a stand-alone basis. This includes, but is not limited to, the discussion of risks of each of these ideas as well as all of the disclaimers throughout the book. The material is presented with a goal of encouraging thoughtful conversation and rigorous debate on the risks and potential benefits of the concepts between you and your advisors based on your unique situation, risk tolerance, and goals.

Chapter 9

Conclusion

Lots of Tricks and Tools

I have a low tolerance for people who complain about things but never do anything to change them. This led me to conclude that the single largest pool of untapped natural resources in this world is human good intentions that are never translated into actions.

—Cindy Gallop

We've covered a lot of ground. We started out by laying the foundation about who should consider the benefits of strategic debt and why they might consider it. We discussed the tenets of a strategic debt philosophy and the benefits of strategic debt. We provided an overview of conventional wisdom and reasons why it might be time for a new approach. We then roughly framed out the different types of debt—oppressive, working, and enriching—and established the seven rules for being a better debtor. We discussed how longer life expectancy might impact retirement planning, making it essential that your money last longer. This led to the discussion of the importance of a holistic approach that factors in both your assets and your debts.

With this foundation in place, Part II focused on what debt may be able to do for you. We began with a discussion on distribution rates, the importance of using the right number and considering whether your distribution rates will change throughout your retirement. Table 4.1 showed historic confidence ranges that you could use as you plan for your retirement, and we suggested that you would have to take some risk if you need a higher rate of return. If you don't need a lot from your portfolio, then forget about a debt strategy and don't take a lot of risk. If you do need to take risks, you will want to take the least risk possible. We proved that there are two ways to get a certain rate of return, such as 9 percent, and we proved that debt could increase your rate of return. I illustrated that you can buy assets that deliver a 9 percent rate of return or leverage a 6 percent rate of return. I concluded that, all things equal, a lower-volatility portfolio with debt might be less risky than a high-volatility portfolio without debt.

I illustrated that for some people, utilizing a proper debt strategy might be able to nearly eliminate their taxes. That section's appendix shows multiple examples of people across the net-worth spectrum that are paying virtually no taxes. I showed that debt is just one part of the picture and that retirement could generally be much more tax efficient than you think, depending on how you organize your life.

Chapter 6 showed how debt might actually reduce your risk. I then made the controversial statement that your risk tolerance may not matter because it's secondary to your needs. Your needs are what matter! If you *need* a rate high rate of return, you either have to take risk or lower your needs. Those are your only two options.

I proved that the odds of a 6 percent rate of return during your retirement are zero. Even if we know your average rate of return and inflation and your distributions, we still won't know your ultimate net worth because we do not know your sequence of returns. From here, I argued that risk is equally if not more important in determining your long-term net worth and whether or not you will have a successful retirement. I compared and contrasted a high-return high-risk portfolio with a lower-return, lower-risk portfolio and showed why it would be smart to choose a lower-return, lower-risk portfolio over a higher-risk portfolio with a higher return in retirement. This is true regardless of your debt strategy. I then overlaid the power of a debt strategy and a low-volatility portfolio and showed how that may in fact be the best combination.

In Part III, I focused on how to do this. I discussed the risks of being debt-free and/or rushing to pay down your debt as well as investing risks. I don't want you to read this book and go out and lever up a portfolio of U.S. stocks and bonds, both of which are trading near record highs. I explained that nobody knows what's going to happen, but if you apply lessons from math, history, and valuation, those assets look risky. The question of what you should be investing in is fodder for a different kind of book and thoughtful conversations with your financial advisor.

In this book, I tried to transcend time and geography to provide topical information that you can use in setting your strategy. I suggest that you apply the same framework to every asset class. I encourage you to have an aversion to expensive assets and a bias toward inexpensive assets. I talked about the importance of a world-neutral approach to asset allocation and the importance of protecting from extreme shocks—especially when you are implementing a debt strategy!

I then gave a more detailed review of the types of debt—oppressive, working, and enriching—and how they can evolve over time. I discussed the need to eliminate oppressive debt but that you may not want to rush in and eliminate working debt. I gave you a glide path of debt ratios to think about throughout retirement, trying to consistently target a debt ratio between 15 and 35 percent. I gave you strategies to consider if you are not on track and we talked about the risks of sudden movements versus a gradual glide path.

A Checklist Review

Let's review briefly.

The strategic use of debt may enable you to reach these three goals:

1. Decrease your taxes
2. Increase your rate of return
3. Reduce your risk

Five Tenets of a Debt-Inclusive Philosophy

1. Adopt a Holistic—Not Atomistic—Approach
2. Explore Thinking and Acting Like a Company
3. Understand Limitations on Commonly Held Views of Personal Debt
4. Set Your Sights on an Optimal Personal Debt Ratio
5. Stay Open-Minded, Ask Questions, and Verify What Works

The Four Key Qualities, or Indebted Strengths, of a Strategic Debt Philosophy

1. Increased Liquidity
2. Increased Flexibility
3. Increased Leverage
4. Increased Survivability
5. And the fifth strength: Increased Perspective!

A Checklist: Four Ways to Determine If You Are Prepared to Take on Debt

1. Do you have adequate resources?
2. Are you psychologically disposed to making wise use of better debt?
3. Are you truly open-minded and willing to see what works (or doesn't)?
4. Are you willing to put in the effort to find and work with qualified experts to make sure your situation and circumstances are a good fit?[1]

The Seven Rules for Being a Better Debtor

1. Honestly assess whether you can handle any debt at all, including better debt.
2. Never overextend yourself, even for better debt.
3. Make sure any new debt you take on is high-quality (better) debt, that is, either working or enriching debt.
4. Only take on better debt in the context of a thoughtful, holistic, professionally vetted plan.
5. Get rid of all low-quality oppressive debt as soon as it's feasible.
6. Don't necessarily rush to pay off existing debt.
7. If you do take on debt be conservative and scientific.

Six Strategies for Minimizing Risk in Investing

1. Use a goals-based approach to your asset allocation.
2. Adopt a world-neutral view to your asset allocation.
3. Stress test your portfolio for a range of outcomes.
4. Play offense and defense. For your defense, as in American football, make sure you have a safety playing deep so that you are protected if things go really wrong.
5. Be familiar with valuations and how they impact expected returns.
6. Study economic history—passionately.

This Book in Tweets

- Healthcare, diet, personal finance, and debt cannot be reduced to a tweet. Or maybe they can: "Moderation is key and avoid absolutes."
- If you need a rate of return over 4 percent, you have to take risk. Faced with risk, choose whatever path you feel is the least risky.
- There is risk to having debt. There is risk to not having debt. You need to compare these risks against each other.
- Many times, not having debt increases your risk.
- You have an optimal debt ratio. Chances are high that you are not at that level now—you are too high, too low, or there by accident.
- Liquidity is more valuable than you think. On Planet Earth we pay for things that are valuable.
- Rushing in to pay off your mortgage may not be optimal—think before you do this.
- All debt is not created equal. Know the difference between oppressive, working, and enriching debt.
- Avoid oppressive debt! Working debt is good. Enriching debt is best!
- People are not as rational or disciplined as we would like them to be. I do not want people to abuse and misapply the strategic use of debt.

Even with all this, there are more questions than answers. It's impossible for a book like this to serve as a "how-to" guide. It is intended to be a thought-provoking book that will trigger more questions than answers and topics to explore with your advisors. For a clearer path on how to apply these ideas to your individual situation, consider one more story.

Bringing It All Together: A Strategic Debt Strategy in Action

The following is a hypothetical scenario for you as you move into your retirement. Let's learn from somebody who's possibly a few years ahead of you. Their net worth is higher than average, but this case easily demonstrates the power of a holistic approach to a balance sheet. The guides that follow describe the mechanics of how to implement these strategies.

Our situation begins with a couple in their mid-50s. Their taxable assets are $1 million, and their tax-deferred assets are $1.5 million. They're eligible for a $500,000 line of credit and live in a nice house in the Midwest. Their four children recently finished school and are in the process of purchasing homes. Two are financially independent and good savers, but they face a hurdle coming up with a down payment for their homes. The parents lend each of the children $50,000 for down payments. One child found a compelling business investment, and the parents lend her $50,000. One child had $25,000 of credit card debt at 20 percent, which the parents refinance at 3 percent. The parents help their kids to the tune of $175,000 without disrupting their balance sheet. The kids all move forward in their lives, and each repays their loans in full over the next five years.

How did the parents accomplish all this? They realized that their debt ratio was low and that instead of paying down their mortgage they could put all of their excess savings into a globally diversified portfolio, which gave them the flexibility and liquidity to help their family. Between growth in the market and their continued savings in both tax-deferred and taxable accounts, their portfolio grew considerably when they were between 55 and 65.

When the couple is 58, the husband's parents need to move into an eldercare facility. The older couple own their house but don't have enough assets to put money down to secure the unit. With siblings who aren't in a position to help out, this causes tension in the family. So the couple uses their portfolio line of credit to put down $200,000 and purchase the unit. The parents move in. Six months later, the elderly couple's house sells and the loan is repaid. The total cost of the interest was $3,000, which the couple happily pays to make their parents' life easier in a time of need.

At age 60 the couple decides to purchase a $500,000 second home. They use 100 percent financing on a floating-rate LIBOR loan at a cost of 1.75 percent. Their monthly cost of $729 is fully tax-deductible for them. Because their assets have grown, their debt ratio is still under 15 percent (after all, they picked up an asset when they purchased the home). The couple has no outstanding balance on their securities-based line of credit, a mortgage on their Midwestern home, and a large mortgage on their new second home.

After three years, the couple decides to move into a larger second home a few blocks away in a slightly different neighborhood. This home costs $1 million. They again do 100 percent financing to buy the new home using an interest-only mortgage locked in at 3 percent for seven years. Their monthly payment is $2,500, and a large portion of it is tax-deductible. A big reason they are able to get this mortgage is because they put it in place while they are still working. They move in, temporarily owning three homes using the power of their balance sheet. They eventually sell the initial second home, and the proceeds are exactly enough to pay off their mortgage.

Just before they retire, the couple receives a significant payout on the sale of their business, triggering taxable income of $1.5 million that they cannot defer. They use their line of credit to fund a $250,000 charitable contribution split between a charitable gift annuity and a charitable account from which they can make future contributions. This lets them take advantage of the tax deduction while their income-tax rate is high. They receive almost $100,000 back in tax benefits in that year alone.

They retire at 65. Their situation now looks a lot like the Websters', but their net worth is a sliver higher. They start taking out money from their IRA and borrow from their taxable portfolio so that they pay virtually no tax. They travel extensively during this period, and their "burn rate" is running close to $30,000 per month. Because they never paid off their homes, their portfolios have the additional money they would have used to do so, hence this ends up being a reasonable 5 percent distribution. (Had they paid off their homes it would be a 7 percent distribution rate!)

At 66, the couple buys a used RV for $125,000 and finance it 100 percent on their line of credit. Their cost of the line is 3 percent, so their monthly cost of the RV is $250. The first summer they use it all the time, but then they decide they don't love RVing. They sell it two summers later for $80,000 and put the proceeds down on their line of credit. At 69, they buy a boat for $200,000 and again, 100 percent finance it on their line of credit at 3 percent interest only. Their monthly payment for the boat is $500, but they choose to not make the interest payments and instead let the interest "cap and roll." They keep the boat for three years and then sell it for $150,000 and put the proceeds down on their line of credit. At 71, they buy the dream car they always wanted, using $85,000 from their line of credit. The cost is $212 per month, but they never pay any of it and again let the interest build up.

At 72, the couple realizes that they have spent about eight years with the big house in the Midwest and the large second home, enjoying both properties. But they're getting tired of maintaining both places. They decide to purchase a smaller "crash pad" up north, which they're able to 100 percent finance on their line of credit. They temporarily own three homes again. Before long they sell their primary home and have enough proceeds to pay off the mortgage and pay down the line of credit with the balance.

At 80, the couple has a health scare and determine that they need to move into a facility that has independent living but offers assisted living in the future. They use their line of credit to put down money to secure the new unit. They then sell the big second home and pay off the mortgage. Now they have no mortgage and their only debt is on their portfolio line of credit. At 85, they sell the "crash pad" and use the proceeds to pay down their line of credit. Obviously, their cost of living (distribution rate) falls considerably throughout the later years of their retirement.

One Sunday afternoon the couple sits around the kitchen table and determines that they paid only $4,000 per year in taxes throughout their entire retirement!

Then the financial crisis of 2008 hits. The couple had always hoped to have a 9 percent rate of return on their portfolio, but the world went through some crazy times. Their globally diversified portfolio averages less than expected at 7 percent. The good news is that their greater focus on risk means they were able to have a standard deviation of 7. When the big shock comes, they have a type of portfolio insurance where they hedged their investments from major shocks (the use of options or other strategies I mentioned earlier) that kicks in and protects them from a deep loss. They never run out of money and live to be 100—never crossing into assisted living until the last couple of months—and pass on their accomplishments to their community and their children.

They die with debt. But they also die with assets. As a result of constantly drawing on their line of credit, their amount of debt grew over time but so did their portfolio. How much? Well, you know that even though I know their average rate of return, their standard deviation, and inflation, I don't know because we don't know their sequence of returns! (For more detail, you can see the math on this example at www.valueofdebtinretirement.com or www.vodr.com..)

Debt was a tool that they used in multiple ways throughout their retirement. It is a holistic, integrated part of their financial picture. It isn't something that is bad or evil—it is a tool that let them retire comfortably, minimize taxes, buy the things they wanted and do the things they wanted to do, help their family, and help their charities.[2]

To apply these strategies to your specific situation, I encourage you to spend time with the three guides that follow this chapter. The first is all about ways to use debt to leave a legacy. The second looks at the psychological aspects of retirement and things to consider as you move into retirement. The third reviews ways to help your family and buy the things you want and need.

A Last Word: The Value of Debt in Retirement

I believe that higher liquidity will almost always create more flexibility, which is valuable in good times and in bad times. Striving for lower risk can be, well, lower risk. Liquidity, flexibility, and risk are perhaps your most important considerations as you plan retirement.

We have wrapped up with the big picture concepts I wanted to communicate, and, in Part IV, the book becomes a bit of a "choose your own adventure." Please turn to the sections that are of most interest to you. The first guide is on some charitable giving strategies that I hope will blow you away. The second guide is on the "ROI" of retirement—thoughts on maximizing your resources, outer dynamics, and inner pragmatics. The third guide borrows heavily from *The Value of Debt* and offers ideas on how to use debt with respect to specific topics in your life such as buying a second home, helping your family, eldercare needs, or luxury items. From there the book moves into a series of Appendices where you can find more detail on the ideas that we covered earlier in the book. These are primarily written for professionals, academics, and people who love detail. In aggregate these are all designed to be tools to really help you throughout your retirement.

My goal in life is to give people more financial freedom through more thoughtful strategies. Financial freedom reduces fear, uncertainty, and doubt in retirement, creates a more relaxed state of mind, and lets you worry less and enjoy more. The ideas in this book can help you work with your advisors to increase your return, minimize taxes, and reduce risk. I believe they will leave you better positioned to retire comfortably, buy the things you have always wanted, do the things you have always wanted to do, and leave a bigger legacy—for your family and your charities. You can spend more time figuring out the meaning of life—and do let me know when you discover the answer.[3]

Notes

1. As a part of working with qualified experts, they'll review a number of important aspects of your situation and investing experience, including, but not limited to, your risk tolerance, time horizon, investment objectives, and liquidity needs.
2. Case studies are for educational and illustrative purposes only. They assume eligible assets and that funds are available on the facility. All client situations are unique, and all loans are subject to eligibility and approval by the lender. A lender may deny an advance on an ABLF, preventing the scenarios. Pledging assets reduces and may eliminate liquidity. A market correction could impact market values and/or security eligibility, which could impact the facility size and/or trigger a margin call and/or forced liquidations of assets. See complete disclosures and risks to using an ABLF in Appendix F.
3. Author's Note: The information in this chapter is to be considered in a holistic way as a part of the book and not to be considered on a stand-alone basis. This includes, but is not limited to, the discussion of risks of each of these ideas as well as all of the disclaimers throughout the book. The material is presented with a goal of encouraging thoughtful conversation and rigorous debate on the risks and potential benefits of the concepts between you and your advisors, based on your unique situation, risk tolerance, and goals.

Part IV

GUIDES

It's the little details that are vital. Little things make big things happen.

—John Wooden

Success is the sum of details.

—Harvey S. Firestone

The true secret of happiness lies in taking a genuine interest in all the details of daily life.

—William Morris

Guide 1

Leaving a Legacy

Everybody can potentially benefit from the ideas in this section, though it is primarily written for people who have significant philanthropic intent, a net worth of more than $1 million, or need to make less than 3 percent annually from their portfolios. If you're fortunate enough to have a significant pension that covers your monthly needs when combined with your Social Security benefits, for example, you're in a great position to pass on your assets to your family or charities. If you have enough assets and conservatively believe you won't run out of money, you could increase your annual giving to family, religious institutions, and other charities—or a combination of all three—by making strategic use of debt.

I will cover three broad topics in this guide:

1. General giving philosophy
2. The benefits of giving while you're working
3. Giving to create income

General Giving Philosophy

Nobel Laureate Daniel Kahneman's Nobel Prize–winning Prospect Theory[1] states that two good things are better than one good thing and, similarly, two bad things are worse than one bad thing. Why is this simple concept worthy of a Nobel Prize? Because Kahneman proved that people like two good things so much more than one that they're willing to make irrational choices.

Stores lure consumers with this theory all the time. They'll mark down items by 20 percent, then take an additional 10 percent off that. They don't just mark things down by 28 percent because people are drawn to the perception of a "double sale." A percentage off a percentage is twice as exciting.

How does this relate to your money? Imagine I give you $1,000, just to have. You'd probably be stunned at first, but you'd be happy! Then I give you $10,000. You'd be happier—much happier. But interestingly, you wouldn't quite be 10 times happier. Frankly, it's difficult to be 10 times happier.

We can continue this to the next level. If I give you $1 million, you will be happier for sure. But it becomes difficult to differentiate levels of happiness in this range. The difference between $839,500 and $859,500 appear to be in the same range. The difference of $20,000 is not as significant when compared to the $839,500.

If we were robots, our happiness scale might be perfectly linear. But we're human, and happiness doesn't follow a straight line. It levels off. Figure G1.1 is a sample of what the diminishing returns to happiness look like.

How does this relate to leaving a legacy to your family or charities? Well, it points to the most important thing to know and understand:

Don't give it all away at once!

All too often I see people let money sit in their account, cooking, cooking, cooking. When they die, they leave a big lump-sum pot to their charities and children. Instead of doing this, Professor Kahneman's Nobel Prize–winning theory shows that there are benefits to giving throughout your life.

Giving and Distribution Rates

As we've determined, it's highly likely that you will live a long time. Accordingly, I'm much more defensive with younger clients because I

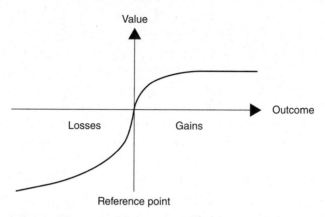

Figure G1.1 "Happiness" Curve

Source: Daniel Kahneman and Amos Tversky, "Prospect Theory: An Analysis of Decision under Risk," *Econometrica* 47, no. 2 (1979): 263.

Note: Figure titled "A Hypothetical Value Function" in original material.

want to be sure that they will have enough money to make it to the end of their lives. Older people, particularly those in their 80s, tend to have a very good sense of whether they'll have sufficient assets to live out their lives. They're in a position to take more risks.

Let's say that a couple, both 82 years old and with a net worth of $3 million, are spending $90,000 per year—a 3 percent distribution rate—from their portfolio to supplement their Social Security benefits. Increasing their distribution rate to 6 percent with an additional $90,000 per year as distributions to their family, religious institution, and charities as annual, recurring gifts would let them make an impact *now*—rather than after they have died—for each one of these entities that is special to them. If their assets fall to a level where they no longer feel comfortable making these donations, they could suspend the giving and lower their annual distributions.

If the couple got a zero rate of return on their assets for five and a half years, their portfolio's value would fall to around $2 million when they're 87. If they're concerned about not having enough money, they could stop giving. At a zero rate of return, they would have enough money to cover $90,000 of living expenses for about 22 more years. This simple example doesn't account for inflation, but the big-picture point is clear.

Many people I know want to help their family and charities but give in amounts that are significantly above or below what's prudent at different parts of their life. The Trinity Studies reviewed earlier in the book (Chapters 4, 6, and 7 and later in Appendix D) give us some ideas that we could consider:

- If you're under 70 and anticipate you will need more than 5 percent from your portfolio, be conservative with your charitable and family gifts.
- Between 70 and 80, you're in a more flexible zone.
- When you're over 80 and spending less than 6 percent of your portfolio's return, perhaps consider increasing your annual gifting.

The key takeaway for many baby boomers is that it may make sense to give more conservatively early in retirement and give more aggressively later.

Giving Strategies Using Debt

If you end up having a low debt ratio when you're in your 80s, you might consider giving to family and charities from your securities-based line of credit. This enables you to keep assets, get the immediate benefit of a tax deduction, and have an impact today. The key question is whether you will earn a rate of return higher than your after-tax cost of the debt. If you do capture that spread—and you can—this strategy may add tremendous value over time.

This hybrid approach brings together many of the ideas we've already discussed. If you are within the glide path for an optimal debt ratio, you could write a check from your line of credit against your portfolio to fund your annual gifts and reap tax benefits that could offset the cost. Borrowing from the previous example, say their net worth is $3 million, they have no debt, and they are only spending $90,000 from their portfolio on an annual basis. They determine that they like the idea of making a bigger impact during their life rather than giving it all away when they die. Rather than sell additional assets to raise money for gifting, they could consider writing a check from their line of credit. This is an alternative way to embrace the "hybrid vigor" of Chapter 5. This can be an exceptional, flexible way to stay within optimal debt ranges.

Quick Thoughts on Giving to Your Children

Giving early and often to your children can be good and bad. On one hand, you can make a bigger impact on their lives and long-term savings by giving them money earlier. If you live to be 100 and die with an estate of $2 million, your "kids" wouldn't collect their inheritances until they're entering their own retirements. On the other hand, giving early and often could create what economists call a "moral hazard;" you could encourage dependency and expenditures the children can't actually afford. An "early and often" giving strategy works if the children save but destroys value if the kids squander their inheritance.

There isn't an easy way to address this moral hazard because it depends so much on your children and their unique circumstances. The key is to be aware of it. If you feel that giving is creating a problem or enabling bad behavior, consider an incentive system where you are encouraging good behavior. I have seen the spectrum including:

- Not giving to the child directly but rather funding a retirement account or taxable savings account on their behalf.
- Funding a college savings plan (a 529 plan) for the grandchildren so that the grandparents can still control the money and its use in the future.
- Direct incentives as extreme as a parent who would give $10,000 if the child showed they put $5,000 into a Roth IRA.

There isn't a right answer except knowing that sometimes funny things happen when large checks are deposited into checking accounts without a clear plan in place for those funds. The best plan is an honest and open conversation with your family on your intentions for the gift, as well as your concerns.

The Benefits of Giving While You're Working

Because your income tax rate is generally much higher when you're working than when you are retired, you may want to consider the potential impact of giving while you're working. If you're 62 years old and making $300,000 per year, giving $100,000 per year to charity could be very beneficial in maximizing your tax deductions. For example, you could save up to $45,000 in making the gift while you are working, compared to potentially nominal savings when you are retired. Remember that the Websters received considerable benefit on their gift but they would not really receive much benefit at all if they increased their giving above these levels.

If you don't want to give that much to charity at one time, there's an easy solution. Instead of giving it directly, you can build up a pot to allocate to charities in the future. This can be accomplished through a donor-advised fund, which enables you to give the money and receive the deduction in a particular year but allocate the money to be distributed in future years. You can learn more about how these funds work by typing "donor-advised funds" into Google where you will see a lot of information from organizations such as Fidelity, Vanguard, Schwab, the IRS, and others.

Using debt to accomplish these objectives is an even more sophisticated approach to consider. If your debt ratio is low and on track to be below the suggested 15 to 35 percent range, you could fund your charitable gifts through borrowing. Depending on your tax bracket, placing $100,000 per year for three years into a donor-advised fund could garner more than $130,000 in tax benefits and a charitable pot of $300,000 to allocate in the future. This means that for a cost of $170,000,[2] you could allocate $300,000 to charities. The benefit of building up this pot is that it may reduce the amount you need to take from your portfolio in the future. Charitable giving is often one of people's biggest retirement expenses.

These strategies can bring even more extreme opportunities when a significant liquidity event or the payout of a large taxable event occurs. The bottom line is, it's worth discussing debt strategies for charitable giving with your tax, legal, and financial advisors as a way to optimize your debt ratio and maximize tax benefits at key times in your life.

Giving to Create Income

We all have fears that we could either "live forever" or die tomorrow, but none of us knows how long we'll live. This makes it difficult to determine how much—and when—we can give to charity. The following strategy could let you have your cake—income, guarantees, and a significant charitable legacy—and eat it, too.

Charitable gift annuities are a way to give money to a charity in return for their commitment to give you a fixed payment for the rest of your life. You get the tax deduction the year you set up the annuity, and the remainder value goes to the charity when you die. This transfers the investment risk to the charitable organization, which enters into a contract guaranteeing it will continue to pay you, no matter how long you live. The better the charitable organization does with its investment returns, the more they get after you (and/or your spouse) die. You may want to consider donating to only large organizations that have big endowments (deep pockets) and qualified professional staffs to minimize the risk of the organization running out of money and not fulfilling its obligation to pay you. It is also a best practice to know the organization well, including its asset base and payment history record. You will definitely need professional advice from your tax advisors on the amount you donate.

A deferred payment charitable gift annuity is structurally very similar to a charitable gift annuity, but you can make the contribution now and have the fixed payments start later. Let's look at an example of how this could be an effective tool.[3] Consider a 60-year-old couple who believe they are on track for retirement. At ages 60, 61, 62, 63, and 64, they give $100,000 per year to a series of deferred payment gift annuities. At age 65 they have a significant taxable event from the sale of their business and give an additional $500,000, for a total of $1 million. They set each gift to start payment at age 90. Depending on their tax bracket, they would receive a total tax savings of approximately $290,000, meaning that the gift in effect cost them approximately $710,000. At age 90, the couple would receive total payments of approximately $215,000 per year until the longest surviving spouse dies. They have a safety net, and their remaining assets need to last them only until they're 90. Of course, the best part is that they can pass on $1 million to an organization that they care about.

To make this even better, let's say the couple's debt ratio is not optimal (it is below the 15 percent range). In this case, they could consider borrowing to fund these gifts. To use a simple, albeit a bit extreme example, let's say that their assets are $5 million and they have no debt. They could give $1 million as indicated above from their line of credit. As they use their income tax deductions, the potential tax refunds could help pay down the line to $710,000. Their debt ratio would be approximately 15 percent. Their $5 million would really only have to get them through age 90, and from 90 forward they would have $215,000 coming in for the rest of their life plus social security. If they don't need that much money they could give it away at that time. Again, the best part is that they would know that they are passing $1 million on to their charity.

There are an infinite number of iterations around this. Here are three more examples:

1. A 65-year-old couple in a high tax bracket borrows against their portfolio to fund a $200,000 deferred gift annuity. This would garner approximately $71,000 in tax benefits right away, meaning that their net cost of the donation is $129,000. The couple is confident their savings will last them at least 30 years, and then they would receive a lifetime income payment of $55,000 per year starting at age 95. In the event that one spouse lives to be 105, he or she would have received $550,000 in income from what was effectively a $129,000 investment. (The impact of inflation could considerably erode the purchasing power of this income, but it's a powerful way to have a strong safety net in place.)

2. A couple is both 60 years old and in a high tax bracket. They borrow against their portfolio to fund a $500,000 deferred gift annuity. This would garner approximately $75,000 in tax benefits right away, meaning that their net cost of the donation is about $425,000. The couple chooses to start the income stream at age 80. They would receive a fixed payment for their lifetime of $59,000 per year starting at age 80.

3. A couple is 70 years old and has one 45-year-old child that they are particularly concerned is not financially responsible. The adult child has no savings, $10,000 in credit card debt, and just can't get ahead. The parents are most concerned about the child later in life, when they are in their 70s and beyond. They know how expensive life is and know their child is not on track. They could give $500,000 to a deferred charitable gift annuity on behalf of the child. This would give them a tax savings up to $59,000, give the charity $500,000, *and* the charity would make fixed payments to the child of $89,000 per year starting at age 75 for the rest of his or her life. Although the

child will have to get to age 75, the parents can rest assured that there is a safety net in place for the later stages of the child's life, when work may be more difficult.[4]

Detail note: The aforementioned examples assume that you are donating cash or via your line of credit. It is essential to know that you will almost always receive better benefit by donating highly-appreciated securities. Together with your advisors, you should consider the possibility of maximizing your benefits by using highly-appreciated securities and then repurchasing the securities later. If your ABLF is a non-purpose facility this may be restricted. To overcome this you could alternatively consider using your ABLF to cover things like taxes or vacations (expenses where you would have otherwise used cash) and then use that cash to repurchase your securities. All of this becomes complicated and the big picture goal is to get the conversation started.

Each of these ideas have significant tax, legal, and financial considerations that you will want to vet with your tax, legal, and financial advisors—as well as with the charitable organization's planned giving department. Do remember this is a "giving guide" and that the primary goal is to make an impact on the charities that are most important to you. That said, I would suggest that you approach the conversation with your advisors with an open mind and a "dream" mentality of what you would ideally like to accomplish. Tell them your fears. What would be the worst case for *you*? Tell them your dreams. What would be the best case—for *you*? It is ok to be selfish when you are talking to planned giving professionals. The more they know, the more they can help you with effective strategies. Work with your advisors to look at multiple scenarios and with some luck you can come up with a win for you *and* for your nonprofit. As long as you are on track to be within your optimal ranges, you should be sure to always factor in how debt may help make the pie larger.[5,6]

Notes

1. Daniel Kahneman's Nobel Prize–Winning Prospect Theory. The Prospect Theory originated with a highly influential paper about decision making under uncertainty by D. Kahneman and A. Tversky, "Prospect Theory: An Analysis of Decision under Risk," *Econométrica* 47 (1979): 263–291. The ideas in this theory and in behavioral finance are important to understand and overlap with the ideas in this book. Combining behavioral finance with traditional finance can help an advisor gain a better understanding of individuals' feelings toward debt, their risk reward objectives, and their optimal debt ratio. Also see www. princeton.edu/~kahneman/docs/Publications/prospect_theory.pdf.

   For information on behavioral finance I recommend the following: Ziv Bodie, Alex Kane, and Alan Marcus, *Investments*, 9th ed. (New York: McGraw-Hill, 2011), Section 12.1, "The Behavorial Critique in Investments." Implicit in this section are the ideas of behavior finance. Investors may accept the financial theory outlined in these ideas but be unwilling to implement them. This can occur due to a number of reasons. The discussion in this section of the text is largely based on Nicholas Barberis and Richard Thaler, "A Survey of Behavioral Finance," in *Handbook of the Economics of Finance*, ed. G. M. Constantinides, M. Harris, and R. Stulz, (Amsterdam: Elsevier, 2003), 1053–1128.

2. To calculate the total cost you would of course also need to include interest expense. Interest rates are subject to change daily. However, if you are borrowing, versus liquidating, then it brings you right back to the concept of capturing the spread and if you are earning a rate of return higher than your after tax cost of debt or not for your bottom line true cost of the strategy. The ideas expressed here are to provide a path of potential options to consider and review with your tax, legal, and financial advisors.

3. The numbers for the following case studies have been prepared using a calculator provided by Washington University. It may be accessed at this site: https://www.glpresents.com/epres_link.jsp?WebID=80. The calculator was run in December 2014. Neither the completeness nor accuracy of this information can be guaranteed by the author, publisher, or Washington University. This information was put together independently of anybody at Washington University and any errors are the author's alone. Figures are not guaranteed and are subject to change without notice. This educational illustration is not professional, tax, or legal advice; consult a qualified tax advisor about your specific situation. Different institutions may—and likely will—provide different figures. Please e-mail plannedgiving@wustl.edu for specific questions on how their calculator arrived at these figures. Donors need to carefully consider the credit risk of the institution that offers the payouts discussed in this chapter. Default by the institution is a possibility you need to consider. Inflation risk is another significant risk when you have a fixed payment. Speak with your specific charities and tax, legal, and financial advisors about these risks and others you should consider.

4. This case study is particularly complicated because you have gifting laws as well as estate laws and state-by-state laws to consider. The deduction for charitable contributions is generally limited to 30 percent or 50 percent of your AGI with the remainder carried over for five years. The goal here is to plant a seed of what may be possible and the types of things that you can discuss with your advisors. Implementation of any of these strategies will require advice from your tax, legal, and financial advisors. This educational illustration is not professional, tax, or legal advice; consult a qualified tax advisor about your specific situation.

5. Case studies are for educational and illustrative purposes only. They assume eligible assets and that funds are available on the facility. All client situations are unique, and all loans are subject to eligibility and approval by the lender. A lender may deny an advance on an ABLF, preventing the scenarios. Pledging assets reduces and may eliminate liquidity. A market correction could impact market values and/or security eligibility, which could impact the facility size and/or trigger a margin call and/or forced liquidations of assets. See complete disclosures and risks to using an ABLF in Appendix F.

6. Author's Note: The information in this guide is to be considered in a holistic way as a part of the book and not to be considered on a stand-alone basis. This includes, but is not limited to, the discussion of risks of each of these ideas as well as all of the disclaimers throughout the book. The material is presented with a goal of encouraging thoughtful conversation and rigorous debate on the risks and potential benefits of the concepts between you and your advisors based on your unique situation, risk tolerance, and goals.

Guide 2

Managing the ROI
of Retirement

The only way to make sense out of change is to plunge into it,
move with it, and join the dance.

—Alan Watts

T his section's holistic but pragmatic guide to retirement is also
meant to challenge your assumptions and beliefs. Perhaps Yogi
Berra was speaking about retirement when he said, "90 percent
of the game is half mental." This guide will have succeeded if it helps
you to take more seriously the climate of massive, accelerating change
that all of us now live in and are seemingly permanently subject to, especially as you approach or move further into retirement. Note that this is
not, and never was meant to be, a *fully comprehensive* guide to retirement
but rather offers up some important things to consider.

Retirement "ROI": Resources, Outer Pragmatics, and Inner Dynamics

Act as if what you do makes a difference. It does.

—William James

Americans are pragmatic and naturally focus on what works, regardless of who validates or approves of it or where it came from. ROI—return on investment—is a well-known concept. How much do you get back for what you put in? This term usually applies to the growth of your financial and business investments. In fact, from a bottom-line perspective, that's exactly what this entire book is about. But from a holistic perspective, the other elements of ROI—**R**esources, **O**uter Pragmatics, and **I**nner Dynamics—are just as important.

The goal is simply this: for all three of these categories or elements—resources, outer pragmatics, and inner dynamics—to directly feed into each other in a reinforcing, potentially very beneficial, positive feedback loop—and to avoid a negative feedback loop (see Figure G2.1)!

Retirement Is Coming: A Holistic Roadmap of the Territory before You Retire

The map is not the territory.

—Alfred Korzybski

Positive (or Negative) Feedback Loops among the Major ROI Categories

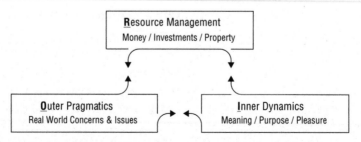

Figure G2.1   Retirement ROI

In a world of longer—potentially much longer—lifespans, some people will push down the average length of retirement by postponing the big day, in some cases indefinitely. Driven by economic necessity or simply the love of what they do, more and more people are likely to work into and through their 70s and beyond. However, we also conclude that given increasing life spans—especially those who have a reasonable amount of resources at their disposal to begin with—the overall trend will be not just toward longer life but toward longer retirements.

So sooner or later, retirement *is* coming, and if you want that retirement to be the way you'd always hoped it would be—then you have to begin with a reasonably comprehensive and holistic map of the territory you will likely travel through. And while it's true that the map is not the territory—so no matter what map you're using, it's likely that various mistakes and miscalculations might be made—it's also true that having no map at all is usually even worse. For now, then, we'll use the *Roadmap* in Figure B.2 to guide us in our explorations of how to best approach retirement.

The term "holistic" can refer to the wellness of the whole person, including physical, emotional, and even spiritual dimensions, as well as to referring to whole systems generally—that is, to the comprehensive big-picture perspective. In this case, it refers both to the wellness of the whole person in retirement, very importantly including emotional health and issues of meaning and purpose, and a wide range of subjects that you are pragmatically required to think about and pay attention to as retirement approaches, including money and cash flow, estate planning, legal issues, health and residence, and so forth.

Meta-Management against a Background of Accelerating Change

Start with the end in mind.

—Steven Covey

The first thing to notice about our holistic *Retirement Roadmap* (Figure G2.2) is that all of these activities take place against a background of *accelerating change in nearly every conceivable domain*. We are without a doubt facing unprecedented change in nearly every area of human life.

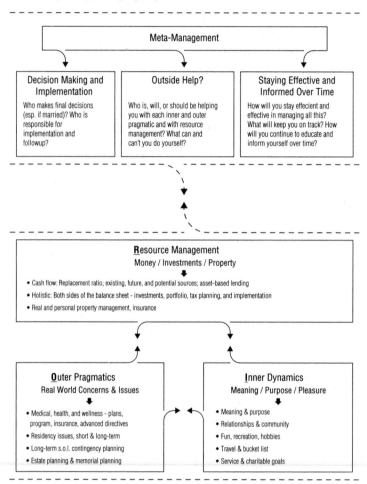

– <u>R</u>esources / <u>O</u>uter Pragmatics / <u>I</u>nner Dynamics –

A background of **accelerating change** in nearly every conceivable domain.

Financial change / Technical change / Biomedical change / Media change / Social change / Climate change / the approaching singularity...

Meta-Management

Decision Making and Implementation

Who makes final decisions (esp. if married)? Who is responsible for implementation and followup?

Outside Help?

Who is, will, or should be helping you with each inner and outer pragmatic and with resource management? What can and can't you do yourself?

Staying Effective and Informed Over Time

How will you stay effecient and effective in managing all this? What will keep you on track? How will you continue to educate and inform yourself over time?

<u>R</u>esource Management
Money / Investments / Property

- Cash flow: Replacement ratio; existing, future, and potential sources; asset-based lending
- Holistic: Both sides of the balance sheet - investments, portfolio, tax planning, and implementation
- Real and personal property management, insurance

<u>O</u>uter Pragmatics
Real World Concerns & Issues

- Medical, health, and wellness - plans, program, insurance, advanced directives
- Residency issues, short & long-term
- Long-term s.o.l. contingency planning
- Estate planning & memorial planning

<u>I</u>nner Dynamics
Meaning / Purpose / Pleasure

- Meaning & purpose
- Relationships & community
- Fun, recreation, hobbies
- Travel & bucket list
- Service & charitable goals

Figure G2.2   Roadmap for Measuring the ROI of Retirement

Financial change, technical change, biomedical change, media change, social change, climate change, and a variety of other types of change are all very real and already very much in progress.

We may be approaching technological breakthroughs that will change everything in ways we cannot now even imagine. Breakthroughs in info-tech, biotech, and nanotech could start to reinforce each other, leading to beneficial or disastrous scenarios that are right out of—or even stranger than—science fiction.

There are two things, in particular, to note about this background of inescapable change. First, it is placed at the top of the *Retirement Roadmap* so that we always keep it in mind as the ongoing background, the biggest of big forces that shape all our lives. You can't effectively plan for retirement if your head is in the sand and you are not aware of the sweeping changes impacting every level of societal and individual experience. Second, the change we are experiencing is seemingly accelerating. As David Schilling wrote for *Industry Tap*:

> Buckminster Fuller created the "Knowledge Doubling Curve"; he noticed that until 1900 human knowledge doubled approximately every century. By the end of World War II knowledge was doubling every 25 years. Today things are not as simple as different types of knowledge have different rates of growth. For example, nanotechnology knowledge is doubling every two years and clinical knowledge every 18 months. But on average human knowledge is doubling every 13 months. According to IBM, the build out of the "internet of things" will lead to the doubling of knowledge every 12 hours.[1]

In the face of such all-pervasive accelerating change, what's an ordinary person—and we are *all* ordinary in the face of such change—to do? Well, the first thing to do is to recognize that familiar ways of going about things—for example, the way your parents may have gone about doing certain things—may no longer be adequate. You need to bring your "A" game if you want to have the retirement you've always desired and deserved.

The first big picture focus is *decision making and implementation*. Basically, you have to know, from the start, *who is in charge*. That is, with regard to the many things that need to be done leading to and then during retirement, who is or will ultimately be in charge of:

- Planning
- Implementing
- Follow-up
- Final decision-making (i.e., who makes the final call if there is any doubt or controversy?)

If you are unmarried or are married and the sole breadwinner and you're used to making all important financial and life decisions and making sure that everything needful is correctly implemented, then this area of decision making and implementation should be pretty straightforward. But if you are married and approach things together, or if you are in a complicated family arrangement with responsibilities either above you (to older generations) or below you (to children and grandchildren)—or both—then you may have to first get very clear about who is in charge of what, who is responsible for what, and how you go forward when there is a disagreement.

It may *seem* that there's no need to figure out what happens when push comes to shove before an issue actually becomes a real-time concern. In reality, however, it's critically important to know who is responsible for what, who gets to make which final calls, and who is ultimately in charge . . . *long before a crisis actually arises.* As you are no doubt well aware, it's vastly more difficult to decide who the ultimate decider is and who is ultimately responsible once there is a major problem. Forewarned is forearmed, and being prepared is just better.

The second big picture focus is *outside help.* This extends beyond the general management of financial resources into managing both the inner dynamics and the outer pragmatics of retirement. Whether you're seeking the right attorney to help you with your estate planning or working with a counselor, minister, or psychologist to help you make the inner meaning-oriented transition to retirement, seek out people who are qualified to assist you in working through any doubts, questions, or concerns or can provide relevant technical expertise. Absolutely consult a caring, open-minded, and technically proficient professional before making any dramatic or drastic changes!

Staying Effective and Informed over Time

> The key is not to prioritize what's on your schedule, but to schedule your priorities.
>
> **—Steven Covey**

The final part of managing the big picture concerns the critical question of *staying effective and informed over time.* At the highest level is what might be managing the whole enchilada, including how you will be able to stay effective (getting the right things done), efficient (getting things done in the right way), and informed (knowing the things that you need to know) over time, from the planning stages of retirement all the way through the rest of your years.

Staying effective and informed over time in any critically important long-term adventure—such as retirement—is just not an easy thing to do. To most efficiently move through this area, let's turn to Steven Covey's *Seven Habits of Highly Effective People* (New York: Simon & Schuster, 2013) and associated works. This classic book is chock-full of powerful applicable wisdom, such as "be proactive" (the first habit), "begin with the end in mind" (the second habit), and "first things first" (the third habit).[2] This advice can be translated into your holistic retirement plan as:

- Get yourself in gear now, even before you think you need to (first habit).
- Take a close look at all three major areas—inner dynamics, outer pragmatics, and resource management—and how they interact, and make sure you know how you want all of that to end up working together (second habit).
- Make sure you are doing things in a sensible order that will work out (third habit).

Covey brilliantly illustrated the third habit in "The Big Rocks of Life."[3] Suppose you have a wide-mouth gallon jar and are given some sand, some gravel, and rocks of various sizes, the largest of which barely can fit through the opening. If you want to get all these materials in the jar, you *have to start with the biggest rocks first* or everything won't fit. Similarly, by analogy, if you want to make sure you have covered and handled everything of importance relating to your approaching or ongoing retirement, then you *have to start with the biggest and most important issues and decisions first* or you simply won't be able to properly address everything in a way that will work.

Resource Management for the Long Haul

With the importance of the big picture in mind we can transition to a discussion on the importance of resource management. In this book we have discussed the following:

- The importance of getting your numbers right: distribution rates vary greatly for different people.
- That your distribution rates may or may not be constant over time in retirement.
- Social Security strategies.
- Focusing on incoming cash flow and that your taxes may be dramatically different during retirement than they were during your working years.
- Investment decisions governed primarily by your needs, not by your risk tolerance.
- Risk and standard deviation.
- Risks with investing and how debt can magnify your investment decisions—for better or worse.
- What to do if it looks like you are not on track:
  - Lower your projected retirement yearly budget by adjusting the necessary outer pragmatics and inner dynamics inputs.
  - Do better with your financial investments over the long run.
  - Find and access additional potential resources such as the wise use of strategic debt.

To supplement these ideas I want to share quick thoughts on other commonly asked questions that I get with retirees and preretirees.

Partial Retirement/Partial Income

I love income! There are many wonderful things that come with having a partial retirement or a part-time job. There are incredible mental benefits, to be discussed later in this section, but here I want to focus on the financial aspects. To the extent possible, it is best to not have an "on–off" switch but rather a glide path when considering these ideas.

One key benefit borrows from the ideas on efficient income in Chapter 5. The first amounts of ordinary income that you earn are generally very tax efficient. An $80,000 job could substitute for an IRA distribution, which can be huge on a long-term financial plan. The difference between having $30,000 to $100,000 of income and no income for a few years is incredible—not only from a tax perspective but also because it considerably reduces the amount you need to generate from your portfolio. Over five years, this could be the rough equivalent of adding $400,000 directly into your IRA. Do not underestimate the value of some income and benefits on your overall financial plan for a number of years.

To the extent possible, I strongly encourage you to generate some form of income through age 70. To me this is 100 percent true if your required need is over 6 percent. It is a great thing to consider if you need 4 percent to 6 percent from your portfolio. Here are some fun examples:

- Four-day weekends, every weekend.
- Work two weeks on, two weeks off (with Fridays always off, of course).
- A part-time job at your favorite store (not only do you earn some mad money, but you might get a killer discount on things you were buying anyway).
- Become a part-time consultant.
- Teachers may be able to become substitute teachers. Does that idea apply to your profession, too?
- Take a job with your favorite nonprofit organization as a hybrid of charity and some income.
- Leverage remote technology to create a flexible schedule.

Now, I fully understand that everybody does not have these options available but a structure like this can be incredibly mutually beneficial to you and to your employer. They may be paying 30 to 60 percent of what they once paid you and, in my opinion, may be getting more than 80 percent of your value. We all tend to be much more effective when you have a limited amount of time. We are focused with a clear mission and objective. Combine that with technology and your talent, and it's a winning formula!

You Can Test-Run Retirement

The good news is that retirement is one of the few things that you can test-run. You can test it with math, and you can test it in how you live your life.

If you really think you want to stop working cold turkey and never work again, then test it with some simple math. Use the distribution rate table to determine a reasonable rate of return. You may want to use the ideas from Chapter 7 to make those numbers more conservative, perhaps chopping off 1 percent per year. Don't forget to factor in the chances of a longer life expectancy. If you have $1 million and get to a distribution rate of, say, 3 percent ($30,000), then you are likely to be in good shape. This will, of course, depend on your asset allocation.

As to how you live your life, I learned a trick from a couple who "retired" a year before they retired. They put 100 percent of their paycheck into a completely different account and never looked at it. They started living their financial life as though they were retired, seeing how they felt about seeing money come out of their account versus going in. Trust me—the psychological change of money going out instead of money coming in is very, very hard for people. Think about it. If you spend more than 35 years putting money in (saving), to then see it coming out is very difficult. In fact, most of my savers have a hard time spending.

The good news with the test run is that if you find that you aren't ready and don't feel comfortable, you still have your job. If you are ready, you've built up a fun savings account that perhaps serves as a buffer or perhaps as a pot from which to give to charity or do something fun—and maybe even crazy!

Real Estate, Small Business Ventures, and Personal Guarantees

Don't sink the ship! Tread very cautiously with personal guarantees, closely held real estate, and small business ventures. Closely held investments will typically reduce your liquidity. This automatically increases the riskiness of the venture. If they say that they are offering a high rate of return please know that from my experience many do not deliver the results they anticipate. Note that you should receive a higher rate of return to compensate you not only for the risk, but also for the reduction in liquidity! Typically you would not want to allocate more than 5 percent of your net worth in any single venture, and 1 to 2 percent is a much better range.

I cannot think of a situation where I would sign a personal guarantee for anything in retirement. So often retirees get sucked into real estate deals where they put down a relatively small amount and then borrow the rest from the bank, with a personal guarantee of 100 percent of their assets. This also happens with start-up businesses, restaurants, and other similar ventures. The risk/reward is skewed too much toward the risk side of the equation. If the upside is a 15 percent return on $50,000 and the downside is that you are on the hook for $500,000, I don't know why you would sign up for that. Yet it happens all the time. Bottom line: I have seen too many retirements sunk by investments in what was supposed to be the next home-run. Invest small amounts of money and do not personally guarantee anything, ever.

Medicare

Just as with Social Security, you should work with a professional and spend a minimum of 20 hours understanding the system. You should do this when you are 64 and be mindful that there are essential enrollment dates that you cannot miss because they have considerable consequences.

Long-Term Care Insurance

This is such an emotional topic. From my experience, people typically take math and logic and throw it out the window . . . or, they simply *guess*! This brings us back to the theme of Stop Guessing With Your Money^{TM}! Consider applying a mathematical and logical framework first and then overlaying the emotional aspects—which are equally important! I bought a $15 martini the other night. It was an awful financial decision. But emotionally, it was great. I had a wonderful night, and I slept well. So remove "right and wrong": Nobody knows what's right or wrong for you.

There are so many factors that go into whether or not long-term care is right for you that it's impossible to give you individual advice. What I can do is give you some questions to talk about with your advisors. Advisors typically word questions in a sales-oriented process, and I recommend that you turn some of these around. Honest people who are acting on your behalf should have no hesitation in answering any of these.

- What percentage of people never need long-term care?
- What percentage of people need long-term care for more than six months? One year?
- Am I in a position to self-insure? Why or why not? (Don't accept a guess or a hunch—require your advisor to do the math and examine the assumptions in detail.)
- If I have sufficient assets and am mathematically on track, am I purchasing insurance to not deplete my assets? (Sometimes people buy policies out of fear that long-term care costs will eat away their life savings. Purchasing a policy is a guaranteed expense and therefore a guaranteed depletion of your assets. So, what is the breakeven? How much long-term care would you need at what cost for it to have been a good, profitable decision? Don't just compare the raw numbers. You need to apply a time value of money/rate of return comparison to do the real math.)
- What are the potential cost savings of applying a 6-month or 12-month exclusion period (meaning the policy does not cover your needs for the first 6 or 12 months and then kicks in)? This is a lot like a car insurance deductible in which you may have a $500 or $1,000 limit before insurance kicks in. (For example, compare and contrast a policy with a 12-month exclusion that covers you for 24 months versus a policy with no exclusion that covers you for 60 months.)
- What are the potential risks, benefits, and costs of having a policy for a period of one to three years?
- What are the potential risks and potential benefits of insuring one spouse versus two spouses?
- What kind of facility does this policy cover?
- Do I need to cover the full amount with insurance? (After all, if you are prudent with your investments, they should be there to cover your expenses during this time. You may want to consider the risks and benefits of coverage for perhaps as low as 30 percent to 50 percent of the anticipated average daily cost versus the full daily cost. You should also consider what other expenses you may or may not have if you are in a long-term care facility.)
- The old rule of thumb in insurance is that high-probability events are best self-insured and insurance works well for low-probability events. In your opinion, how does this framework apply to long-term care?

For what it is worth, I have a $5,000 deductible on my home and car insurance, but I own earthquake insurance on my home in the Midwest.

Thoughts on Life Insurance

This is a very complicated topic that depends on so many personal factors. I have found the following list of questions helpful to discuss with one's advisors.

If You Feel You Have Sufficient Assets

If there is enough money for two people to live on, mathematically there should be enough money for one person to live on. The question that I would ask, then, is, "Absent estate-planning reasons, if we have sufficient assets to have the retirement we want to have, what exactly are the costs and potential benefits of continuing to maintain coverage?"

If You Do Not Have Sufficient Assets or Do Not Feel As Though You Are on Track

In this case, you have to make difficult decisions with respect to your resource allocation. What is the cost versus the expected benefit? When would that "benefit"—the expected payoff from the policy—take place? Who is the beneficiary and at what likely point in their life? What is their alternative? Rule number one to any process is to compare it to your best alternative. What is the best alternative to continuing coverage? What are the potential risks and benefits?

Paying for insurance is a guaranteed immediate depletion of your assets and therefore depletion of your liquidity. You have to overlay the guaranteed cost with the potential benefit.

Reverse Mortgages

Conceptually they can be very beneficial but they are so complicated and regulated by so many entities that the honest answer is that I am prohibited from discussing them in a lot of detail. I can, however, provide you with a list of questions to consider:

- What is the worst thing that can happen?
- How could that happen? Is it by outside parties or by actions of my own doing?
- What are the interest rate risks?
- Under what circumstances do you get kicked out of your house?

In a perfect world reverse mortgages could be avoided. You could consider not paying down your house, protecting the liquidity, and turning the liquidity into an income stream, either via borrowing or without borrowing. To me it doesn't make sense to rush in, pay down, and then turn around and borrow it back.

I just dealt with a scenario where a client insisted on owning their house outright so they paid it all off. After a couple of years they wanted to embrace the strategies from Chapter 5 and began borrowing from their portfolio. Debt grew against their portfolio and they worried about the floating interest rate risk and they worried about a market downturn. They wanted to instead have the debt against their house. The problem is that they were already retired. Doing a cash-out refinance against a house to refinance that debt against the portfolio is very complicated— and sometimes prohibited. They would have been better off if they had placed a mortgage on their house while they were working and left it in place during the early years of their retirement. This would have increased their liquidity and decreased their risk considerably.

How You Should (or Should Not) Factor in Inheritance

The aggressive strategy is to factor it in. The conservative strategy is to leave it out. My advice is that you are better off being surprised to the upside than disappointed on the downside. If you do decide to factor it in I recommend that you do the following:

1. Assume that the gifting party (likely your parents) live to be 105 years old. Do they have enough to make it or will what you thought would be an inheritance turn into the need to support them?
2. Assume that their expenses later in life are higher and that they live the dignified glorious life they deserve—remember, it is their

money, not yours. *Never* compromise their lives or lifestyle for your potential benefit.

3. If you don't know their intentions, then assume that they give 20 percent of it to charity.

4. Assume that there is a significant market correction that you can't control since you don't have the assets.

Discount it a sliver more to be conservative, and then you can decide if you want to factor it in at all. I also have a personal philosophical belief that it is best for us to be financially independent. It creates so much more mental freedom and flexibility. I have a huge problem with people making decisions to maximize their expected inheritance.

Outer Pragmatics: Real World Concerns, Issues, and Details

The outer pragmatics of retirement and retirement planning—the "O" of our ROI—can be daunting. A brief glimpse at the *Outer Pragmatics Planning Table* (OPPT) (see Table G2.1) will remind you that life in the modern world is very complex. (And, like it or not, for the most part it is getting more complex all the time.)

Even if you had all the money in the world, you still have a whole lot of work ahead of you when it comes to identifying, making decisions about, and taking appropriate actions with respect to how your retired life will play out over time. Very importantly, even though things are unlikely to happen exactly the way you want them to, no matter how carefully you plan, there's still no excuse for not doing the planning. Why? Because failing to pay attention to any particular category or issue in the outer pragmatics planning table *can have substantial personal, financial, medical, legal, or other consequences,* both for you and your close and extended family members.

When considering the quality of life and standard of living that you hope to maintain throughout retirement, *the weakest link is exactly where things will fall apart* and where a little bit of thinking and planning ahead of time may have made a big difference. It's like the game of chess, in which novice players will place their seemingly unimportant pawns without much thought early in the game while advanced players know that exactly where a pawn is or isn't often makes all the difference. Well, if

Table G2.1   Outer Pragmatics Planning Table (OPPT)

Category/Issue	Subcategory/Issue	Help? Who?	Status	Next Steps
Legal				
	Proper titling of all assets			
	Adequate liability and other insurance			
	Estate and wealth transfer planning			
	Memorial planning			
Medical				
	Health-care options			
	Advanced directives			
	Adequate insurance			
Residency				
	Primary residence			
	Second and vacation homes			
	Long-term residency and assisted living			
Life Planning				
	Maintaining standard of living generally			
	Transportation, shopping, meals			
	Recreation, travel, fun, bucket list			
	Community, religious affiliation, charitable involvement			

Source: © Tom Anderson, Timber Wolf Publishing, 2014, 2015.

you think of life as a big game of chess, you will understand that the planning and preplanning you do in all of these areas is likely to make a huge difference for your personal experience of retirement in the long run.

Legal Planning

The first category in the OPPT is Legal. Whether or not you already work with one or more attorneys, no doubt you will indeed need the services of an attorney for a variety of different OPPT issues. In the Legal category, however, we have included only subcategories that are legal in nature.

The first of these is making sure all your assets are properly titled, that is, that the official paperwork showing *everything you own of value* is just the way you want it. Real estate, cars, investment funds, retirement accounts, bank accounts, insurance policies—all of it should be checked, and you very well may need help from your attorney as well as officials from other involved entities (like banks, or insurance companies, or title companies) to get it all straightened out. Don't simply assume that all of your assets are properly titled; you really and truly have to have it checked out.

A second explicitly legal area is estate and wealth-transfer planning. If you have significant assets, are your holdings already part of a family trust? What about your will? Have you determined how you are going to ensure a satisfactory "wealth transition" once you (or you and your spouse) are no longer here? Research consistently shows that a shockingly high percentage of estates do not transfer as planned, with greed, bickering, and backbiting ruling the day or entitled children receiving far too much money all at once and in effect never developing their own financial life and resources, or unexpected, unintended tax consequences taking a horrendous bite out of the entirety of your estate.

Picking the right executor or executors is critical here, and once you are gone this is not something you can change. Also, of course (although this more properly falls into the resources element of ROI), you want to do everything you can to make your estate transfer as tax efficient as possible. The rules here are always subject to change, so you may need help from both an attorney and ideally a CPA or other accountant.

A legal area related to estate and wealth transfer planning is *memorial planning*. How, exactly, do you want your funeral, if any, to go down? How will your memorial service be paid for? Who will be in charge?

Will you be buried or cremated? It may seem a bit morbid to plan for this, but once again, failing to plan for it can lead to a whole lot of confusion and unhappiness when the time actually comes and you are no longer there to straighten things out. An ounce of prevention...

The last legal-related issue concerns making sure you have legally protected your assets by having *adequate liability and other insurance*. This applies to your car insurance as well as to your homeowner's and umbrella policy. If you don't have an umbrella policy, you should consider speaking with your insurance agent right away. You should also make sure you have enough coverage. If you have one from a few years ago for $1 million, there is a chance it should be doubled or tripled. There is also the brave new frontier of identity theft insurance, something that may become more and more necessary as our individual, social, and online worlds continue to merge.

Medical Planning

The next major category in the OPPT is Medical. How will you have your health attended to as your retirement proceeds and as illness and old age take their toll? It takes a good deal of work to get even a broad feeling for the changing landscape in health care. Then there's the question of paying for all of this, which begins with making sure you have adequate insurance that you can afford.

On top of all that, you want to make sure that you have advanced medical directives in place. Do you or don't you want to stay alive for as long as possible regardless of what type of vegetative state you end up in? Who gets to make the call about whether you are conscious and aware enough to make your own medical decisions? And what, if anything, have you decided about organ donation? (Do you carry one of those cards in your wallet, and, if so, is it signed, current, and valid?)

Residency Planning

The OPPT next discusses residency planning, or *where you will want to physically live and reside over time*. If you own your primary residence, how important, if at all, is it for you to remain there until you die? Can you afford to keep your primary residence, or will you need to sell it at some point to fund your retirement? And what about upkeep on the home? Will you need someone to help you do things around the house as you get older?

Related are questions of second and vacation homes. If you have a second property, is it an investment or mainly for recreation and pleasure purposes? Perhaps your extended family comes to vacation with you in the woods or at the beach and this time together is worth whatever it will cost you to hold onto the property. Or perhaps you simply intend to eventually pass it on to your children … or then again, maybe you will hold it in reserve in case you need more assets later on. You may also need to consider assisted living or other types of residency options for the long run. Is it worth investing in a retirement facility of some type, especially one that has various levels of assistance available?

Life Planning

This question of assisted living segues us into the last outer pragmatics category, Life Planning. The questions here concern how you will generally maintain your standard of living as you move into and through your retirement years. At some point you may need help with transportation, shopping, meal preparation, and so forth. Individuals who are forced to no longer drive (for vision-related or other reasons) often experience this as a depressing, sometimes devastating, turn of events. But if you know this might happen and prepare for it by arranging other types of transportation, it likely won't be nearly as distressing.

An interesting and enlightening perspective on how to maintain your general standard of living as you get much older and experience various types of decline is presented by the psychologist Ellen Langer in her award-winning book *Counterclockwise: Mindful Health and the Power of Possibility* (New York: Ballantine Books, 2009). As a simple example, she suggests that if you return from the grocery store and find that it has become difficult to put the groceries on the floor and then pick them up after you've unlocked your door, you may want to put a bench outside your door so you don't have to bend down as far. (Which is easier: regaining full back flexibility through stretching, yoga, therapy, Pilates, and perhaps surgery, or just putting in a bench?) Langer discusses many ways that older adults can regain a sense of personal self-mastery and efficacy despite the increasing challenges that come with very old age.

The next Life Planning subcategory concerns recreation, travel, fun, and your "bucket list." You don't have to plan out any or all of this in detail, but you should have an idea of what you will do to have fun and enjoy yourself, and roughly what it is going to cost to do this. The cost will feed into your general assessment of the resources you need as your retirement progresses through the years and decades. Also, simply keeping in mind that you will not be alive forever should motivate you to do everything you want to do that you haven't done and to find a way to afford it even during retirement.

The last Life Planning category—community, religious, and charitable involvement—is something to take pretty seriously. The evidence is clear that those who are involved in an active community life live happier, longer, lives. No man or woman is an island, and the emotional and physical support from a community as well as the opportunity to give something of value back to others is extremely valuable. The sixth and final "happiness imperative" from author Henry Miller is "Make a meaningful contribution" (to others, to community).[4] When all is said and done, people who find ways of giving back to the greater community and the greater good are happier than those who do not, so you may want to begin planning for the kind of long-term community, religious, or charitable involvements that will provide you with these kinds of opportunities.

Inner Dynamics: Meaning, Purpose, and Pleasure in Retirement

The *Retirement Roadmap* (Figure G2.2), you will note, shows the "R," the "O," and the "I" interconnecting. The three together create a continuous feedback cycle, and the inability of any one of these to inform or be informed by the other two is suboptimal and could be disastrous. Just because you can't necessarily measure or externally point to inner dynamics doesn't mean that they're not of pivotal importance. In fact, inner dynamics may very well comprise a life and death issue. Many people believe that early retirement leads to an earlier death, and if you search online for "early retirement" and "death," you'll find a large number of articles, reports, and studies indicating that yes, indeed, retirement and death sometimes are directly, perhaps even causally, linked.[5]

You will find references to people "losing the will to live," to the "broken-heart syndrome," and to the idea that loss of routine and *too little stress* both lead to early death.[6] It's difficult to tease out the ultimate scientific truth here (not all the studies agree), but this line of thinking makes intuitive sense. If you aren't living in a meaningful and purposeful way, then you have less to live for, and if you have been working your entire life and suddenly are no longer working—and you haven't planned for that—then you could find yourself unhappy, de-energized, depressed, and lacking the kind of gusto and enthusiasm that makes life worth living.

When most people start focusing on retirement, they first focus on managing money and making sure they'll have enough resources to retire at the standard of living they aspire to, and perhaps they also start attending to outer pragmatics. In a somewhat cruel twist of fate, the energy and focus that it takes to approach and deal with both resources and outer pragmatics take away from the focus on the inner dynamics of meaning, purpose, passion, and pleasure that are every bit as important, or perhaps even more important, than the other two areas.

But they won't take care of themselves. Only you can do this kind of inner work if you make it a priority. Now, you may be one of those people who is interested in and excited by almost everything, who has many hobbies and interests, and who has been looking forward to lots of sleeping and napping, media, reading, fishing and golf, and so on, for a very long time. But even if you *are* one of those people, it still behooves you, very early in the process of approaching or being in retirement, to take a detailed inner inventory and delve into the following questions:

- Now that I am retired, where will I find meaning and purpose in life?
- What relationships and community opportunities am I currently involved in or would I like to further be involved in when I retire?
- How am I likely to actually spend my days when I retire? What would an ideal day look like? An ideal week?
- How will things change in my home, with my wife (and other family members who are living with me) once I retire?
- What will I do for fun and recreation? What hobbies do I have or do I want to develop and pursue? Music? Reading? Sports? Computers? Filmmaking? What used to interest me or have I always had a yearning to get involved with?

- Do I have a bucket list? If so, what's on it, and is it complete? If not, why not, and when will I create or complete it? When will I start checking off items?
- What are my community service or charitable goals? Is there anything I would like to volunteer for? What would I like to contribute to my world?

Essentially, you must figure out who you are outside of work, what you truly enjoy doing on a daily basis, where you want to make additional contributions to the greater community (if at all), and perhaps, ultimately, what your life purpose is.

If this all seems a little soft or unimportant, consider again that you are much more likely to be happy while approaching and during retirement if you have a handle on these issues.

Sharpening the Saw

Happiness, true happiness, is an inner quality. It is a state of mind. If your mind is at peace, you are happy. If your mind is at peace but you have nothing else, you can be happy. If you have everything the world can give—pleasure, possessions, power—but lack peace of mind, you can never be happy.

—Dada Vaswani

Let's turn back to the late, great Steven Covey and his seventh habit, Sharpening the Saw:[7]

Sharpen the Saw means preserving and enhancing the greatest asset you have—you. It means having a balanced program for self-renewal in the four areas of your life: physical, social/emotional, mental, and spiritual. Here are some examples of activities:

Physical: Beneficial eating, exercising, and resting
Social/Emotional: Making social and meaningful connections with others
Mental: Learning, reading, writing, and teaching
Spiritual: Spending time in nature, expanding spiritual self through meditation, music, art, prayer, or service

. . . As you renew yourself in each of the four areas, you create growth and change in your life. . . . Without this renewal, the body becomes weak, the mind mechanical, the emotions raw, the spirit insensitive, and the person selfish. . . .

Feeling good doesn't just happen. Living a life in balance means taking the necessary time to renew yourself. It's all up to you.

Covey is exactly right: It's all up to you. And, very important, the same sort of practices that will help you sharpen the saw will help you to explore the inner dynamics of meaning, purpose, and pleasure and will also help you stay on top of how you manage your retirement process.

To keep on top of things during retirement, you have to work at it in a balanced, ongoing, and proactive manner. If you want to keep yourself informed about things, you have to keep seeking out, reading, and digesting information. If you want to make sure that you have the right level of outside professional help assisting you, you have to keep evaluating whether what you are currently doing is or isn't working. There is no shortcut here.

Particular Considerations on Retirement and ROI for the LGBT Community

Members of the LGBT community face particularly unique and complex issues with respect to retirement planning. There are some key specific challenges that the LGBT community faces with respect to resources, outer dynamics, and inner pragmatics. The topics we are discussing— aging, family structure, and self-actualization—all fall into this space but with nuanced twists. The LGBT community has added retirement challenges due to marginalization and discrimination in the workplace, as well as other institutions that have limited available financial options. These factors, along with some unique health-related challenges, have led to a community that is less prepared, if not entirely, unprepared, for retirement.[8] The ideas of making sure you have a comprehensive, holistic plan apply here more than perhaps anywhere else.

Life Expectancy

For many reasons the LGBT community has generally accepted a thought process that they will have a shorter life expectancy than their straight peers. It is time to wake up! It is my belief that the greatest advances in life expectancy will transpire within this demographic over the next 20 and 30 years.

You need to have a plan that will get you well past your 90s and into your 100s. Who or what is the fallback if you run out of money? Regardless of whether you have a partner, you may want to consider the benefits of having a solid plan for self-sufficiency, particularly in the unfortunate event your partner predeceases you.

Health Care

With respect to health care, there are numerous issues to consider. Although many members of the community are incredibly successful, oftentimes they don't have the same system to protect them and to provide health care. What makes this more challenging is that there are community specific health issues that often require particular care and attention. The issues are exponentially exacerbated for the large majority of the LGBT community who fall outside the "incredibly successful" class.

Long-term care is of critical importance. What happens if dementia sets in? Do you have kids? Will you be treated with dignity and respect during a vulnerable time? Many in the LGBT community fear institutionalization. Will your nurse treat you with the same care and respect? Will you get the treatment you deserve or will you be discriminated against and marginalized? Will you have an advocate?

The unfortunate fact is that the LGBT community is denied services more than any other population—especially transgender individuals! While some people may have a strong safety net in a worst-case scenario, this is not always the case in the LGBT community. Fractured family relationships and institutional marginalization increase the likelihood of LGBT individuals facing their golden years alone and vulnerable.

What does this mean to you? Tailored health-care solutions, choice, and flexibility all cost money and you need to be prepared. It has to be part of your plan. The earlier you start the better for you and your family.

Family Structure

The younger LGBT community is embracing, if not demanding, a family structure that was not available to people a few years ago. The problem with anything that is relatively new is that there is a lack of folklore to guide people through issues. You can imagine that for "traditional" families a person may bump into a friend at a gym and hear awful stories about divorce and/or the importance of a prenuptial agreement. These same stories are less common—there isn't as much guidance. Regardless if it is from a lack of folklore or ignorance or the overwhelming desire to finally be able to announce a relationship, frankly many people are making terrible decisions.

Who is the beneficiary of your IRA? Your 401(k)? Why? What about your life insurance beneficiaries? What are the potential tax consequences of your selection? Will the marriage penalty apply? Which spouse should claim tax deductions? How is your household set up to receive an inheritance from one side of the family? How does that inheritance pass on? Do you have an estate plan in place? Laws are continually changing from state to state; are you working with someone that understands your state's laws, especially if you just moved to that state? These issues are just some of the numerous and significant challenges facing LGBT individuals.

The previous discussion on Social Security is about 10 times more complicated for the LGBT community, and partners in particular. It is way outside of the scope of this book to get into specifics but suffice to say it is complicated and you have to get advice from somebody that understands your unique situation and the options available to you.

There are wonderful aspects of marriage but there are incredible complexities as well. Your relationship may last forever or it may encounter difficulty and dissolve five years from now. You or your partner may live a long time or die unexpectedly. This can often create conflicting goals and requires a combination of detailed planning before you fully engage in a committed relationship (a prenuptial agreement) and updating throughout the relationship. In many cases there may be a large age gap between partners, which adds an additional level of complexity that needs to be addressed.

There is another important consideration that some people outside the LGBT community do not understand as well and it relates to the importance of pets and pet trusts/pet protection. These subtle needs can

positively be addressed but often they are not addressed or given importance—or understood in the same way.

Philanthropic Considerations

Many of the most generous donors I know come from the LGBT
community. Passionate supporters of their community, they're often dedicated to advancing arts, education, and, most importantly, equality. Often
it is part philanthropy and part of a movement. We all try to balance the
goals of making sure that we have enough money to last our lifetime and
that we are enjoying the present. Please review the philanthropic guide
closely because if you desire to leave a legacy to a nonprofit there may be
a way to have your cake and eat it too.

Working with Your Advisors

You need to work with tax, legal, and financial advisors that understand
your life issues. It would be way too controversial for me to say that
LGBT clients should solely seek out LGBT advisors. I would rather
suggest that you find someone who will be your advocate: someone
who will be your cheerleader, get you to where you want to be in
life, and will protect you. They need to understand your family and the
family structure, your long-term goals, and that you may not have the
same safety net if things go wrong that other people have. Ideally, your
advisor(s) should be someone that is active in *your* community. This is
particularly important as many laws protecting the rights of LGBT individuals vary from state to state.

Final Checklist

- Master the complexities of LGBT Social Security distributions.
- Be sure your beneficiaries are correct in every single place where
  you need to update them.
- Be sure you have a comprehensive estate plan, focused on your goals,
  with someone who understands your life.
- Plan to have adequate resources so that you have a freedom of choice
  and flexibility with respect to your health care.

- Anticipate and plan that your life expectancy may be very long.
- Consider philanthropic giving strategies and how they can be mutually beneficial.
- Carefully consider having a prenuptial agreement.[9]

Notes

1. See www.industrytap.com/knowledge-doubling-every-12-months-soon-to-be-every-12-hours/3950.
2. See www.stephencovey.com/7habits/7habits-habit1.php.
3. See www.appleseeds.org/Big-Rocks_Covey.htm.
4. Miller, Henry S. *The Serious Pursuit of Happiness: Everything You Need to Know to Flourish and Thrive* (Los Gatos: Wisdom House Media, 2013).
5. See, for example, www.webmd.com/healthy-aging/news/20051020/early-retirement-early-death.
6. See www.slate.com/articles/news_and_politics/explainer/2012/01/joe_paterno_are_people_who_retire_more_likely_to_die_.html.
7. See www.stephencovey.com/7habits/7habits-habit7.php.
8. See http://sageusa.org for more information on SAGE. I have consulted with SAGE and am incredibly impressed with the organization. At the same time, I wrote this section on my own. Any errors, omissions, or problems with tone, style, or direction should be attributed to me and to no other person or institution. Friends have encouraged me to be direct and have encouraged me to provide a "much needed wake-up call."
9. Author's Note: The information in this guide is to be considered in a holistic way as a part of the book and not to be considered on a stand-alone basis. This includes, but is not limited to, the discussion of risks of each of these ideas as well as all of the disclaimers throughout the book. The material is presented with a goal of encouraging thoughtful conversation and rigorous debate on the risks and potential benefits of the concepts between you and your advisors based on your unique situation, risk tolerance, and goals.

Guide 3

How to Help Your Family and Buy the Stuff You Want and Need

A Reference Guide

*T*he *Value of Debt's* theme can be summarized as *What would a company do?* This guide borrows extensively from that framework to lay the foundation for a guide that will help you as you approach different needs in your retirement.

Act Like a Company/Think Like a CFO

Consider what happens when a company needs to buy new desks for all of its employees. Does the CFO of the company walk down the street to the nearest bank and say, "Please tell us about your desk financing options" and then accept whatever interest rate the bank is willing to offer for a loan at that moment? Of course not!

Instead, the CFO looks at the entirety of the company's balance sheet—its assets and its liabilities—and then considers all the plusses and minuses of all the different financing options available. The CFO wants to determine the best way to finance the desks, which means determining the lowest cost of capital that will accomplish the company's objective. It's a holistic and pragmatic approach that considers all of the available loan and financing options in the context of what will be best for the company in the long run.

As an individual or family with some resources and wealth behind you, is there any conceivable reason why you wouldn't want to take the same approach? While it may be true, as discussed in Chapter 1, that individuals and families are not companies and ultimately may have very different goals, there's nothing virtuous about not being as smart with your money as possible.

This guide considers the options available to you when you want to buy something—in particular, expensive items. We'll start by looking at four basic principles and then consider specific scenarios that illustrate how you might buy a boat, a car, a diamond ring, or a second (or even a first) home. The most important thing to keep in mind is that by following these strategies you should not only have access to better rates but also better terms. These terms ultimately should reduce the likelihood you will encounter severe financial distress (or if you do encounter it, that the direct and indirect costs of that financial distress, its severity, and its duration will all be minimized).

Principles When Financing the Purchase of a Desired Item

Keep these two principles in mind when considering how to finance the purchase of an expensive item:

1. The value of an item is 100 percent independent of the financing you have around that item.
2. In my opinion, amortization stinks!

The first principle concerns *the relationship between the type of financing you use to acquire an item and the value of that item*. Now, suppose you own a late-model BMW. The value of that car—the actual worth of the car—remains the same whether you bought it with cash from your savings, came up with the money through a line of credit, or took out a loan from the bank to purchase the car. The structure of the financing, if any, is 100 percent independent of the value of that item.

> The value of an asset is 100 percent independent of the financing in place around that asset.
>
> If you wanted to buy my house, you would not ask about the amount or terms of my mortgage. Similarly, if I sell my car, a prospective buyer wouldn't care if I owned it outright or had a loan against it.
>
> The value you will receive upon selling an asset has nothing to do with whether that asset has a loan against it.

You can think about this in terms of the following question: If you have a car loan today and pay off that loan tomorrow, does the value of your car change? The answer, of course, is no. The car would be worth exactly the same today as it was worth yesterday (except perhaps it might be worth a tiny bit less because there is one more day of depreciation that has to be subtracted from its value). Similarly, your house—or your vacation home or a Renaissance painting or a rare coin collection—will either appreciate in value or depreciate in value regardless of the financing you have in place around it. Delinking the type of financing and the value of an item is an important root principle that allows you to think better—more holistically, more creatively—about the varieties of financing available.

The second principle, plain and simple, is that, in my opinion, *amortization stinks!* Amortization requires the borrower to repay parts of the loan over time. What's the problem with this? If you take on a loan with amortization, you will have *an inflexible minimum monthly payment* (including both interest and principal reduction) that you have to make no matter what else is going on in your life. This cuts directly against the indebted strength of increased flexibility and also amounts to *decreased* liquidity just when you might need it the most. A loan with amortization locks you in until that loan is paid off, ties up capital in fixed assets, and reduces your savings—which is why you should avoid such loans whenever possible. Even items that are considered depreciating assets— which are necessarily worth less as every year goes by—can be financed interest-only. There is no need to link a depreciating asset with an amortization schedule.

> One hundred percent of all publicly traded corporate debt in America is issued on an interest-only basis.[1]

Let's return for a moment to how companies think and act. Have you ever purchased an amortizing corporate bond in which you receive monthly interest payments as well as a locked-in portion of the principal being paid back to you on a monthly basis? The answer is no, you haven't ever purchased such a bond, because 100 percent of corporate debt in America is issued on an interest-only basis (with the principal due at the bond's ultimate call date or maturity). If I purchase a bond from General Electric or Walmart or IBM, I will receive an interest payment every six months, but I will never receive a partial principal repayment until the bond matures.

So if companies issue only interest-only nonamortizing bonds, why do individuals agree to amortizing car loans, boat loans, home loans, and so on?[2] Harkening back to the pervasive knee-jerk antidebt stance that most people have, perhaps the willingness to agree to amortizing loans has to do with the idea that this is a quicker and guaranteed way to be free of debt at the end of the day. Certainly, however, no CFO of any company would agree to amortization unless absolutely forced to, because agreeing to a fixed monthly payment *no matter what else is happening in your life* increases your risk of encountering financial distress and increasing its costs (direct and indirect), its duration, and its impact.

Think about it: Whether you're in good times or bad times, if you have an amortizing loan, you are required to make the same monthly payment *no matter what*. If you have a nonamortizing way of financing the purchase of an expensive item, you can make little or no payment when times are bad or pay down some, most, or all of the remainder of the loan if you get a big bonus (taking into account where you are with respect to your optimal debt ratio, of course).

> An amortization schedule reduces your flexibility in good times and bad, which is just when you will need that flexibility the most!

Here's a quick example. Suppose you have a $500,000 home loan at 4 percent, amortizing over 15 years. Your monthly payment would be roughly $3,700 per month. If you pay down $250,000, your next month's payment is . . . the exact same amount! What if you lose your job? Your next month's payment is still $3,700, and there is nothing you can do to change it.

The bottom line is that you should avoid amortization whenever possible, which means avoiding many common commercially available and bank-originated loans and financing options whenever possible.

Many people might say, "Wait a second! Are you saying I should have interest-only debt on my car? But my car *will* depreciate over time." Here principles 1 and 2 come together. Just because an asset depreciates does not mean that you need to have an amortization schedule for it. Moreover, with an interest-only loan you can choose to pay down any amount of principal any time you want to. Think about it from a CFO's perspective. Do companies own assets that depreciate? Absolutely! If a large company owns 50,000 desks that are good for, say, 10 years, it doesn't go out and issue a desk bond that amortizes over 10 years. It issues debt based on its whole balance sheet, knowing that some of its assets will appreciate over time and some will depreciate over time.

With this foundation in place, let's look at specific examples of how to use a holistic approach to your liabilities.

Managing Credit Card Debt

We discussed this in Everyday Example #1 in Chapter 1.

It is stunning how many high-net-worth individuals I see who carry $10,000 to $20,000 (and much more) of credit card debt. Typically this is because they consider credit cards a separate "bucket" that they don't want to pay off. I get that and feel the same way. Having different buckets can be a very effective way to manage your money. At the same time, you want to consider having that separate bucket be at the lowest possible cost to you. Using a line of credit against your portfolio may be that way!

Helping Your Kids with Their Credit Card Debt

It may turn out that you do not have credit card debt—and I hope that's the case! But the other day I was visiting someone who explained to me that her child had $25,000 of credit card debt running at 20 percent interest. This parent was thinking about stepping in and paying it off because she was concerned that her child would bury himself in debt and destroy his credit, with no way out. The only reason she didn't want to pay it off was because she wanted her son to learn a lesson.

I suggested that perhaps there was a middle ground. She could use her securities-based line of credit (she was well within her optimal debt ratio) to pay off the loan. This would lower the rate from 20 percent to closer to 3 percent. This would save her son $4,250 per year! Her son could redirect just the interest savings and would be on track to pay off the loan in just a few years—instead of all that money going to the bank. Now, of course, the parent is on the hook for the debt; if the son stops paying, the bank that issued the loan is still going to expect payment. If the son is vigilant about making payments, on the other hand, the parent could reward good behavior and (working with her CPA) knock off some of the loan balance.

Helping Your Parents

Everyday Example #2, "A Bridge Loan over Troubled Quarters," in Chapter 2 is one of my favorites. Now, this is a great story, but let's turn back to my grandparents for a minute. You may recall my grandfather's battle with Alzheimer's and that he worked for the federal government. He had a nice pension, but like many Americans, when he needed to move into his eldercare facility he was a bit stuck. He needed to move and then sell his house. But he couldn't get a mortgage. A home-equity line of credit wasn't big enough. What could he do?

Fortunately, my parents had a portfolio that was eligible for a line of credit. They were able to use their assets to secure a spot in the new facility without disrupting their investments. The total cost of bridging this scenario for six months was nominal and certainly wasn't the big issue in their life. Taking care of Grandpa John was the big issue.

Buying a Luxury Car

Everyday Example #5 in Chapter 5 is about "Danny Driver," who spotted a recreational vehicle (RV) that he could have for a "steal" at only $100,000. He is offered a "car loan" from a bank that specializes in used recreational vehicles at 6 percent. Of course, the loan will amortize—always require a monthly payment—with the entirety of the remaining principal due at the end of five years. So his monthly payment is $1,933.

Danny realizes that the $600,000 of taxable investments he has with his brokerage firm gives him access to an assets-based loan at only 3 percent, that is, $3,000 a year of interest. Critically, the loan will not amortize, so if Danny has a slow month or two, he will not be required to make any payments. His monthly payment is $250 per month. His required payment is $0. Danny can do 100 percent financing and can pay down any amount any time he wants to.

Let's apply a few other quick examples to this:

$50,000 car 100% financed at 3% = $125/month

$225,000 car 100% financed at 3% = $526/month

Many people are intrigued by the idea of borrowing to create income in retirement, but are uncomfortable doing that. Instead, start by recalling the glide paths in Chapter 7 that suggest you maintain a 15 percent to 35 percent debt ratio. This is actually harder to do than it sounds. If you are well within your optimal debt ratio (and only if you are well within your optimal debt ratio), to maintain an optimal debt ratio you may want to consider funding large purchases on your securities-based line of credit and never paying it down. Not even paying the interest.

Do you know who else does this? Companies buy depreciating assets all the time, maintain relatively constant debt ratios, and have increasing, not decreasing, amounts of absolute debt.

Buying a Boat/Airplane/Art/Antiques/Jewelry, Paying for a Dream Vacation, Financing a Hobby (Horseback Riding, Car Racing)

For all of these, you can do what "Danny Driver" did in Everyday Example #5. Here are quick examples:

- Buying a \$400,000 boat × 3% = \$1,000 per month—and no required monthly payment
- Buying a \$1 million airplane × 3% = \$2,500 per month—and no required monthly payment
- \$100,000 dream trip around the world without ever making a payment

Never make a payment? That's difficult to understand, but consider that if you are well under your optimal debt ratio, using debt to pay for things such as a vacation can be a great way to gradually nudge your debt ratio toward an optimal range.

Obviously, purchasing assets that have zero residual value increases the risk of these strategies significantly, so it is essential that you pay attention to the risk factors throughout the book. Equally important for you to consider is that these ideas are not about buying things that you can't afford but better ways to pay for things that you already can afford. Taken together, I am assuming that you could pay for and afford the toy or vacation you are considering. Therefore, I am now providing strategies for you to consider weighing the pros and cons of (1) liquidating securities or using cash—which is of course a mathematical guarantee of a reduction of your assets, versus (2) using strategic debt as an alternative, as long as you are within the optimal ranges.

Vacations typically don't offer financing (they are just memories when they are over), but boats and planes do occasionally offer interesting and relatively low-cost fixed-rate terms, sometimes with amortization schedules of 15 or 20 years. The fixed rate may be beneficial and offer tax advantages (consult your CPA), but amortization schedules make me so nervous because there's nothing you can do to change them in good times or bad. They can squeeze you at the worst time. The power of securities-based lines of credit is not just about the rates, it is about the flexibility of the terms and that, as long as the loan is in good standing, you can choose how much you want to pay down and when you want to pay it down. You can pay as much or as little as you like, any time that you choose.

It is worth mentioning again that in a perfect world, I like seeing long-term debt against a house because it can't be called in the event of a market downturn. For example, I would typically not like to see somebody pay off a $500,000 mortgage and then go get a $500,000 securities-based line of credit. Not only is there potentially more risk in a securities-based line of credit, but regardless whether you choose fixed or floating rate debt the rate will generally be higher. This is another reason to carefully consider if you should pay down your mortgage and another reason that your balance sheet should be looked at in a holistic perspective.

A final thought: Immediately after purchasing any item, it is worth perhaps 10 to 20 percent less (0 percent in the vacation example!), so you need to look at what accountants call your "pro forma" debt-to-asset ratio. This is a fancy way of asking the question, what does your debt-to-asset ratio look like after taking on the debt and buying the asset (including the asset's depreciation)? To be extra conservative, always proactively apply a market shock to be sure your coverage ratios have plenty of safety margins.

Paying for Fractional Ownership (Home/Plane/Boat)

Using a securities-based line of credit may sometimes be the only way to finance these holdings. Same math applies: $200,000 interest in a fractional home ownership program, 100 percent financed at 3 percent interest only = $500 per month. $100,000 interest in a boat = $250 per month.

Fractional ownership programs financed on a securities-based line of credit can be a great combination of the rent-versus-buy math when considering a second home or toy. This can be particularly beneficial if you will have your head on the pillow for less than 60 nights per year and/or during one particular season. See the pluses and minuses of purchasing a second home in the section that follows.

Helping Out Our Kids and Student Loans

Everyday Example #4 in Chapter 4 is about getting rid of student loans once and for all. John went to school later in life and still had $100,000 of debt. A surprising number of people in their fifties have student debt, or, more commonly, have kids who have student debt. In many cases, this debt might have been at a good rate during school but the payments may be increasing or the rate may be higher.

In this case, a securities-based line of credit may be a good solution as the rate may be lower and the terms may be better. Do keep in mind that some student debt has federal subsidies that may make it more attractive. Many times I've seen it make sense for parents to keep the powder dry on their line of credit rather than refinance their child's student debt even if they could save them 1 percent or 2 percent. To be clear, if the rate and terms are only slightly better on a securities-based line of credit, you may not want to use that line to refinance the debt.

Let's do some math. If you have a $500,000 taxable portfolio, I recommend that you never borrow more than $125,000 on the line (50 percent of the available capacity). If you refinance $100,000 of your child's debt, you may have only saved them $2,000 per year but have used up the capacity on your line, which may reduce the flexibility you need to do the things you want to do.

Make no mistake, saving $2,000 is better than a poke in the eye. But you want to weigh the trade-off in flexibility versus savings. You should do this same exercise with all of these scenarios.

Homes: Downsizing/Moving/Building

Many people tend to move as they enter retirement. This happens for a lot of reasons: a desire to be close to family, the freedom and flexibility they didn't have before, the desire to try something new, downsizing, and so forth. This is an essential point to realize as I often see people in their late 50s refinance on 30-year fixed loans, yet they know that their goal is to move to a different place in five, seven, or 10 years. Always remember that with a 30-year loan you are not protecting rates for 30 years but rather for the length of time that you intend to be in the property. You should always overlay the cost of fixed versus floating rate debt and look at the potential risks and potential benefits.

In Everyday Example #6: Taking Big Advantage of a Housing Opportunity, in Chapter 6, we discuss a way that a loan can be taken out against a portfolio to bridge the purchase of a lot or other construction until you sell your current home. This rhymes a lot with the eldercare bridge loan story. From a big picture perspective you should consider the flexibility that a line of credit against your portfolio may afford you in facilitating these goals.

For example, I know someone who lived in a $750,000 house but wanted to move into a $300,000 condo. They were worried about qualifying for a mortgage and, more important, knew that they didn't want to have a mortgage long term. They accessed $300,000 from a line of credit against their well-diversified portfolio of $1 million. They purchased the house and took an additional $50,000 from the line to do improvements/updates. They moved into the new property and then sold their old house. They used the proceeds to pay off the loan and were mortgage-free. Here the debt just acted like a bridge loan rather than structural debt.

Purchasing a Second Home: Pluses and Minuses

For some people, there's no question that their primary residence should be free and clear—with no debt on it—as this is emotionally important to them. However, as a way to add desirable debt into your overall financial equation, buying a second home may prove very promising.

Before considering how you might go about purchasing a second home, let's start by reviewing some of the disadvantages of owning a second home and whether you might want to just rent a vacation home instead. That is, before even beginning to look for a second home for vacation, investment, or adding good debt into the mix, you want to be well aware of the expenses and other factors typically associated with owning a second home. Let's go through these one by one.

Depreciation

Homes have multiple expenses associated with them that are often not fully factored into the cost of ownership and the likely rate of return on the property, starting with depreciation. If you were to build a new house and leave it in the middle of a cornfield for 50 years, you would not be able to use any part of the property. You'd essentially have to replace everything—the house would need a new roof, windows, carpet, appliances, bathrooms, and so on. With a 50-year time horizon, this implies a 2 percent annual depreciation just to maintain the house and keep it exactly the same; if you assume a 30-year period, that means approximately a 3 percent yearly depreciation cost.

It's important to apply this to the value of the building and not the land. So, let's say that you have a $1 million house on a lot worth $100,000 for a total value of $1.1 million. In this example, it's reasonable to assume that you will have somewhere between $20,000 and $30,000 a year of maintenance expenses just to keep the building in the same condition. Alternatively, if you have a $2 million structure and a $3 million lot, then your depreciation may run closer to $60,000 per year (3% × $2 million). Separating the land value from the building value is particularly important in areas with high land values (coasts and cities) and less important where the land value is less than 30 percent of the property's value.

Clearly, these expenses won't be evenly distributed. With new construction, the first two years tend to be expenses related to finishing work versus maintenance. Years three to 10 don't have as much maintenance, but homeowners tend to underestimate the deferred maintenance that is building up. Years 10 to 20 tend to have a lot of expenses: most everything that plugs in, carpets, potentially the roof, and certainly the paint, and let's not forget that the entire decorating scheme will become outdated. Years 20 and beyond tend to normalize in the 2 percent to 3 percent range. Normal may be a $10,000 expense one year and a $30,000 driveway the next, but over a three-year period a total of 6 percent to 9 percent will most likely be the total cost that was reinvested into the property.

Do remember to factor in a homeowners' association fee or condo fee, if you have it; in effect, it will typically cover a part of the depreciation because the association is keeping up certain areas such as the exteriors, the roof, and the common elements that you might otherwise be maintaining on your own.

Taxes and Operating Costs

Property taxes tend to run between 1 and 2 percent, depending on where you live (although there are places where it's higher and places where it's lower).[3] You will also have operating expenses that could range from .5 to 2 percent or more, which includes everything from insurance to heating, gas, utilities, cleaning, lawn care, and so on. (Again, if you are in a condominium situation with a homeowner's association, they may cover some of these expenses, but then, of course, you also have the homeowner's association fee to consider.)[4]

Cost of Funds (Direct or Opportunity Cost)

It's important to consider the actual cost of debt (the cost of debt after all tax implications) for the financing that you have in place vis-à-vis the *opportunity cost* of any equity that you have in the property. Perhaps it goes without saying, but any equity that you choose to tie up in a second home could be invested and, therefore, could return whatever the average return will be for the rest of your portfolio. Bottom line: There's a cost to using debt and a cost to using equity. Companies look at this through their weighted average cost of capital (WACC).

Up-Front Transaction Costs

Unlike the other expenses, this is not recurring but should be factored in as it is still significant. Closing costs, of course, range by area but are generally between 1 and 2 percent of the property's value. These can include appraisal, inspection, title insurance, legal fees, and so on. Many markets now have mansion taxes and/or mortgage taxes on mortgages over a certain size that need to be included in the equation as well. Regardless of whether a property that you purchase is a brand-new construction or a historic home, it's unlikely to be 100 percent perfect. If it's 97 percent perfect, you will have to put about 3 percent of the purchase price into the home to make it what you wanted. Typically, this 3 percent is related to decorating or personal taste and adds little to the property's value. Expenses associated with moving and furnishing can be considerable and may also factor into a rent versus buy decision.

Liquidity (The Ability to Sell at a Good Price When You Want or Need)

When you close on a property, unless you were very lucky, it's likely that you paid the highest price for that property at that point in time. If you wanted to turn around and resell the property immediately, not only would you typically have a roughly 5 to 6 percent real estate commission, but you would also most likely sell it for 2 to 3 percent less than you paid for it. In other words, one problem with residential real estate is that right after you buy it, if you want to turn around and sell it, you will take an approximately 7 to 9 percent hit, in addition to the roughly 4 to 8 percent in annual expenses.

But what about *appreciation* on second homes? Isn't real estate among the best investments you can make in the long run? Well, residential real estate certainly has the possibility of being an investment that can keep pace with inflation over time. Think about a home that your parents or grandparents lived in during the 1950s or 1960s and what that house was later sold for in the 1980s or is worth today. Over long periods of time, it can appear that residential real estate has been a great inflation hedge.

However, this notion of real estate's increasing value over time can also be misleading. Unlike a stock or bond where you purchase the asset and have nominal tax consequences along the way (generally the only taxes due are on income or dividends that have been received, which is in effect a net reduction of the gross amount you have received along the way), you will pay various state and local taxes (along with the above-outlined expenses) all the way along. Moreover, residential real estate does not generate income or pay dividends to the owner unless it is rented, which both changes the characteristics of what we are discussing and requires further injections of capital to maintain and manage the asset.

It can be tricky to determine a property's actual appreciation in value over time, in part because there's a distinct human tendency to deceive ourselves. We all want to think we've done better than we've actually done. Consider the following example: if you buy a home for $500,000 and sell it for $1 million 10 years later, there is an appearance that you doubled your money or had an approximate annual return of 7.2 percent. However, if you paid a total of $60,000 in property taxes (factoring in any potential tax benefits) and invested $150,000 in the property for maintenance, upkeep, and remodeling, your actual basis is $710,000, a 3.5 percent rate of return (less the opportunity cost of the equity or any interest expenses).

Rent versus Buy a Second Home

If you really have a desire to spend some time at a second home, for vacation or other purposes, the question then comes to whether you should *rent or own*.[5] In a typical rental contract, the property owner is responsible for all repairs, maintenance, taxes, and homeowners association fees, and provides the property (meaning you have no debt or equity tied up in it), which frees up the renter's capital. You are trading one fixed cost to replace several direct and indirect expenses.

Ultimately, the most important factor is *how many nights you are likely to be in a rental property a year*. In general, the math works out roughly as follows. Consider renting if:

- You are at a property less than 30 nights per year.
- You are only at a property for a consecutive series of dates and not in and out throughout the year (e.g., winter or summer only).
- You plan on being at that property for less than three years (too many transaction costs to recover in too short of a time).
- You do *not* intend to rent the property (not renting effectively increases the cost).

Consider buying if:

- You intend to rent out the property.
- You will be there more than 30 nights (especially if you will be there more than 120 nights) per year.
- You will be there throughout the year.
- You believe there is a likelihood of appreciation at least equal to (or greater than) inflation.

MATH NOTE

You can take the total after-tax cost of all the expenses mentioned earlier, subtract your appreciation assumption, and divide by the number of nights you will be at a second home to get an estimated cost per night. This can be represented by the formula:

Estimated annual cost/number of nights you anticipate being there

The estimated annual cost = (appreciation + income) − (recurring expenses + (one-time costs/number of years in the property))

☺ **For example:**

Appreciation and income
+ appreciation assumption
+ rental income (if any)
= approximate annual gain

☺ **Recurring expenses**

− 2.5% depreciation
− 1.25% property taxes
− 1.5% operating expenses
−   % after tax cost of funds (ideally factoring in your WACC)
= recurring annual expenses

☺ **One-time costs**

−   % transaction costs
−   % liquidity costs
= one-time costs

Compare this figure to your rental alternatives. Rental income, appreciation, cost of funds, the number of nights you will be there, and your anticipated holding period are big drivers of the formula.

RENT VERSUS BUY EXAMPLE

In Candace Taylor's *Wall Street Journal* article "End of the Road: Miami area house on Private Peninsula seeks $60 million," she references a house that is for sale for $60 million but is also on the market for $50,000 a month.[6]

Now, $50,000 per month may sound like a lot, but let's apply the formula above. I think you will find the rental option compelling. Of course, the property could go up perhaps $10 million in value, but it could go down $10 million in value as well. If it were me, I would rent all day long.

One Hundred Percent Financing: The No-Down-Payment Real Estate Purchase Option

Let's assume that you have decided that you do, in fact, want to purchase a second home. You can, of course, follow the conventional route and find the best possible mortgage through a bank or a mortgage broker. There's another option, however, whereby many major financial services firms can offer you a 100 percent financing option against the home's value. Basically, the firm takes a security interest in the home—like any bank or mortgage owner would do—as well as an interest in a pledge account that you make with your existing assets at the firm, a pledge that covers the down payment on the home.

Here's what this looks like. Suppose you want to purchase a $1 million residence with 100 percent financing along these lines. A traditional mortgage for a second home at this dollar amount will typically be at about 70 percent. Instead of putting down $300,000, you could do 100 percent financing—all as a first mortgage at the same terms as a traditional loan. To do this, in addition to having the property as collateral, the firm could also ask you to pledge, for example, 200 percent of the $300,000 down payment, or a $600,000 pledge account. (Note that you are *not* allowed to use the same assets that you may have pledged to get an asset-based loan facility (ABLF) and the exact pledge amount can and will vary by firm.)

With this kind of 100 percent financing, instead of coming up with a separate down payment—say, by selling $300,000 of assets—you are pledging assets that you already have invested with the company. Instead of disrupting your portfolio or finding some way to come up with enough liquid cash, you are able to cross-collateralize your existing portfolio, thereby making good use of your Indebted Strength of Increased Leverage to move into a mortgage (which may have tax-favored deductions) at an attractive rate.

Let's continue the math on this $1 million, 100 percent-financed example. As discussed with fixed versus floating rates, if you own your primary house outright and your debt ratio is less than 25 percent (with the mortgage), you might choose to get a mortgage that floats at a spread over LIBOR. These loans are available for around 2 percent in the current interest-rate environment. After you figure in the tax deduction (if you are in the 33 percent tax bracket), you would effectively be paying about $1,100 per month (2% × (1 − .33) = 1.32%. 1.32% per year × $1 million = $13,200/12 = $1,100) while enjoying a million-dollar home—and you didn't put any money down. Of course, there will still be the taxes, maintenance, and so on. But this can give you a tremendous amount of flexibility as you go forward in life. Further, if you had sold $300,000 of your assets and had a 50 percent gain, you would owe the government $15,000 (assuming all of the gain was long term)!

At this point nearly everybody asks two questions: What if the value of the property falls? And what if interest rates rise? This is why the foundation we have built is so important. As we learned, the property's value is independent of the financing in place around it. Its appreciation or depreciation is an independent event from the financing in place around that asset. If you maintain a debt ratio of 25 percent, then by definition you have the ability to step in and *pay off the loan any time you do not like the strategy*. At the same time, it's imperative that you study how your portfolio is positioned for the risks of a rising rate environment.

HELPING OUT YOUR CHILDREN—PURCHASING A HOME

Many firms offer a version of 100 percent financing that enables parents to do the same thing for their adult children.

Parents can pledge assets that will enable a child to avoid having to come up with a down payment. If the child wants to purchase a $300,000 home, he or she would need to come up with approximately a 20 percent down payment of $60,000. Alternatively, depending on the institution, the parents can pledge roughly $120,000 of assets. This pledge will enable the child to have a 100 percent loan with no PMI (private mortgage insurance), and the parents' accounts stay fully invested in their investment strategy.

The parents are not cosigners, and they are only at risk in the event that the child stops paying the loan. In essence, they are there as a backstop or additional collateral in the worst-case scenario. The parents' assets continue to be invested, and whatever returns they generate go exclusively to the parents' account. The parents can typically continue to buy and sell investments, just as they normally would, as long as the assets they are buying and selling conform to ABLF requirements and they maintain the minimum amount required by the firm in the pledge account. This is a very powerful tool for families to discuss and consider (but read Appendix F, first!).

This can enable the purchase of a $300,000 property at, say, 4 percent fixed: $300,000 × 4% = $12,000 per year/12 = $1,000 per month. This $1,000 would be a tax deduction to the child. Additional savings from this strategy should not go to paying down the mortgage. They should go to building up cash, retirement plans, and liquid investments.

The family should work together to determine whether a fixed or floating mortgage is a better decision. If you choose fixed, remember that you are only trying to insure against rate movement during the time period the child anticipates owning the property. It can generally make sense for conversations to start around loans that are fixed for five to seven years (interest only) and adjust up or down from there.[7,8]

Notes

1. Stephen A. Ross, Randolph Westerfield, and Jeffrey Jaffe, *Corporate Finance*, 10th ed. (New York: McGraw-Hill, 2013), Chapter 15. This is true with respect to corporate bonds. There are examples of certain asset-backed securities such as equipment trust certificates that railroads have used (among others) that either have direct amortization or a toggle feature that can trigger amortization.

There also are mortgage-backed securities that contain an income stream that is comprised of both principal and interest payments. Many private company bank loans are subject to amortization terms. The fact that these loans and securities exist does not exclude the fact that publicly traded corporate debt is issued on an interest-only basis.

2. While no public traded companies issue bonds with built-in amortization, there are indeed amortizing bonds issued in the private equity markets. Also, corporations will establish sinking funds for their bonds where the money needed to repay the principal is put into escrow. However, the company still controls the cash and the ongoing payments they make on their debt will be interest only, that is, the only time you will receive a repayment of the principal is when the bond is called or matures. An individual can, of course, create a sinking fund as well.

3. "Median Effective Property Tax Rates by County, Ranked by Taxes as a Percentage of Household Income, 1-Year Average, 2010," The Tax Foundation, July 27, 2012. See http://taxfoundation.org/article_ns/median-effective-property-tax-rates-county-ranked-taxes-percentage-household-income-1-year-average.

4. Yingchun Liu, "Home Operating Costs," HousingEconomics.com, National Association of Home Builders, February 8, 2005. See www.nahb.org/generic .aspx?sectionID=734genericContentID=35389&channelID=311.

5. Ross, Westerfield, and Jaffe, *Corporate Finance*, Section 21.9: Companies lease many assets.

6. See http://online.wsj.com/articles/a-florida-home-on-private-peninsula-will-list-for-60-million-1409948247 (September 5, 2014).

7. Case studies are for educational and illustrative purposes only. They assume eligible assets and that funds are available on the facility. All client situations are unique, and all loans are subject to eligibility and approval by the lender. A lender may deny an advance on an ABLF, preventing the scenarios. Pledging assets reduces and may eliminate liquidity. A market correction could impact market values and/or security eligibility, which could impact the facility size and/or trigger a margin call and/or forced liquidations of assets. See complete disclosures and risks to using an ABLF in Appendix F.

8. Author's Note: The information in this guide is to be considered in a holistic way as a part of the book and not to be considered on a stand-alone basis. This includes, but is not limited to, the discussion of risks of each of these ideas as well as all of the disclaimers throughout the book. The material is presented with a goal of encouraging thoughtful conversation and rigorous debate on the risks and potential benefits of the concepts between you and your advisors based on your unique situation, risk tolerance, and goals.

Part V

APPENDICES

Appendix A

About the
Companion Website

S ome of the ideas in this book require more detail to better understand. Other ideas are controversial and merit a healthy amount
of debate and discussion. Some of the information is better in a
different format (such as Excel) or in an interactive format (debt ratio
calculators and tools).

To address the need for detail and to facilitate more conversation, discussion, and debate on this important topic, we have created
a website with supplemental information that can be found at www
.thevalueofdebtinretirement.com or www.vodr.com.

Please join me online, where you will see calculators, spreadsheets,
details, links to additional resources, and more discussion on the topics
covered throughout the book.

Appendix B

Details for Chapter 4

Understanding the Ideas of Chapter 4, with Charts and Tables

Let's look at the exact same situations but with some charts and tables. Consider a scenario—we'll call this Jane Scenario A: No Debt!—where an individual named Jane is renting a house, has no material assets, has just inherited $1 million, and is close to retirement. Jane is debt-averse and decides she wants to buy a home worth $500,000 outright, with no mortgage (after all, that is what all the popular authors told her to do!). This would leave her with a $500,000 investment portfolio.

(It is essential to note that one could arrive at the following balance sheet over time through any number of different ways outside of inheritance. Inheritance just makes it easy to understand exactly how this hypothetical situation came to be.)

At this point Jane has no debt, no possessions valuable enough to include in these calculations, and a net worth of $1 million, as shown in the balance sheet in Table B.1.

Table B.1 Balance Sheet—Jane Scenario A

Original Scenario A Balance Sheet

Assets		Liabilities
Real estate	$ 500,000	—
Investments	500,000	—
Total	1,000,000	—
Net worth	$1,000,000	**0%**
		debt ratio

What about income? If Jane's investment portfolio returns an average of about 6 percent, she would be making roughly $30,000 in income per year, as shown in the income statement in Table B.2. (For purposes of illustration, Jane's other income sources will be ignored. Also, all of the illustrations throughout the book are hypothetical and not intended to demonstrate the performance of any specific security, product, or investment strategy.)

Now let's consider a different scenario for Jane, that is, a different version of what her finances could have looked like had she made different choices along the way and embraced a Strategic Debt Philosophy.

In this case, Scenario B, Jane could have purchased the same house with a mortgage of 80 percent loan to value, that is, a $400,000 mortgage. This would have allowed her to keep her money invested, without having changed her net worth—unfortunately, you can't change your net worth through finance. (For those following along at home, that is a finance joke. Sorry, finance doesn't give me better material.)

Jane now has $1.4 million of assets and has a 29 percent debt-to-asset ratio ($400,000 divided by $1,400,000 equals about .29). This is illustrated in the balance sheet in Table B.3.

Table B.2 Income Statement—Jane Scenario A

Scenario A Portfolio Income

Portfolio		$500,000
Portfolio return	6%	30,000
After tax cost of debt	0%	—
Net income from portfolio		**$ 30,000**

Table B.3 Balance Sheet—Jane Scenario B

Scenario B Balance Sheet

Assets		Liabilities
Real estate	$ 500,000	$400,000
Investments	900,000	—
Total	1,400,000	$400,000
Net worth	$1,000,000	**29%**
		debt ratio

What happens to Jane from an income perspective in Scenario B? Assuming Jane has the same portfolio return of 6 percent, and assuming her mortgage was at a 3 percent rate and she is in the 33 percent tax bracket (so that the cost of that additional $400,000 in her portfolio is effectively 2 percent, resulting in an $8,000 cost), then what happens to her net income?

As the income statement in Table B.4 shows, Jane now receives a net income from her portfolio of $46,000, or $16,000 more than she received in Scenario A. So without having changed her net income, by taking on the mortgage at 3 percent she has increased her portfolio income by $16,000 a year, which is over 50 percent more compared to $30,000. (Of course, this is all assuming a hypothetical 6 percent portfolio return.) Note, too, that by taking on the mortgage debt Jane has increased her overall liquidity substantially—she is eligible for a larger line of credit and can better implement the ideas from Chapter 4.

Table B.4 Income Statement—Jane Scenario B

Scenario B Portfolio Income

Portfolio		$900,000
Portfolio return	6%	54,000
Aftertax cost of debt on $400,000	2%	(8,000)
Net income from portfolio		$ 46,000
Additional income compared to A		**$ 16,000**

Another way to look at this is that while in Scenario A Jane would have to have over a 9 percent return on her investments to generate a $46,000 return ($500,000 × 9% = $45,000), in Scenario B Jane can get to the same place with just a 6 percent average return.

What is perhaps most exciting is that once you know your required rate of return, you can then attempt to create that return through one of two ways: (1) The traditional way of reaching for assets that may be able to deliver that rate of return or (2) The sophisticated—potentially lower-risk way—of figuring out if there might be safer, lower-risk assets that you could leverage to get the same effect. All of the iterations of where this can go of course get to be complicated. The main point is to concentrate on the central idea and to discuss it with your advisors.

ADVANCED AHA! ADVISOR HIGHLIGHT ANSWER

Question: Two part question: (1) Is this a strategy that high-net-worth individuals can use, too, and (2) could this strategy be done in reverse to lower the required return of a portfolio?

Answer: Yes! and Yes! I love the way you are thinking and want to pull from late in Appendix D of *The Value of Debt* to highlight one of my favorite case studies.

Statistically speaking, this scenario may not apply to a lot of families or individuals, but reviewing the strategies appropriate to those in the higher net-worth range—sometimes called ultra-high-net-worth—can provide important insights for those at all levels of investing.

In the base case, the family owns a $5 million primary home and a $5 million second home, and they have an investment portfolio of $20 million for a net worth of $30 million. Many such families may feel as though they do not need additional income, and that their home or homes may protect them from inflation and potential weakness in the dollar. (The idea here is that if one's local currency—in this case, the dollar—falls by a great deal, high-end homes hold value as foreigners step in to buy, which indeed has historically been the case in some situations.)

Ultra-High-Net-Worth Investors Also Tend to Lack a Debt Strategy

You might be surprised to find out that based on my professional experience, high-net-worth, higher-net-worth, and even ultra-high-net-worth investors have something in common with average investors—they usually do not have any inkling about Strategic Debt Philosophy. What I've seen time and again is that they, too, tend to either be far too highly leveraged, or they are completely debt averse. Here, too, I would urge these individuals and families to seek an optimal middle ground.

Many feel that in a worst-case scenario they could sell their home for around 30 percent less than it is worth, or in this case, for around $3.5 million, which would provide plenty of flexibility, especially considered on a relative basis as the world at large would be in much worse shape. Along the way—and if there is never an emergency need to sell it—the family gets to enjoy a great home. They recognize they are taking some risks here but feel that they have similar risks with regard to their other assets without those other assets providing the same lifestyle benefits. Similarly, second homes also have a utility aspect to them that a municipal bond portfolio, for example, just does not offer. I'm not saying that I totally agree with this thinking, but I am saying that a lot of people do implement this type of a philosophy (or justification).

Now, since this family's net worth is $30 million, they could say that they don't want to have any debt, as shown in Scenario A. But let's look at a more optimal Scenario B for them. They could:

- Structure their balance sheets so that they had $3 million of debt versus each of the homes.
- Leverage their core portfolio by $4 million.
- This could be accomplished over time by paying for their taxes, cars, improvements, and renovations to their properties, and so on, through their asset-based loan facility (ABLF).
- Their net worth is $40 million − $10 million = $30 million.
- Again, net worth will never change based on financing.

- $10 million divided by 40 million is a 25 percent debt ratio.
- Notice that 25 percent ($10 million) of their balance sheet is in residential real estate and the other 75 percent ($30 million) could be in a globally diversified portfolio comprised of all assets that one can invest in.
- In Scenario B they will generate approximately $400,000 a year of excess income.
- That is a 33 percent greater return than the base case Scenario A.
- It is equal to increasing the return of Scenario A by 2 percent per year on a net basis.
- They will gain considerable tax benefits.
- Any time they don't like their strategic debt strategy, they can pay off their debt.

Is there another alternative for this family? After presenting Strategic Debt Philosophy and Practices to a client, I'll often hear something like the following: "Tom, these are neat ideas, but personally, I'm much more concerned with protecting the downside versus having additional upside." How could we apply the ideas found in this book with this goal in mind?

For one thing, this family could reach for a lower yield with the levered portfolio and target the same return![1] What I mean is that you could have debt and a lower returning portfolio and hit the same objective. Let's look at the math. For example, in Table B.5, the family in Scenario B could have their investment portfolio target a return of 4.67 percent and they would have the same net return as Scenario A. After all, 4.67 percent × $30,000,000 = $1.4 million, less the $200,000 after-tax cost of debt = $1.2 million, which is the same as 6 percent of $20,000,000. They may feel more comfortable with more debt, a larger portfolio targeting a lower return, and a lower standard deviation.

Notice as well that since they have debt against two properties and their portfolio, they could do a very interesting, and potentially powerful, combination of fixed and floating rate debt.

This thinking can be applied to each of the scenarios previously presented in this appendix and throughout the book.[2]

Table B.5 Scenario 4: Ultra–High Net Worth

Ultra–High Net Worth—Scenario A

Assets		Liabilities
Real Estate		
Home	5,000,000	–
Home 2	5,000,000	–
Investments		
Portfolio	20,000,000	–
Total	30,000,000	–
Net worth	$30,000,000	0% debt ratio

Income Perspective

Portfolio income	6%	$1,200,000
After tax cost of debt	2%	–
Net Income		$1,200,000

Ultra–High Net Worth—Scenario B

Assets		Liabilities
Real Estate		
Home	5,000,000	3,000,000
Home 2	5,000,000	3,000,000
Investments		
Portfolio	30,000,000	4,000,000
Total	40,000,000	10,000,000
Net worth	$30,000,000	25% debt ratio

Income Perspective

Portfolio income	6%	$1,800,000
After tax cost of debt	2%	200,000
Net Income		$1,600,000
Additional income compared to existing		$ 400,000

Notes

1. Case studies are for educational and illustrative purposes only. They assume eligible assets and that funds are available on the facility. All client situations are unique, and all loans are subject to eligibility and approval by the lender. A lender may deny an advance on an ABLF, preventing the scenarios. Pledging assets reduces and may eliminate liquidity. A market correction could impact market values and/or security eligibility, which could impact the facility size and/or trigger a margin call and/or forced liquidations of assets. See complete disclosures and risks to using an ABLF in Appendix F.

2. Author's Note: The information in this appendix is to be considered in a holistic way as a part of the book and not to be considered on a stand-alone basis. This includes, but is not limited to, the discussion of risks of each of these ideas as well as all of the disclaimers throughout the book. The material is presented with a goal of encouraging thoughtful conversation and rigorous debate on the risks and potential benefits of the concepts between you and your advisors based on your unique situation, risk tolerance, and goals.

Appendix C

Chapter 5 Detail

The purpose of this appendix is to highlight some tax issues for people in retirement and to showcase a few more scenarios of how I am able to offer my clients no taxes in retirement. I will preface this by stating that I am not a CPA, but I have had the assistance of a CPA with this book and particularly with this appendix.

Understanding RMDs

Retired people are always worried about their RMDs, which stands for Required Minimum Distributions. I am going to explain RMDs in simple terms and describe how they work.

RMDs are the minimum amount that you must take from your tax-deferred accounts as mandated by the IRS. This is the *minimum* you can take from your tax-deferred account; you can always take more. But if you fail to take your RMD or take too little, then the IRS will slam you with a 50 percent penalty on the amount that you didn't take.

RMDs generally start when you turn age 70.5, but there are some exceptions if you are still working and have an employer plan. There are no distribution requirements for Roth IRAs. The RMD amount is calculated based on your current age and the prior year-end account balance. Since both of these change, your RMD must be recalculated every year. There are two tables for calculating your RMD. The first one is called the IRS Uniform Lifetime Table and the second one is called the Joint Life and Survivor Expectancy Table. You should use the IRS Uniform Lifetime Table unless your spouse is the primary beneficiary of the account and is more than 10 calendar years younger than you. I am including the IRS Uniform Lifetime Table (see Table C.1) since it is the most common table used. I found this table in the IRS Publication 590 (www.irs.gov/pub/irs-pdf/p590.pdf).

Let's study an RMD example. Fred is age 72. He uses the IRS Uniform Lifetime Table because the beneficiary is his wife and she is his same age. His prior year-end IRA balance was $1,000,000. So look at Table C.1. The factor next to age 72 is 25.6 so you take the $1,000,000 divided by 25.6 for $39,062.50, his current year RMD.

Table C.1   IRS Uniform Lifetime Table

Table III (Uniform Lifetime)

For Use by:
- Unmarried Owners
- Married Owners Whose Spouses Are Not More Than 10 Years Younger
- Married Owners Whose Spouses Are Not the Sole Beneficiaries of Their IRAs

Age	Distribution Period	Age	Distribution Period
70	27.4	93	9.6
71	26.5	94	9.1
72	25.6	95	8.6
73	24.7	96	8.1
74	23.8	97	7.6
75	22.9	98	7.1
76	22.0	99	6.7
77	21.2	100	6.3
78	20.3	101	5.9
79	19.5	102	5.5

Table C.1   (*Continued*)

Age	Distribution Period	Age	Distribution Period
80	18.7	103	5.2
81	17.9	104	4.9
82	17.1	105	4.5
83	16.3	106	4.2
84	15.5	107	3.9
85	14.8	108	3.7
86	14 1	109	3 4
87	13.4	110	3.1
88	12.7	111	2.9
89	12.0	112	2.6
90	11.4	113	2.4
91	10.8	114	2.1
92	10.2	115 and over	1.9

Source: IRS, www.irs.gov/pub/irs-pdf/p590.pdf.

The Liger at Work Again

People argue with me all of the time that you should place all of your money into a tax-deferred IRA or 401(k) versus a taxable investment account. And I completely agree with the fact that it takes $1,389 to invest $1,000 after tax (assuming a 28 percent bracket) and dollar for dollar $1,389 will grow to be more than $1,000 all other things equal. *But*, I also see all the time people who have no liquidity and flexibility to weather hard times when all of their money is tied up in a tax-deferred account. I also know it is impossible to predict what your tax rates are going to be in retirement, but many times they are significantly *less* than your taxes in your working years. In my opinion, these conflicting data points demand a balanced and holistic approach. Again, I will refer to the liger example. The most powerful, tax-efficient, and flexible portfolios are those with a combination of taxable and tax-deferred investments.

I showed you in Chapter 5 how the Websters were able to generate $240,000 in annual incoming cash flow with a $5,500,000 net worth and pay less than $4,000 in taxes. Was it a freak accident that their tax bill was nearing zero? Nope! I can run these scenarios all day long! The key is a hybrid of after-tax and tax-deferred money and can be enhanced by embracing a strategic debt strategy.

Here are a few more examples I ran using Intuit's TurboTax Tax-Caster tool:

- $1,250,000 net worth, draws $50,000 incoming cash flow and pays 0 taxes
- $4,500,000 net worth, draws $180,000 incoming cash flow and pays 0 taxes
- $2,300,000 net worth, draws $90,000 incoming cash flow and pays 0 taxes

Alice: $1,250,000 Net Worth/$50,000 Incoming Cash Flow/Zero Taxes

Alice is a 65-year-old divorcee. She has $500,000 in an IRA and $500,000 in a tax-efficient investment account. She takes an "annual draw" of 4 percent, which is $40,000 and receives Social Security of $10,000 per year. She is in great health and lives in a condo valued at $250,000 that is paid for. After running several scenarios in TurboTax and talking with her CPA, I advise her to take $10,000 from the IRA and $30,000 from the investment account. Therefore, her annual draw is comprised of $10,000 of interest and dividends, $10,000 IRA distribution, and $20,000 from proceeds from her sale of stock.

Her total incoming cash flow of $50,000 is composed of:

Social Security benefits $10,000
Interest/dividends $10,000
   (assume 2% of the investment account)
IRA distribution $10,000
Proceeds from sale of stock $20,000
   (assume $10,000 basis, therefore a long-term capital gain of $10,000)

Her tax deductions are:

Real estate taxes $5,000
Donations $7,500
Investment management fees $10,000
   (assume 1%, all paid out of taxable account)

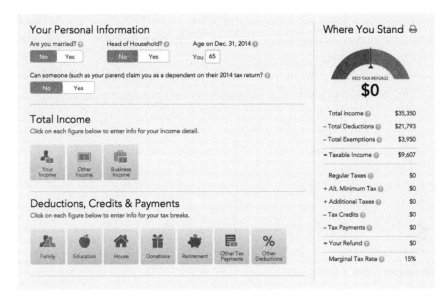

Figure C.1   Summary of Inputs for Alice

Reprinted with permission © Intuit Inc. All rights reserved.

I input all of this information in the TurboTax TaxCaster. You can reference Figures 5.4 through 5.8 for more details on the inputs. You will see the end result is zero taxes. That's right! Alice has a $1,250,000 net worth, has an annual incoming cash flow of $50,000, and pays zero taxes (see Figure C.1).

Fred and Joanne: $4,500,000 Net Worth / $180,000 Incoming Cash Flow / Zero Taxes

Fred and Joanne are both 72 years old and their tax status is Married Filing Jointly. They are in great health and are still traveling and enjoying life to the fullest. They are Florida residents so they pay no state income tax. They have a $3 million investment portfolio, and Fred has a $1 million IRA for a total of $4 million in investible assets. They take an annual draw of $180,000, which is 4.5 percent of their total portfolio. The annual draw is comprised of interest and dividends, IRA distributions, and proceeds from the sale of securities that have appreciated.

They still have two homes—a $500,000 house and $1,000,000 condo. The house is paid for and the condo is 100 percent financed with an interest-only loan. If you add the value of their homes to their investment assets, then their total assets are $5.5 million, their liabilities are the mortgage on the condo of $1 million for a net worth of $4,500,000.

I ran several scenarios in TurboTax and discussed them with their CPA. Due to the lower tax rates for long-term capital gains they took only their required minimum distribution (RMD) from the IRA and the remaining amount from their taxable account.

Incoming Cash Flow

Social Security benefits $20,000
Interest/dividends $60,000
   (assume 2% of investment account)
IRA distribution $40,000
   (rounded up his RMD from 2013 IRS Uniform Lifetime Table which was $39,063)
Proceeds from the sale of stock $60,000
   (assume $40,000 basis, therefore a long-term capital gain of $20,000)

Expenses

Real estate taxes $25,000
Mortgage interest $30,000
   (assume 3% on the $1 million condo)
Investment management fees $30,000
   (assume .75% paid out of taxable account)
Donations $30,000

I input all of this information in the TurboTax TaxCaster and you will see that with their $4,500,000 net worth and $180,000 annual incoming cash flow, they pay *zero* taxes (see Figure C.2).

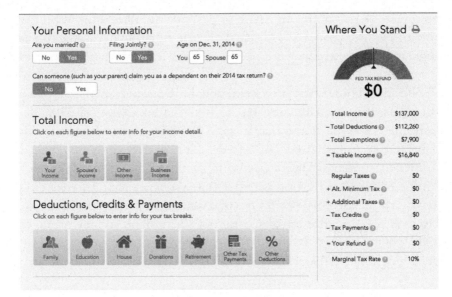

Figure C.2 Summary of Inputs for Fred and Joanne

Randy: $2,300,000 Net Worth/$90,000 Incoming Cash Flow/Zero Taxes

Randy recently retired as a software engineer at age 60. He never married and lived simply, and now he is ready to enjoy his retirement traveling. He was a good saver and has a $1,000,000 IRA and a $1,000,000 investment portfolio. I talked to him about his Social Security options and he has decided to defer taking it, due to his expected long life. He needs $90,000 per year cash, after taxes. That is a 4.5 percent draw, and I warn him that this higher distribution rate combined with his lower age may lead to him running out of money.

He has decided to downsize and lists his house for sale. He anticipates he will net $300,000 after paying off his mortgage.

While traveling he finds a perfect condo in Costa Rica that he wants to buy for $300,000. He calls his local banker who tells him that he cannot finance international properties. Randy calls me, and I go through some rent versus buy scenarios with him. He is determined to buy so we discuss using an ABLF to purchase it. Ultimately, Randy is able to buy the property without the hassle of an international mortgage and is able to finance it at 100 percent interest only at a rate of 3 percent.

Randy's house eventually sells, and he does net $300,000. Since Randy has financed his property, he now has an additional $300,000 from the sale of his house that he could invest or use to pay down his debt. Randy feels that he can capture a spread over time and decides to invest the money. This brings his investment account to $1,300,000 combined with his IRA of $1,000,000. I feel better about the $90,000 draw on his $2,300,000 portfolio—that is less than a 4 percent burn rate. His total assets are investment accounts of $2.3 million and the condo of $300,000 for total assets of $2,600,000. When you subtract the debt on the condo of $300,000, his net worth is $2,300,000.

Incoming Cash Flow

Social Security benefits $0
Interest/dividends $20,000
   (assume 2% of investment account before house sold)
IRA distribution $20,000
Proceeds from the sale of stock $50,000
   (assume $25,000 basis, therefore a long-term capital gain of $25,000)

Deductions

Mortgage interest $9,000
Real estate taxes $6,000
Investment fees $23,000
   (assume 1% paid out of taxable account)
Donations—zero this year

Once again, I input all of this information in the TurboTax Tax-Caster and you will see he has a $2,300,000 portfolio, $90,000 of annual incoming cash flow, and pays zero taxes (see Figure C.3).

Important note: Many CPAs will tell you that (1) you cannot deduct ABLF interest as mortgage interest, even if the use of proceeds is for buying a house and (2) the mortgage interest on an international

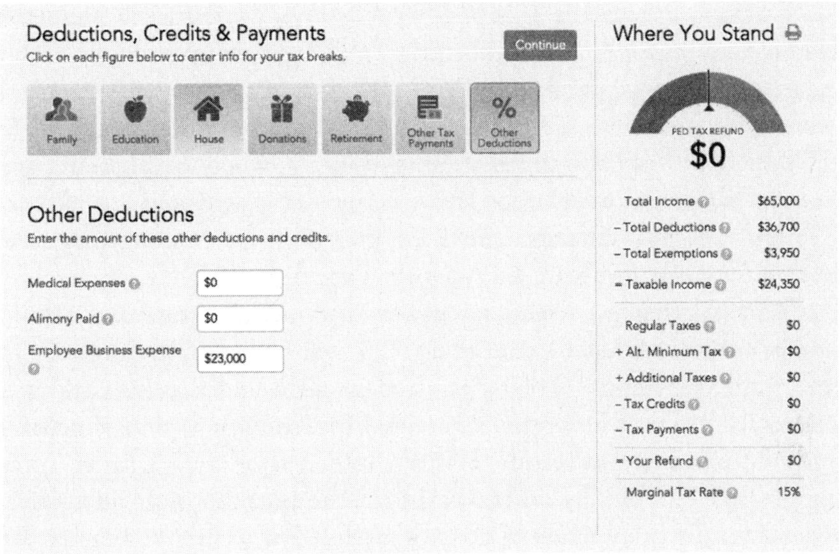

Figure C.3 Summary of Inputs for Randy

property is not tax deductible or, more likely, that it depends on the jurisdiction (country) where the home is located. Some CPAs may let you take this deduction using what are called tracing rules. Others may have you deduct it as margin interest or interest expense.

Based on years of experience, I am confident that five CPAs would write me that they "absolutely know the answer"—and I am confident I would get five different answers, all from very experienced and educated professionals (because I have). The tax code of the United States is about as thick as 55 of these books. There aren't easy or clear answers, so you should seek multiple opinions if your situation is complicated.

You will see that in our tax scenarios I generally assume the investment management fees are paid from the taxable account, and we deduct them. You should read this great article about deducting IRA investment fees and discuss the various strategies with your financial advisor and CPA: www.kitces.com/blog/irs-rules-for-paying-investment-fees-from-taxable-and-retirement-accounts/.

I obviously love the TurboTax TaxCaster and use it daily with my clients modeling scenarios, but want to point out that it is not perfect. I can think of several instances when I modeled a tax estimate for a client, who then paid their CPA to run a tax estimate and the numbers were the same. But I can also think of some examples when the outcome was not as I had expected. The tax law is very complicated, and I would say that TurboTax has amazing calculators and tools for running scenarios, but please work with your CPA for final verification.

This information is general and educational in nature and should not be considered legal or tax advice. Tax laws are complex and subject to change. This book is being released in 2015 and is using 2013 tax information. Tax information contained in this presentation is general and not exhaustive by nature. It is not intended or written to be used, and cannot be used, by any taxpayer for the purpose of avoiding U.S. federal tax laws. This material was not intended or written to be used for the purpose of avoiding tax penalties that may be imposed by the taxpayer. Individuals are encouraged to consult their tax and legal advisors (a) before establishing a retirement plan or account, and (b) regarding any potential tax, ERISA, and related consequences of any investments made under such plan or account. These materials and any statements contained herein should not be construed as tax or legal advice. Tax advice must come from your tax advisor.

Understanding Cost Basis and a Step-Up in Basis

One of the benefits of the strategic debt strategy is that upon your death your heirs will receive a "step-up in basis" on the assets they inherit. Well, what does that mean and how does that work? Let me show you.

First you must understand what cost basis means. Investopedia.com defines "cost basis" as:

> The original value of an asset for tax purposes (usually the purchase price) adjusted for stock splits, dividends, and return of capital distributions. The value is used to determine the capital gain, which is equal to the difference between the asset's cost basis and current market value. Also known as "tax basis". . . [1]

Here's an example: Let's say you purchase 10,000 shares of XYZ in 1990 at $3 per share for a total investment of $30,000. You hold this stock and today the value is $300,000. If you sell the stock you will pay tax on gains. Now if the stock would have split, if you would have reinvested dividends or paid a commission to sell the stock, that would have affected the cost basis, but for this example let's assume none of those scenarios occurred. In this case the gain is $270,000, which is the $300,000 proceeds less the $30,000 cost basis. Now the tax on that gain would be somewhere between 0 and 20 percent, depending on your tax bracket. For this example we will use 15 percent so you will owe the IRS $40,500 in taxes for this gain and potentially some state taxes too.

Now, let's talk about a "step-up in basis," which Investopedia.com defines as:

> The readjustment of the value of an appreciated asset for tax purposes upon inheritance. With a step-up in basis, the value of the asset is determined to be the higher market value of the asset at the time of inheritance, not the value at which the original party purchased the asset.[2]

So in the above example assume you never sell the stock. You implement Strategic Debt Philosophy and borrow against it. As I stated earlier in this book and in *The Value of Debt*, there are no tax consequences for borrowing against your assets.

Now, you pass away and your daughter inherits the stock. A step-up in basis means that your daughter's basis in the stock is now the fair market value on your date of death, which is $300,000. So if she sells the stock, her taxable gain will be zero, which means her tax on the transaction will also be zero. The proceeds will be $300,000, less her basis $300,000, since she received a step-up in basis upon inheritance.

Disclaimer: The value of property that is included in the gross estate is its fair market value of the date of the decendent's death. The executor may elect to use an alternate valuation date or in certain circumstances a special use valuation. The 2013 Estate and Gift Applicable Exclusion amount is $5,250,000.[3]

Professional/detail notes on the Websters

- Property taxes would most likely be higher in most markets. Higher taxes may make this scenario better.
- It doesn't really matter if they have one $2 million house, two $1 million houses, or one house for $1.5 million and one for $500,000.
- For mortgage interest to only be $10,000, their mortgage would have to be at 2 percent, which is likely to be low. A higher mortgage rate will likely make this better.
- Professional fees could be lower but this is 0.75 percent, which is below industry average. Lower fees might not make this as optimal.
- Capital gains can be determined by actions that the portfolio manager takes. It is possible to have zero gains by not selling, and you should try running it with $100,000 of gains to see the impact. You then should also take out the $80,000 of IRA distributions and run it with all capital gains.
- Medical expenses were assumed at zero. If small they likely won't have an impact, but if large they could make this scenario better.
- Social Security is likely to be higher, perhaps closer to $40,000, or more.
- As cited previously, at most institutions they could pay the IRA fees from their taxable or tax-deferred accounts. This is an important decision and should be factored into the ultimate model you create for your client.
- For a very technical level of detail, I counted capital gains as part of their income. While one could make an argument that $20,000 is being double counted it is in fact an attempt to reflect a change in the value of their assets. Factoring in the movement of the portfolio adds an additional layer of complexity. For the purposes of this exercise, I am trying to illustrate the big picture idea of tax efficiency, but a professional should factor in the changes in asset values on a consistent basis.
- There are endless iterations and each person is unique. The key is to leverage the concept for your own maximum benefit.[4]

Notes

1. See www.investopedia.com/terms/c/costbasis.asp.
2. See www.investopedia.com/terms/s/stepupinbasis.asp.

3. Case studies are for educational and illustrative purposes only. They assume eligible assets and that funds are available on the facility. All client situations are unique, and all loans are subject to eligibility and approval by the lender. A lender may deny an advance on an ABLF, preventing the scenarios. Pledging assets reduces and may eliminate liquidity. A market correction could impact market values and/or security eligibility, which could impact the facility size and/or trigger a margin call and/or forced liquidations of assets. See complete disclosures and risks to using an ABLF in Appendix F.

4. Author's Note: The information in this appendix is to be considered in a holistic way as a part of the book and not to be considered on a stand-alone basis. This includes, but is not limited to, the discussion of risks of each of these ideas as well as all of the disclaimers throughout the book. The material is presented with a goal of encouraging thoughtful conversation and rigorous debate on the risks and potential benefits of the concepts between you and your advisors based on your unique situation, risk tolerance, and goals.

Appendix D

Details for Chapter 6— A Study of Withdrawal Rates in Retirement

A retiree who is withdrawing from a lower volatility portfolio with debt may have a higher probability of success (defined as not running out of money in retirement) than a retiree who is withdrawing from a higher volatility portfolio and no debt. This is true when looking at historical returns in U.S. markets as well as when looking at a simulation of potential returns that a retiree could face looking forward. A lower volatility portfolio that incorporates the thoughtful use of debt in retirement differs drastically from previous popular studies that emphasize a heavily equity-weighted portfolio in retirement with no debt.

A major issue with implementing a debt philosophy in varying interest-rate environments is that conventional thinking suggests that leverage and one's ability to capture a spread only "works" when rates are low. If rates are high, however, as in the 1970s and 1980s, or portfolio returns are below average, as in the 2000s, then many investors believe it is impossible to capture the spread and therefore believe that borrowing over the long run is a suboptimal strategy due to the risks of these interest rate and market cycles repeating in the future.

People that make this case are typically comparing two things: historical interest rates and the U.S. large-cap equity market (usually the S&P 500). When doing this, it's easy to look at specific years or periods of history and come to the conclusion that leverage decreased value. For instance, in 1973 and 1974 when borrowing rates were close to or over 10 percent and equity markets were experiencing a significant bear market, one could conclude that markets were bad and borrowing made things even worse. On the flip side, in 2008 when rates were much lower and equity markets were also down over 40 percent, borrowing made things worse as well. Thus conventional wisdom may conclude that a borrowing strategy is ineffective and decreases portfolio returns more than it increases them by only examining specific years and then making broad, sweeping conclusions.

The premise of this study is to assess the validity of conventional wisdom as it pertains to capturing the spread by testing retirees' portfolios both with and without debt across various market cycles since 1946.

Background: How the 4 Percent Rule Came to Life

William Bengen's studies in the mid-1990s of sustainable withdrawal rates have been hugely influential.[1] Bengen looked at portfolios using historical U.S. return data, testing different asset allocations to determine which asset allocation supported a withdrawal rate with a high degree of success. (Success is defined as the retiree not running out of money during their retirement.) Bengen concluded that a portfolio of at least 50 to 75 percent stocks would be able to sustain a 4 percent inflation-adjusted distribution rate for a U.S. investor over any 35-year period since 1926. Any portfolio with less than 50 percent stocks proved to be counterproductive—both reducing long-term wealth and minimizing retirees' probability of a successful retirement. Equally, Bengen argues that allocations over 75 percent of stocks, especially in the early years of retirement, have the same counterproductivity due to sequence risk of poor returns in the beginning. This resulted in William Bengen being labeled in the popular press as "Mr. 4 Percent" and began the debate over whether or not the 4 percent rule of thumb is the best methodology.

The withdrawal rate discussion continued to evolve into the (likely) most famous publication on the topic by three Trinity University professors, Philip Cooley, Carl Hubbard, and Daniel Walz, titled, "Sustainable Withdrawal Rates from Your Retirement Portfolio," or what is more commonly known as the Trinity Study.[2]

The Trinity Study's main objective was to calculate the success rates of a variety of portfolio allocations over various time periods, dating back to 1926. The portfolio allocations tested are a mix of U.S. stocks, U.S. Treasury Bills, and Long-Term U.S. Corporate Bonds. As a representation of each asset class, they used the Standard & Poor's 500 Index (S&P 500) for U.S. Large Cap Equities, the Salomon Brothers Long-Term High-Grade Corporate Bond Index, and U.S. 30-day Treasury bills. The study examined the monthly returns in each asset class in conjunction with making withdrawals from the portfolio at the end of each month, as well as, rebalancing the portfolio back to its original asset allocation on a monthly basis.

To address inflation, the Trinity Study ran two different scenarios: (1) the withdrawal rate as a fixed annualized percentage amount and (2) the withdrawal rate as a percentage based on the starting value and inflation adjusting throughout retirement. For example, suppose an individual starts retirement with $100,000 and desires a $4,000 (4 percent) annual withdrawal from their portfolio. In the fixed-percentage scenario, the individual draws $4,000 for the entire retirement. In the inflation-adjusted scenario, the $4,000 initial draw is increased each year at the previous year's inflation (Consumer Price Index) rate.

The biggest difference between Trinity and Bengen, and likely why Trinity is used more widely than the Bengen studies, is that the Trinity Study offers retirees a menu of options of different portfolio allocations and withdrawal rates instead of just presenting the one that is most optimal.

Trinity Study Results

After running all scenarios, the Trinity Study concluded that, on an inflation-adjusted basis, a portfolio of at least 50 percent stocks and a 4 percent withdrawal rate delivered a probability of success of 95 percent or higher. Therefore, the typical takeaway from the study is that, based on historical information, a retiree should have at least 50 percent of their portfolio in (large-cap) U.S. equities. Although they do not argue that a 100 percent stock portfolio is counterproductive (as Bengen does), their data (from 1926 to 1997) show that a 75 percent/25 percent (stocks/bonds) portfolio had higher success rates than 100 percent stocks. See Tables D.1 and D.2.

The Trinity Study updated their results in 2010 to show rolling 30-year periods from 1926 to 2009.[3,4] Although this added a decade with the lowest U.S. equity returns in history, portfolio success rates actually increased. While this may seem counterintuitive, notice that the latest retirees represented (those retiring in 1980) experienced the best bull market in the history of both U.S. stock and bond markets for the first 20 years of their retirement.

Table D.1 Portfolio Success Rate with Inflation-Adjusted Monthly Withdrawals: 1926 to 1997 (Percentage of All Past Payout Periods Supported by the Portfolio)

Payout Period	Annualized Withdrawal Rate as a % of Initial Portfolio Value									
	3%	4%	5%	6%	7%	8%	9%	10%	11%	12%
100% Stocks										
20 years	100	100	91	77	66	57	42	32	28	19
25 years	100	100	85	69	56	42	33	29	25	15
30 years	100	98	81	65	56	44	33	33	19	7
75% Stocks/25% Bonds										
20 years	100	100	94	77	66	51	38	19	17	6
25 years	100	100	85	65	50	33	25	13	4	0
30 years	100	100	86	63	47	35	14	7	0	0
50% Stocks/50% Bonds										
20 years	100	100	92	75	55	30	17	9	2	0
25 years	100	100	79	52	31	15	4	0	0	0
30 years	100	95	70	51	19	9	0	0	0	0
25% Stocks/75% Bonds										
20 years	100	100	89	51	28	15	9	4	0	0
25 years	100	96	48	19	17	6	0	0	0	0
30 years	100	74	26	19	7	0	0	0	0	0
100% Bonds										
20 years	100	96	57	23	15	13	9	0	0	0
25 years	100	52	19	15	10	0	0	0	0	0
30 years	79	19	16	12	0	0	0	0	0	0

Table D.2 Portfolio Success Rate with Inflation-Adjusted Monthly Withdrawals: 1946 to 1997 (Percent of All Past Payout Periods Supported by the Portfolio)

Payout Period	Annualized Withdrawal Rate as a % of Initial Portfolio Value									
	3%	4%	5%	6%	7%	8%	9%	10%	11%	12%
100% Stocks										
20 years	100	100	91	73	64	55	39	33	27	21
25 years	100	100	82	61	46	39	32	29	29	21
30 years	100	100	74	57	48	43	35	35	22	13
75% Stocks/25% Bonds										
20 years	100	100	91	70	61	45	36	21	21	9
25 years	100	100	75	50	39	29	25	14	7	0
30 years	100	100	74	48	35	35	13	9	0	0
50% Stocks/50% Bonds										
20 years	100	100	88	64	42	27	15	3	0	0
25 years	100	100	64	36	25	11	0	0	0	0
30 years	100	91	48	35	13	0	0	0	0	0
25% Stocks/75% Bonds										
20 years	100	100	82	48	21	0	0	0	0	0
25 years	100	93	36	4	0	0	0	0	0	0
30 years	100	65	9	0	0	0	0	0	0	0
100% Bonds										
20 years	100	100	58	9	0	0	0	0	0	0
25 years	100	54	4	0	0	0	0	0	0	0
30 years	91	0	0	0	0	0	0	0	0	0

Even though the last 10 years of their retirement were not nearly as favorable, the earlier years' returns (when more money was invested) when withdrawing are far more important than returns in the later years.

Methodology

The objective of our study was to test varying annual inflation-adjusted withdrawal rates for 30 year rolling periods, spanning from 1946 to 2013, across various asset allocations, using a combination of stocks and bonds and in some cases commodities as well. The principle focus was to compare these exact same withdrawal rates and asset allocations using a leveraged portfolio. Although 15-, 20-, and 25-year studies were also shown, we've chosen to focus on 30-year rolling periods since those retiring between the ages of 60 and 65 today have a high probability of being retired for 30 years.[5]

Most aspects of our methodology are meant to compare our results to those of the Trinity Study, although we also incorporated aspects of Bengen's study—mainly the use of the U.S. Government 10-year Treasury Bond as a proxy for our bond allocations rather than the Long-Term High-Grade Corporate Bond Index. This was simply a decision of what we have found is most representative of a typical retiree's bond portfolio today, both from a duration and risk standpoint.

For equities, we chose to use the S&P 500 Index as a proxy. An important disclaimer—investments may not be made directly in an index. The closest thing to tracking an index is through the use of an investment vehicle that has the goal of tracking an index, such as an exchange-traded fund. This does create tracking error risk, so actual investments may slightly differ from the returns of the actual index. For cash equivalents we use 3-month U.S. Government Treasury Bills. This is slightly different from the Trinity Study, which uses 30-day Treasury Bills.[6]

For inflation adjustments, we use the Consumer Price Index for an Urban Consumer.[7]

For borrowing costs, we use the after-tax cost of the Bank Prime (Prime) rate dating back to 1946.[8] For taxes, we assume a 25 percent marginal tax rate.[9] We chose the Prime rate and a 25 percent tax rate because we feel it is very close to the middle of where an individual can borrow, regardless of net worth. For perspective on taxes, the top bracket—postwar—was at 91 percent for almost 20 years. For interest rates, in some cases an individual's borrowing rates may be higher, but in many cases, especially in recent history, many individuals can borrow well below Prime, especially when borrowing for a house.[10] As an example, in late 2014 the Prime rate was at 3.25 percent, but a qualified borrower could get an interest-only mortgage at 1.75 percent, fully tax deductible up to $1,100,000. Even in 2012 an individual could get a 30-year fixed mortgage at 3.35 percent, or just over the Prime rate.[11]

For year-end values, we used a similar equation as the Trinity Study for a non-borrowing portfolio:

Equation #1: The Non-Borrowing Portfolio Withdrawal Equation

Ending Value = Beginning Value × Market Return
          − Inflation Adjusted Withdrawal

For the borrowing portfolio, we assume the exact same equation as equation #1 and simply insert one additional subtraction component: the annual cost of debt.

Equation #2: The Borrowing Portfolio Withdrawal Equation

Ending Value = Beginning Value × Market Return
          − Inflation Adjusted Withdrawal − Interest Cost[12]

Debt Ratios

For scenarios without debt, we assume that their assets are composed of 50 percent in the value in their home and 50 percent in the value in their investment portfolio.

For all scenarios with debt, we assume an initial debt ratio of 33 percent and that assets are composed of one third of the value in the retiree's home and 67 percent of the value in their portfolio. We also assume that all debt is borrowed on an interest-only, floating-rate basis.

Another way to look at this is that the Johnsons and Smiths are next-door neighbors. They have the exact same house and the value of their homes is always exactly the same. They have the exact same net worth, exact same expenses throughout retirement, are born and die on the same days, and so on and so forth. The only difference is that the Johnsons chose to pay off their house and have no debt in retirement, and the Smiths chose to keep their house 100 percent financed on their interest-only floating-rate mortgage and keep their assets in their portfolio. Their respective balance sheets look like the following (see Figures D.1 and D.2).

The Johnsons			The Smiths		
Assets		**Liabilities**	**Assets**		**Liabilities**
Real Estate			Real Estate		
Home	$ 500,000	–	Home	$ 500,000	500,000
Investments			Investments		
Portfolio	500,000	–	Portfolio	1,000,000	–
Total	1,000,000		Total	1,500,000	500,000
Net Worth	$1,000,000	**0% Debt Ratio**	Net Worth	$1,000,000	**33% Debt Ratio**

Figure D.1   Example Balance Sheets—The Johnsons and Smiths

Or:

The Johnsons				The Smiths		
Assets		**Liabilities**		**Assets**		**Liabilities**
Real Estate				Real Estate		
Home	$200,000	–		Home	$200,000	200,000
Investments				Investments		
Portfolio	200,000	–		Portfolio	400,000	–
Total	400,000			Total	600,000	200,000
Net Worth	$400,000	**0%** **Debt Ratio**		Net Worth	$400,000	**33%** **Debt Ratio**

Figure D.2   Additional Example Balance Sheets—The Johnsons and Smiths

The actual amounts do not matter since ratios are held constant and withdrawals are at the same percentages, but hopefully this provides a strong frame of reference for the differing balance sheets that were tested.

Results

Table D.3 shows the success rate of various portfolios without and with debt from 1946 through 2013 for 30-year rolling periods. These portfolio allocations can be compared and contrasted to allocations used in previous studies. As you can see in the "no debt" success rates, the numbers are not drastically different from the original Trinity Study numbers even when updated through 2013. There are years that are better and years that are worse.

The key data points come from the comparison between a borrowing portfolio in retirement and a nonborrowing portfolio. With the exception of a 100 percent bond portfolio, *a borrowing portfolio had a higher success rate in every portfolio allocation.* This demonstrates that by utilizing strategic debt within the optimal ranges outlined in this book, even through a period of the highest inflation and borrowing rates in the history of the United States, it may be possible to increase the chance of success—the chances of not running out of money—more effectively than a retiree's portfolio with no debt.

Another interesting observation, as shown in Table D.3, is that there are many cases where one could take less risk and achieve a higher success rate through borrowing. For instance, if a retiree needed a 5 percent distribution and wanted to be as close to a 75 percent probability of success as possible, they would need to be in 100 percent stocks

Table D.3   Returns without and with Debt, 1946–2013

Portfolio Allocation	Annualized Withdrawal Rate as a % of Initial Portfolio Value									
	3%	4%	5%	6%	7%	8%	9%	10%	11%	12%
100% Stocks										
30 years – No Debt	100	95	74	62	54	44	41	33	23	13
30 years – With Debt	100	100	87	74	72	59	59	51	52	49
75/25 Stocks/Bonds										
30 years – No Debt	100	95	69	54	46	41	28	18	3	0
30 years – With Debt	100	100	87	72	59	54	51	43	41	39
50/50 Stocks/Bonds										
30 years – No Debt	100	87	56	46	33	15	13	3	3	0
30 years – With Debt	100	95	77	59	51	46	39	28	23	18
25/75 Stocks/Bonds										
30 years – No Debt	100	72	31	18	15	13	8	3	0	0
30 years – With Debt	100	80	54	36	21	15	13	13	10	10
0/100 Stocks/Bonds										
30 years – No Debt	95	31	18	13	13	8	3	0	0	0
30 years – With Debt	46	31	21	15	13	13	10	8	5	3

according to the Trinity study numbers. However, if they had a borrowing portfolio, they could withdraw at a 5 percent rate and only allocate 50 percent of their portfolio to stocks, all while achieving a 77 percent success rate.

Finally, it is important to look at the more extreme withdrawal rates and how debt may have a major positive affect. Take a 12 percent withdrawal rate, for example. Although it is not recommended to withdraw at this rate by any measure, some circumstances may force a retiree to take a 12 percent distribution. Without debt, the only portfolio that survived on a 30-year horizon was a 100 percent stock portfolio at a 13 percent success rate. However, *a borrowing portfolio comprised of 100 percent stocks survived nearly half the time.* Put another way, a borrowing portfolio was four times more likely to survive when looking at the 1946 to 2013 time period. While this potentially is good news for those who need a higher distribution, it is worth a word of caution. Knowing what we know about the importance of your sequence of returns (Chapter 6), it is also of course possible that the borrowing portfolio could cause the individual to run out of money faster. Remember, there is no free lunch when implementing a borrowing strategy.

Trinity Study: Unfortunate Timing

The original Trinity Study was published in 1998. This date is important to consider, as it was a very interesting time in U.S. markets—equities were in the middle of the greatest bull market of all time. I remember those days as an advisor—it was very hard to prove value. Investors looked at the world and saw repeated 30 and 40 percent annual returns in the S&P 500 and Nasdaq and didn't want someone telling them how important it was to be diversified. After all, these "stupid diversification strategies" were costing them 10+ percent a year by only generating mid-teen returns. It was a deceptive world.

As a result, the confidence of investors was at an unprecedented high, mirroring portfolio values they likely had never seen in their lifetime. In many people's minds, the markets in the 1980s and 1990s were the "new normal," and the almost 13 percent *annualized* rate of return the S&P 500 just experienced from 1969 to 1999 was something they could now expect. I remember advisors in my office running financial plans assuming a 12 percent annualized rate of return for people thinking about retiring, and giving them the confidence that they could make it by withdrawing "only" 8 percent to account for an inflation adjustment.

Although not nearly at the extreme of the advisors encouraging an 8 percent withdrawal rate, the Trinity Study also gave investors confidence that the higher the percentage in equities in their portfolios, the higher the probability of success in retirement. This was especially the case for those looking to retire at a 4 percent withdrawal rate or greater.

Unfortunately, we all know how this story plays out. Beginning in 2000, the market completely changed and U.S. equities experienced the worst decade performance they had seen in the past 110 years.[13] Yes, that includes 1930 to 1940, the heart of the Great Depression. The "retirement classes" of 1999 and 2000 are, as a consequence, currently off to the worst 15- and 14-year starts if they were invested in 100 percent stocks and withdrawing at a 4 percent rate in postwar time. If starting with $100,000 and withdrawing an inflation-adjusted 4 percent, the balances for these retirees at the end of 2013 would be $70,287 for the 1999 retiree and $46,877 for the 2000 retiree. For perspective, the worst 15-year snapshots of previous retirees are $85,379 and $77,634. These are taken from the 1966 retiree and the 1969 retiree. Coincidentally, this happens to be the only two retirement classes in the postwar era who experienced unsuccessful retirements when investing 100 percent in stocks at a 4 percent withdrawal over 30 years. This by no means implies that the 1999 and 2000 retiree who has been invested 100 percent in U.S. stocks this whole time will not make it. Rather, it shows the magnitude of how tough the market cycle they've experienced has been thus far.

The question then becomes, how could they have anticipated this? Should this have been in their base case, or is this simply a very unfortunate start that they could never have predicted? The unfortunate answer is that the market cycle they have faced has simply been a slightly more extreme example of something they could have anticipated—that the historical return at the start of their retirement would *not* be their future return. In fact, since 1928, if one looked backward at the average annual returns at any given time of the S&P 500 and guessed the next 30 years' average annual returns would look the same, they would have only been within 1 percent of being correct five times (5 out of 56). For perspective, the 1999 retiree's historical, annualized average return on the S&P 500 was 10.76 percent and the 1970 through end of 1999 period averaged an annualized 13.5 percent. The next 15 years? An average of 3.56 percent.

The reason this is very important is that historical returns may give perspective on the behavior of asset classes, but they give absolutely no guarantee of what the future may hold. Making decisions based simply on historical returns can have massive implications, especially when starting in a completely different economic environment, as I discussed earlier in the book. For this reason, we have expanded our study to include the following:

- Historical withdrawal rates with borrowing portfolios that include different combinations of stocks and bonds as used in this appendix, while also incorporating asset classes not used in previous studies.
- Success rates of various portfolios on a go-forward basis using Monte Carlo simulations. This is done by looking at different risk/return

characteristics using leverage and testing them in different inflation and interest rate environments.

• Withdrawal rate comparisons between lower volatility portfolios with debt and higher volatility portfolios without debt. As an example, can you take a higher withdrawal rate with a lower risk/return portfolio using debt than with a higher risk/return portfolio without debt?

All of these scenarios have been tested and will be published in an outside whitepaper. For those of you who want to explore this topic further and relate it to your personal balance sheet and retirement plans and for more information please visit www.valueofdebtinretirement .com or www.vodr.com.[14, 15]

Notes

1. The Four Percent Rule, a study by William P. Bengen. See "Determining Withdrawal Rates Using Historical Data," www.retailinvestor.org/pdf/Bengen1. pdf.
2. The Trinity Study a study by Philip L. Cooley, Carl M Hubbard, and Daniel T. Walz. See "Sustainable Withdrawal Rates From Your Retirement Portfolio," www.afcpe.org/assets/pdf/vol1014pdf.
3. See www.onefpa.org/journal/Pages/Portfolio%20Success%20Rates%20Where% 20to%20Draw%20the%20Line.aspx.
4. Decade is defined here as 10-year periods starting with a "0," e.g., 1930-1939, 1940-1949, etc. The worst rolling 10-year period since 1900 was from 1928-1937 with a -4.16 percent annualized rate of return, and the second worst was 1999-2008 with a -3.21 percent annualized rate of return. For two good articles on this see www.wsj.com/articles/SB10001424052748047862045746079 93448916718 and www.theirrelevantinvestor.tumblr.com/post/94001444648/ the-2000s-was-the-worst-decade-for-investors.
5. It is essential to note that although the "without debt" portfolios' results will look very similar to that published in the Trinity Study, they are our own numbers and differ slightly because they are updated through 2013.
6. Returns: www.pages.stern.nyu.edu/~adamodar/New_Home_Page/datafile/ histretSP.html.
7. CPI: www.bls.gov/cpi/#tables.
8. Prime rate: www.federalreserve.gov/releases/h15/data.htm.
9. Tax rates: www.taxfoundation.org/sites/taxfoundation.org/files/docs/fed_ individual_rate_history_nominal.pdf.
10. The true borrowing costs of an individual dating back to 1946 is extremely difficult to accurately track since individual circumstances differ drastically. Variables such as lending products, credit scores, tax brackets, and so on, add

to the complexities of after-tax borrowing rates. As an additional example, in 1985 a 30-year fixed mortgage had an average rate of 12.42 percent and the Prime Rate averaged 9.93 percent (www.federalreserve.gove/releases/h15/data.htm). The highest marginal tax bracket was also 50 percent then (www.irs.gov/pub/irs-soi/85inintxr.pdf). Our proxy of Prime times a 25 percent marginal tax rate equals 7.44 percent, whereas an individual borrowing on a 30-year fixed mortgage in the 50 percent tax bracket would have an after-tax cost of 6.21 percent. On the flip side, if one was in the 20 percent tax bracket, their after-tax cost of the debt on a 30-year fixed mortgage in 1985 would be 9.9 percent. This is what leads to our conclusion of being "close to the middle."

11. 30-year fixed mortgages: www.federalreserve.gov/releases/h15/data.htm.
12. For the academics out there, a more detailed equation:

$$V_t = V_{t-1}(1+R_t) - W_{t-1}(1+ ((CPI_t - CPI_{t-1})/CPI_{t-1}))$$

where:

V_t = The year-end value after the annual return on the portfolio and withdrawal

V_{t-1} = The beginning balance of the portfolio

R_t = The rate of return on the portfolio for that year

W_{t-1} = The withdrawal amount for the previous year

CPI_t = CPI for the end of the year

CPI_{t-1} = CPI for the beginning of the year

For a borrowing portfolio, we assume the exact same return and withdrawal equations as above, we just add one more subtraction component: The annual cost of debt (interest payment).

$$V_t = V_{t-1}(1+R_t) - W_{t-1}(1+ ((CPI_t - CPI_{t-1})/CPI_{t-1})) - (L_{t-1} \times I)$$

where:

L_{t-1} = The beginning of the year liability principal balance

I = The average monthly after-tax Prime rate for the year

13. See note 4.
14. Special thanks to Charles J. Cuny, Senior Lecturer in Finance, Olin Business School, Washington University in St. Louis, for his help with this study. His contributions were invaluable to ensuring the validity of the data.
15. Author's Note: The information in this chapter is to be considered in a holistic way as a part of the book and not to be considered on a stand-alone basis. This includes, but is not limited to, the discussion of risks of each of these ideas as well as all of the disclaimers throughout the book. The material is presented with a goal of encouraging thoughtful conversation and rigorous debate on the risks and potential benefits of the concepts between you and your advisors based on your unique situation, risk tolerance, and goals.

Appendix E

A More Detailed Discussion on Risk, Return, and Correlation

I frequently find that when I discuss the benefit of decreasing risk in a portfolio with investors, many have a great deal of fear that they will be sacrificing too much return by taking on less risk. They believe that by decreasing risk, they will then equally decrease the likelihood that they achieve the necessary returns for a successful retirement. After many back-and-forth conversations on this, I finally discovered that there is a misperception by many investors, both individual and professional advisors, on the relationship between risk and return. Many believe that risk and return have a "lock-step" relationship. For instance, if I have a portfolio that has a goal of averaging a 10 percent return with a standard deviation of 20 and I decrease my risk in half to a standard deviation of 10, then I can expect a 5 percent rate of return by doing so.

For many, a 5 percent average return will not allow them to attain their return and retirement objectives.

I completely understand the math logic behind this and why investors come to this conclusion, but it is a very important part of portfolio theory that all investors must grasp. *The trade-off between risk and return is not a lock-step relationship and you can, in many cases, drastically decrease the risk in a portfolio and give up only a fraction of the return.* To demonstrate this, let's take a look at two assets' returns over the past 20 years. The only importance is their risk and return characteristics and not what they actually are, so we will call them "Asset A" and "Asset B."

From 1994 to 2013, Asset A had an average return of 11 percent with a standard deviation 19.5 and Asset B had an average return of 7.0 percent with a standard deviation of 16. Most would look at these and assume that if they blended the two assets and were 50 percent in Asset A and 50 percent in Asset B, you could expect a return of 9.0 percent with a standard deviation of 17.75 by averaging the two. When they get their investment statements in the mail from their advisor and flip through to the "Risk/Return" chart, they would expect to see something like Figure E.1.

However, when these assets were blended together, investors actually saw something like Figure E.2.

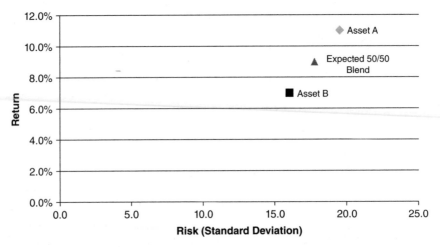

Figure E.1   Risk/Return Trade-Off: Expected

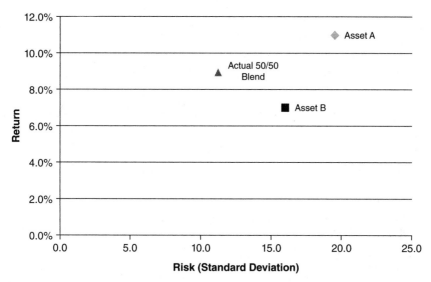

Figure E.2   Risk/Return Trade-Off: Actual

The average return when blending these two remained 9.0 percent, however, the standard deviation of the blended portfolio was drastically lower than either of the two assets' standard deviation individually, coming in at 11.25. Compared to Asset A, the blended portfolio had 84 percent of the return and about *half of the risk*. Some may be asking, "How could this be? You must have done some sort of math trick somewhere!" Don't worry, there were no math tricks done here. The only thing that is missing is that there was a major characteristic of these two assets that *frequently* gets overlooked—correlation.

Asset A and Asset B had a negative correlation over this time period. This means that typically when Asset A was going up, Asset B was going down, and vice versa. As an example, in a year like 2002 when Asset A was down 22 percent, Asset B went up 24 percent. Conversely, in 2013 when Asset A was up 32 percent, Asset B was down approximately 28 percent. Again, the two assets went through quite volatile times in these years. However, the blended portfolio's volatility was much lower.

The same phenomena can occur by blending a portfolio across multiple asset classes as well. From 1994 to 2013, a blended portfolio of U.S. and international equities, U.S. bonds, and cash experienced an average return of 7.4 percent with a standard deviation of 9.4, whereas an

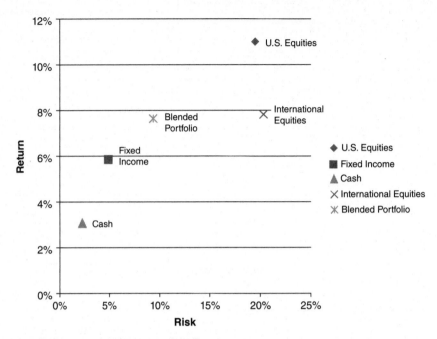

Figure E.3   Asset Class Return 1994–2013

all-equity portfolio of U.S. and international equities had a 9.4 percent average return and a standard deviation of almost 20. Again, the blended portfolio had about 80 percent of the return and took about half the risk, proving that you can drastically reduce risk without drastically reducing return (see Figure E.3).[1]

Notes

1. Author's Note: The information in this appendix is to be considered in a holistic way as a part of the book and not to be considered on a stand-alone basis. This includes, but is not limited to, the discussion of risks of each of these ideas as well as all of the disclaimers throughout the book. The material is presented with a goal of encouraging thoughtful conversation and rigorous debate on the risks and potential benefits of the concepts between you and your advisors based on your unique situation, risk tolerance, and goals.

Appendix F

More Detail on ABLF, Risk Details, and Official Statement of Disclosure and Understanding[1]

More Detail on ABLF

As for the ABLF, or the asset-based loan facility, this kind of loan facility was at the heart of *The Value of Debt* and is of central importance here as well. One of the great things about an ABLF is that money borrowed is generally not taxable, and is generally not amortizable; that is, you don't have to make a fixed monthly payment (or any payment at all until you are ready to do so). Importantly, an ABLF can be defined in both a narrow sense, as I usually use it here, as well as in a broad sense, as follows:

- **Broad definition of ABLF:** Any loan facility based on pledged assets, which can include an ABLF based on your taxable stock portfolio, a margin loan based on your taxable portfolio, and even a home equity loan or line of credit.
- **Narrow definition of ABLF:** A loan facility provided to you by your brokerage firm or another firm that is based on pledging assets in your taxable portfolio, not in tax-deferred (qualified) accounts such as an IRA or 401(k).

Throughout this book, most references to ABLF are to the narrow definition. And with regard to this kind of ABLF, it's important to know that it can only be put into place on the parts of your investment portfolio that are considered taxable assets or after-tax money. For example, you won't be able to get an ABLF by pledging the investments you have in your IRA or 401(k).

Note that most of the financial pundits and retirement gurus who are out there will tell you from the very start that you should put every bit of your extra money into tax-deferred vehicles—that is, into vehicles that are *not* eligible for an ABLF. Why is this? Sadly, blinded by antidebt ideology, they just don't know any better, and unfortunately, if you follow (or have followed) that advice it will be difficult to implement these ideas.

Statement of Disclosure and Understanding

This book does not provide individually tailored investment advice. It has been prepared without regard to the circumstances and objectives of those who receive it. This book contains general information only, does not take account of the specific circumstances of any reader, and should not be relied upon as authoritative or taken in substitution for the exercise of judgment by any recipient.

Each reader should consider the appropriateness of any investment decision as it regards to his or her own circumstances, investment objectives, investment experience, risk tolerance, liquidity needs, time horizon, the full range of information available, and appropriate professional advice.

The author recommends that readers independently evaluate particular investments and strategies, and encourages them to seek a financial advisor's advice. Under no circumstances should this publication be construed as a solicitation to buy or sell any security or to participate in any trading or investment strategy, nor should this book, or any part of it, form the basis of, or be relied on in connection with, any contract or commitment whatsoever.

The value of, and income from, investments may vary because of changes in interest rates or foreign exchange rates, securities prices or market indexes, operational or financial conditions of companies, and geopolitical or other factors.

Past performance is not necessarily a guide to future performance. Estimates of future performance are based on assumptions that may not be realized. The information and opinions in the book constitute judgment as of the date of publication, have been compiled and arrived at from sources believed to be reliable and in good faith (but no representation or warranty, express or implied, is made as to their accuracy, completeness, or correctness), and are subject to change without notice.

Investing with leverage contains multiple risks, including, but not limited to, interest rate risk, greater volatility risk, liquidity risk, call provision risk, rollover risk, and the risk of a total loss of capital.

The information provided is based on tax laws currently in effect and is subject to change. There is a possibility that current tax legislation will be amended or repealed in the future. In that case, the outcome of these planning ideas may not be as advantageous. None of the information herein is to be considered tax advice. All ideas are intended to represent tax facts at the time of publication and are subject to change without notice. All ideas must be reviewed by your tax, legal, and financial advisors based on your individual situation.

Tax information contained in this presentation is general and not exhaustive by nature. It is not intended or written to be used, and cannot be used, by any taxpayer for the purpose of avoiding U.S. federal tax laws. Pursuant to the rules of professional conduct set forth in Circular 230, as promulgated by the United States Department of the Treasury, nothing contained in this book was intended or written to be used by any taxpayer for the purpose of avoiding penalties that may be imposed on the taxpayer by the Internal Revenue Service, and it cannot be used by any taxpayer for such purpose. Federal and state tax laws are complex and constantly changing. Investors should always consult their tax advisor for information concerning their individual situation.

No one, without the express prior written permission of the author, may refer to any of the debt, investment, or tax strategies found in this book.

The author does not accept any liability whatsoever for any loss or damage arising from any use of this book and its contents. All data and information and opinions expressed herein are subject to change without notice.

With Respect to ABLFs

Asset-based loan facilities (ABLFs) are securities-based loans, which can be risky and are not suitable for all investors. Before opening an account, you should understand the following risks:

- The firm can call the loan at any time and for any reason.
- Sufficient collateral must be maintained to support your loan(s) and to take future advances.
- You may have to deposit additional cash and/or eligible securities on short notice.
- Some or all of your securities may be sold without prior notice in order to maintain account equity at required maintenance levels. You will not be entitled to choose the securities that will be sold. These actions may interrupt your long-term investment strategy and may result in adverse tax consequences or in additional fees being assessed.
- Firms typically reserve the right not to fund any advance request due to insufficient collateral or for any other reason.
- Firms can increase your collateral maintenance requirements at any time without notice.
- There may be minimum line sizes and minimum initial draws.
- Disbursements are subject to your available credit and are at the sole discretion of the firm.
- Annual fees typically apply for Standby Letters of Credit, if issued. Standby Letters of Credit carry issuance fees based on the issued amount of the Letter of Credit and are due in advance.

- For brokerage firms, ABLFs are typically offered by the bank affiliated with the issuing brokerage firm.
- Credit lines are often subject to credit approval.
- You should consult your legal and tax advisors regarding the legal and tax implications of borrowing using securities as collateral for a loan.
- For a full discussion of the risks associated with borrowing using securities as collateral, you should review the Loan Disclosure Statement that will be included in your application package.

ABLFs can be either what are called purpose or non-purpose loans. A *non-purpose loan* is a line of credit or loan that is based on the eligible securities held in a brokerage account. It can be used for any suitable purpose except to purchase, trade, or carry securities or repay debt that was used to purchase, trade, or carry securities, and should not be deposited into a brokerage account. A *purpose loan*, or margin loan offered by a brokerage firm, is a revolving line of credit based on securities held in a brokerage account. These loans are primarily used to purchase securities but can be used for any other purpose. The text is not intended to imply that having an ABLF is guaranteed liquidity. It is important to note that many ABLFs are not committed facilities. Therefore, a lender has no obligation to make an advance and can reject any advance request from a borrower in its sole discretion.

ABLFs could in fact actually increase your risk of distress. If you have an ABLF and the market drops (including the securities securing your loan), you could be forced into a margin call with no additional securities/collateral to deposit and in a situation where you don't have liquid funds to pay down the loan. Accordingly, you could be forced to sell the securities collateral at that time, which if the market is depressed, would be at a bad price and potentially trigger tax consequences.

ABLFs generally are structured as demand facilities, which means that the institution offering the loan can demand repayment at any time. Also, the lender usually maintains the right to liquidate the securities-held collateral at any time. You must work with your advisors to understand and mitigate these risks.

All examples within the book assume that the loan is in good standing, credit is available, securities are eligible, and that the lender is willing to continue advancing money.

Securities-Based Loans: Borrowing against securities may not be suitable for everyone. You should be aware that securities-based loans (ABLFs) involve a high degree of risk and that market conditions can magnify any potential for loss. Most importantly, you need to understand the following: An ABLF is not a committed facility, the lender has no obligation to make an advance, and therefore *an ABLF does not offer a guaranteed liquidity solution.*

Although your lender may not have a cost in establishing an ABLF, you must visit with your tax, legal, and financial advisors before implementing any of these ideas. Accordingly, there may be professional advisory fees in pursuing the ideas expressed in this material.

Additional Important Notes

Taxes: Tax laws are complex and subject to change. This material was not intended or written to be used for the purpose of avoiding tax penalties that may be imposed on the taxpayer. Individuals are encouraged to consult their tax and legal advisors (a) before establishing a retirement plan or account, and (b) regarding any potential tax, ERISA, and related consequences of any investments made under such plan or account.

Point of Views: The views expressed herein are those of the author. All opinions are subject to change without notice. Neither the information provided nor any opinion expressed constitutes a solicitation for the purchase or sale of any security. Past performance is no guarantee of future results.

Strategies: This material does not provide individually tailored investment advice. It has been prepared without regard to the individual financial circumstances and objectives of persons who receive it. The strategies and/or investments discussed in this material may not be suitable for all investors. The author recommends that investors independently evaluate particular investments and strategies, and encourages investors to seek the advice of a financial advisor and their tax and legal advisors. The appropriateness of a particular investment or strategy will depend on an investor's individual circumstances and objectives.

Asset Allocation: Asset allocation and diversification do not guarantee a profit or protect against a loss.

Bonds: Bonds are subject to interest rate risk. When interest rates rise, bond prices fall; generally the longer a bond's maturity, the more sensitive it is to this risk. Bonds may also be subject to call risk, which is the risk that the issuer will redeem the debt at its option, fully or partially, before the scheduled maturity date. The market value of debt instruments may fluctuate, and proceeds from sales prior to maturity may be more or less than the amount originally invested or the maturity value due to changes in market conditions or changes in the credit quality of the issuer. Bonds are subject to the credit risk of the issuer. This is the risk that the issuer might be unable to make interest and/or principal payments on a timely basis. Bonds are also subject to reinvestment risk, which is the risk that principal and/or interest payments from a given investment may be reinvested at a lower interest rate. International bonds are subject to these and may be subject to other risks such as risk of default, greater volatility, and currency risk.

Municipal bonds: Interest in municipal bonds is generally exempt from federal income tax. However, some bonds may be subject to the alternative minimum tax (AMT). Typically, state tax exemption applies if securities are issued within one's state of residence, and local tax exemption typically applies if securities are issued within one's city of residence. Bonds are affected by a number of risks, including fluctuations in interest rates, credit risk, and prepayment risk. In general, as prevailing interest rates rise, fixed-income securities prices will fall. Bonds face credit risk if a decline in an issuer's credit rating, or creditworthiness, causes a bond's price to decline. Finally, bonds can be subject to prepayment risk. When interest rates fall, an issuer may choose to borrow money at a lower interest rate, while paying off its previously issued bonds. As a consequence, underlying bonds will lose the interest payments from the investment and will be forced to reinvest in a market where prevailing interest rates are lower than when the initial investment was made.

Note: High-yield bonds are subject to additional risks such as increased risk of default and greater volatility because of the lower credit quality of the issuers.

Equities: Equity securities may fluctuate in response to news on companies, industries, market conditions, and general economic environment. Companies paying dividends can reduce or cut payouts at any time.

Case Studies: The case studies presented are for educational and illustrative purposes only and do not indicate future performance. Past performance is no guarantee of future results. Investment results may vary. The investment strategies and products and services presented are not appropriate for every investor. Individual clients should review with their financial advisors the terms and conditions and risks involved with specific products or services. Neither the information provided nor any opinion expressed constitutes a solicitation for the purchase or sale of any security. All of the illustrations throughout the book are hypothetical and not intended to demonstrate the performance of any specific security, product, or investment strategy.

Home Loan—Mortgage: Proceeds from mortgage loan transactions including initial draws and advances from HELOCs are not permitted to be used to purchase, trade, or carry marginable securities, repay margin debt, or to make payments on any amounts owed under a note or HELOC loan agreement.

LIBOR and Interest-Only Loans: An interest-only LIBOR loan is not for everyone. These loans enable borrowers to make monthly payments of only the accrued monthly interest on the loan during the introductory interest-only period. Once that period ends, borrowers must make monthly payments of principal and interest for the remaining loan term, and payments will be substantially higher than the interest-only payments. During the interest-only period, the total interest that the borrower will be obligated to pay will vary based on the amount of principal paid down, if any. If a borrower makes just an interest-only payment, and no payment of principal, the total interest payable by the borrower during the interest-only period will be greater than the total interest that a borrower would be obligated to pay on a traditional loan of the same interest rate having principal-and-interest payments. In making comparisons between an interest-only loan and a traditional loan, borrowers should carefully review the terms and conditions of the various loan products available and weigh the relative merits of each type of loan product appropriately. Your interest rate can increase and monthly payments can increase every one or six months, depending on the index you choose. On a six-month LIBOR, if you prepay principal during the first 10 years, your required monthly payment may include some principal until your next six-month adjustment.

Life Insurance: Since life insurance is medically underwritten, you should not cancel your current policy until your new policy is in force.

A change to your current policy may incur charges, fees, and costs. A new policy will require a medical examination. Surrender charges may be imposed and the period of time for which the surrender charges apply may increase with a new policy. You should consult with your own tax advisors regarding your potential tax liability on surrenders.

Investments and insurance products are not FDIC insured, are not bank deposits, are not insured by any Federal government agency, are not bank guaranteed and may lose value.[2]

Notes

1. Thomas J. Anderson, *The Value of Debt* (Hoboken, NJ: John Wiley & Sons, 2013), 197–207.
2. Author's Note: The information in this appendix is to be considered in a holistic way as a part of the book and not to be considered on a stand-alone basis. This includes, but is not limited to, the discussion of risks of each of these ideas as well as all of the disclaimers throughout the book. The material is presented with a goal of encouraging thoughtful conversation and rigorous debate on the risks and potential benefits of the concepts between you and your advisors based on your unique situation, risk tolerance, and goals.

Glossary

Note: Many of the terms shown here are from—or are adapted and applied to individuals from—the glossaries that can be found in: Stephen A. Ross, Randolph Westerfield, and Jeffrey Jaffe, *Corporate Finance*, 10th ed. (New York: McGraw-Hill, 2013); and Ziv Bodie, Alex Kane, and Alan Marcus, *Investments*, 9th ed. (New York: McGraw-Hill, 2011). Investopedia.com and the online Merriam-Webster dictionary are also used as sources.

Terms that are part of a definition and have their own definition in this Glossary are presented in *italics*.

ABLF: See *asset-based loan facility.*

amortized loan: Requires the borrower to repay parts of the loan amount over time.

asset allocation: The process and goal of allocating the assets in your investment portfolio so that they are widely diversified.

asset-based loan facility: This is a broad term to represent all types of lines of credit that are secured by assets that are on deposit at financial institutions. It may be a *purpose* or *non-purpose* facility.

available credit: The amount of credit available on your line of credit or *ABLF*. This will typically fluctuate according to the value of the assets securing the line.

average cost of capital: Typically called the *weighted average cost of capital*, or *WACC*. For firms it is the weighted average cost of a firm's common equity, preferred stock, and debt. Individuals need to apply a similar framework and consider the cost of debt compared to the opportunity cost of equity with their investment decisions.

average tax rate: Tax bill divided by taxable income. This is also called your *effective tax rate*.

balloon payment: A large final payment on a loan.

call provision: A written agreement between an issuing corporation and its bondholders that gives the corporation the option to redeem the bond at a specified price before the maturity date.

capital structure: The mix of various debt and equity capital maintained by a firm or individual.

capture the spread: The process of earning a rate of return higher than your after-tax cost of debt.

collateral: Assets that are pledged as security for payment of debt.

correlation: A standardized statistical measure of the dependence of two random variables. Defined as the covariance divided by the standard deviations of the two variables.

cost of debt: The cost of borrowing.

costs of financial distress: There are two types of costs of financial distress, *direct costs* and *indirect costs*.

coupon: The stated interest payment on a debt instrument.

coverage ratio: The available credit compared to the amount that has been drawn on a line of credit. Since available credit is a function of assets, this can also be looked at as the percentage drawn relative to the total assets securing an ABLF. The book suggests keeping your draw under 50 percent of your available credit.

debt: Loan agreement that is a liability of the individual. An obligation to repay a specified amount at a particular time.

debt capacity: Ability to borrow. The amount an individual or firm can borrow.

depreciation: A non-cash expense reflecting the decreased value of an asset over its estimated useful life.

direct costs of financial distress (for individuals): Direct costs of *financial distress* include late payment penalties; filing fees; attorney, accountant, and bankruptcy fees; and a lower credit rating leading to an increased cost of capital. (For companies, the direct costs of financial distress include the legal and administrative costs of liquidation, reorganization, and bankruptcy.)

discount rate: Rate used to calculate the present value of future cash flows.

diversification: Allocating your investments across a wide or diverse array of securities, from different industries and sectors to different countries. Not putting all your financial investment eggs in one basket.

dividend: Payment made by a firm to its owners from sources other than current or accumulated retained earnings.

effective tax rate: Traditionally defined as your total tax paid/adjusted gross income (AGI). I'd suggest that with the ideas expressed in the book AGI can be deferred (reduced) so you could also look at this as total tax paid/gross income.

enriching debt: Debt that may make you wealthier over time, such as debt borrowed through an *ABLF* at a low interest rate that enables a careful investor to leverage that debt and capture the spread over time.

endogenous risk: "From within"; as used in this text it means within your assumptions or risk that you have already factored into your calculations.

exogenous risk: "From outside"; as used in this text it describes events that occur that are outside your assumptions or things you didn't factor into your calculations.

expected return: Average of possible returns weighted by their probability.

financial distress: Events preceding and leading to bankruptcy, including an inability to pay bills, debts, and creditors, eventually potentially leading to bankruptcy for individuals and companies, and personal and family survival issues for individuals.

financial leverage: Extent to which a firm relies on debt.

five indebted strengths: Five key qualities that flow from the strategic use of debt: (1) Increased liquidity—having more ready access to liquid funds or cash; (2) Increased flexibility—having more options for addressing the direct and indirect costs of financial distress; (3) Increased leverage—the possibility of capturing the spread and accelerating the accumulation of wealth; (4) Increased survivability—a diminished likelihood that real survival issues will arise; and (5) Increased perspective—the ability to better see and embrace the big picture as a result of having a comprehensive philosophy.

hedging: Taking a position in two or more securities that are negatively *correlated* (taking opposite trading positions) to reduce risk.

high-yield bond: *Junk bond*—a speculative grade bond.

hostile takeover: A takeover that occurs against the wishes of stockholders in the acquired firm.

impacts of financial distress (for individuals): Five levels of the impact of *financial distress* are described in Chapter 2 of *The Value of Debt*, increasing from negligible to moderate to severe to bankruptcy to survival issues.

income: Earned income, wages, salaries, profits from stocks or real estate sales, stock dividends, interest payments, lottery or gambling winnings, the cash value of bartered items, and anything else defined by statute or case law by the IRS as income.

incoming money (during retirement): The totality of incoming money or cash, including both taxable income and other sources of nontaxable income such as money borrowed against your own ABLF.

indirect costs of financial distress (for individuals): The indirect costs of *financial distress* for individuals include worry, stress, anxiety, distraction, and lifestyle/standard of living diminishment. (For companies, the indirect costs of financial distress include an impaired ability to do business and an incentive toward selfish strategies such as taking large risks, underinvesting, and milking a property or resource.)

inflation: A fall in the buying power of a unit of currency.

inflation risk: Risk faced by investors due to uncertainty about future inflation.

interest rate: The price paid for borrowing money.

interest rate risk: The chance that a change in the interest rate will result in an adverse effect on the borrower.

junk bond: A speculative grade bond.

liabilities: Debts of the individual.

LIBOR: London Interbank Offered Rate. It is the rate the most credit-worthy banks charge one another for large loans of euros overnight in the London market.

line of credit: An agreement that allows individuals to borrow up to a previously specified limit.

liquidity: Refers to the ease and quickness of converting assets to cash. Also called *marketability*.

long-term debt: An obligation having a maturity of more than one year.

marginal tax bracket: The rate at which incremental ordinary income is taxed.

Modern Portfolio Theory (MPT): A theory of financial investing that attempts to maximize the return for any given level of risk, or minimize the risk for any given level of return.

municipal bonds: Bonds issued by a municipality such as a city or state.

non-purpose loan: An *ABLF* that explicitly does not let you buy, carry, or trade securities.

nonqualified money: Money that you have already paid taxes on (think of the money in your investment account, outside of your IRA).

oppressive debt: Low-quality debt that oppresses the debtor and makes them continually poorer, such as high-interest credit card debt.

personal financial ecosystem: The entirety of the financial resources available to an individual or family, including all cash and other reserves as well as all potential debt that can be accessed.

present value: The value of a future cash stream discounted to present day.

purpose loan: An ABLF that enables you to buy securities.

qualified money: Money that you haven't paid taxes on yet, or money that is inside tax-deferred programs (IRA, deferred compensation plans, etc.).

rebalancing: Realigning the percentages or weightings of the assets in one's portfolio, usually by selling certain assets that have done well over time, to return the portfolio to its original desired asset allocation.

rent: A contractual arrangement to grant the use of specific assets for a specified time in exchange for payment.

risk: A peril or danger; the possibility of loss or risk; in financial matters, the chance the return on your investment will become worthless, or just worth less than it cost in the first place or than you expected it to be.

risk tolerance: The degree of variability in investment returns that an individual is willing to withstand; how much *risk* or potential loss of return or value an individual or couple is able to emotionally and psychologically tolerate in the pursuit of reward or return.

ROI: Traditionally defined as return on investment—the benefit of an investment expressed as a percentage of the cost of the investment—or simply, how much you get back from what you put in. Taking a holistic view, the ROI of retirement—Resources, Outer Pragmatics, and Inner Dynamics—is: Resources—money, investments, and property; Outer Pragmatics—real world concerns and issues; Inner Dynamics—meaning, purpose, and pleasure.

securities: Tradable financial investments such as stocks, bonds, and derivatives.

scenario analysis: Analysis of the effect on a project or investment portfolio of different scenarios with each scenario involving many variable changes.

sinking fund: In corporate finance, an account managed by the bond trustee for the purpose of repaying the bonds. In your personal life, a separate savings account you establish to cover a known future obligation.

standard deviation: A measure of the dispersion of a set of data from its mean. The more spread apart the data, the higher the deviation. Standard deviation is calculated as the square root of *variance*.

TIPS: Treasury Inflation Protected Securities. U.S. government securities that promise payment in real, not nominal, terms.

variance: A measurement of the spread between numbers in a data set. The variance measures how far each number in the set is from the mean. Variance is calculated by taking the differences between each number in the set and the mean, squaring the differences (to make them positive) and dividing the sum of the squares by the number of values in the set.

volatility: Refers to how volatile a security is, or how likely it is to move substantially up or down in any given time period. This is typically measured by *standard deviation*.

WACC: Weighted Average Cost of Capital. The weighted average cost of a firm's common equity, preferred stock, and debt.

working debt: Debt such as a mortgage, at a reasonable interest rate and with reasonable terms, that enables you to move forward with important life goals; nonoppressive debt that enables you to access your *Five Indebted Strengths*.

Bibliography

Books

Anderson, Thomas J. *The Value of Debt: How to Manage Both Sides of a Balance Sheet to Maximize Wealth*. Hoboken, NJ: John Wiley & Sons, 2013.

Bach, David. *Debt Free for Life*. New York: Crown Business/Random House, 2012.

Covey, Stephen R. *The 7 Habits of Highly Effective People: Powerful Lessons in Personal Change*. New York: Free Press, 1989.

Graeber, David. *Debt: The First 5000 Years*. Brooklyn: Melville House, 2011.

Hanson, Jon. *Good Debt, Bad Debt—Knowing the Difference Can Save Your Financial Life*. New York: Portfolio Penguin, 2005.

Malkeil, Burton. *A Random Walk Down Wall Street*, 9th ed. New York: W.W. Norton & Co., 2007.

Mundis, Jerrold. *How To Get Out of Debt, Stay Out of Debt, and Live Prosperously*. New York: Bantam Books, 2012.

Orman, Suze. *You've Earned It, Don't Lose It: Mistakes You Can't Afford to Make When You Retire*. New York: Newmarket Press, 1998.

Ramsey, Dave. *The Total Money Makeover*, classic ed. Nashville: Thomas Nelson, 2013.

Schwab-Pomerantz, Carrie. *The Charles Schwab Guide to Finances after Fifty*. New York: Crown Business, 2014.

Shook, R. J. *The Winner's Circle: Asset Allocation Strategies from America's Best Financial Advisors*. Horizon Publishers Group, 2006.

Singer, Mark. *The Six Secrets to a Happy Retirement: How to Master the Transition of a Lifetime*. Medford, MA: ATA Press, 2013.

Zelinski, Ernie J. *How To Retire Happy, Wild, and Free: Retirement Wisdom That You Won't Get from Your Financial Advisor*. Edmonton, Alberta: Visions International Publishing, 2014.

Articles, Research Papers, Studies, and Online Resources

Bengan, William P. "Determining Withdrawal Rates Using Historical Data." *Journal of Financial Planning* (1994). Available at www.retailinvestor.org/pdf/Bengen1.pdf. The four percent rule.

Bennett, Johanna. "S&P 3K? Morgan Stanley Bullish on Rest of Decade." *Barron's*, September 30, 2014. http://online.barrons.com/articles/s-p-3-000-morgan-stanley-bullish-on-rest-of-decade-1412076606. Interview with Adam Parker, chief equity strategist for Morgan Stanley, discussing his market forecast for 2014.

Bonds Online. www.bondsonline.com. Information on current bond prices and yields.

Bordo, Michael D. and Wheelock, David C. "When Do Stock Market Booms Occur? The Macroeconomic and Policy Environments of 20th Century Booms." Federal Reserve Bank of St. Louis, September 2006. http://research.stlouisfed.org/wp/2006/2006-051.pdf. Study by the Federal Reserve Bank of St. Louis on the history of boom and bust market cycles across 10 countries.

Cooley, Philip L., Carl M. Hubbard, and Daniel T. Walz. "Sustainable Withdrawal Rates from Your Retirement Portfolio." *Journal of Financial Counseling and Planning* 10 (1999). www.afcpe.org/assets/pdf/vol1014.pdf. The Trinity study.

Damodaran, Aswath. http://pages.stern.nyu.edu/~adamodar/New_Home_Page/datafile/histretSP.html. Updated January 5, 2015. Table produced by NYU Stern on average returns on stocks, Treasury bonds, and Treasury bills from 1928 through 2013.

Farrington, Robert. "Struggling With Student Loan Debt Over Age 50." *Forbes*, August 20, 2014. www.forbes.com/sites/robertfarrington/2014/08/20/struggling-with-student-loan-debt-over-age-50/. Article on outstanding student loan debt for those over 50

Frazzini, Andrea, Kabiller, David, and Pedersen, Lasse Heje. November 21, 2013. www.econ.yale.edu/~af227/pdf/Buffett's%20Alpha%20-%20Frazzini,%20Kabiller%20and%20Pedersen.pdf. Research paper regarding Warren Buffett.

Goodman, Wes and Worrachate, Anchalee. "Yields Driven Under 1% on Almost Half World's Government Bonds." *Bloomberg, September* 4, 2014. www .bloomberg.com/news/print/2014-09-04/almost-half-of-government-bonds-yield-less-than-1-bofa-ays.html. Article on current world government bond yields.

Hartnett, Michael, Moore, Kate, Leung, Brian, and Putcha, Swathi. "The Longest Pictures." Bank of America Merrill Lynch, June 27, 2012. www.merrilledge. com/publish/content/application/pdf/gwmol/globalstrategyapictureguideto-financialmarketssince1800.pdf. Research paper on the long run.

Hopkins, Jamie. "Planning For An Uncertain Life Expectancy In Retirement." *Forbes*, February 3, 2014. www.forbes.com/sites/jamiehopkins/2014/02/03/ planning-for-an-uncertain-life-expectancy-in-retirement. Article regarding increased life expectancies.

Krantz, Matt. "26 U.S. Companies with No Long-Term Debt." *America's Markets*, May 29, 2014. http://americasmarkets.usatoday.com/2014/05/29/debt-free-26-u-s-companies-shun-debt. Article on the 26 nonfinancial companies in the Standard & Poor's 500 Index that had zero long-term debt.

McCaffery, Edward J. "Why Do the Romneys Pay So Little in Taxes?" *CNN*, September 25, 2012. www.cnn.com/2012/09/24/opinion/mccaffery-romney-tax.

McCaffery, Edward J. "Zuck Never Has to Pay Taxes Again." CNN, September 25, 2012. www.cnn.com/2013/04/09/opinion/mccaffery-zuckerberg-taxes. Two articles by Edward McCaffery on low tax rates for the super-rich.

MorningStar. http://financials.morningstar.com/balance-sheet/bs.html?t=[XXX]. Information on publically traded companies. Note: "XXX" should be replaced with the stock symbol of the company for which you are searching.

Nuwer, Rachel. "Humans Have Been Messing with China's Yellow River for 3,000 Years." *Smithsonian*, June 20, 2014. www.smithsonianmag.com/ smart-news/3000-years-humans-alterations-chinas-yellow-river-created-catastrophic-situation-exists-today-180951815/?no-ist.

Suttmeier, Stephen, and Jue Xiong. "A Closer Look at the Best Bull Markets in Excess of 20%." *Merrill Lynch Global Research* (August 13, 2013). Research piece from Bank of America Merrill Lynch Global Research.

Trading Economics. www.tradingeconomics.com/united-states/gdp. Data showing where the United States stands as a percentage of world gross domestic product.

Wall Street Journal. Market Data Center. http://online.wsj.com/mdc/public/ page/2_3021-peyield.html. Information on current Standard & Poor's 500 Index dividend yields.

Nobel Prize–Winning Theories

Modern Portfolio Theory: Markowitz, Harry. "Portfolio Selection." *Journal of Finance* 7 (1952).

Prospect Theory: Kahneman, Daniel, and Amos Tversky. "Prospect Theory: An Analysis of Decision under Risk." *Econometrica* 47 (1979). www.princeton.edu/~kahneman/docs/Publications/prospect_theory.pdf.

Suggested Readings

Bernstein, William J. *The Investor's Manifesto: Preparing for Prosperity, Armageddon, and Everything in Between*. Hoboken, NJ: John Wiley & Sons, 2010.

Conrad, Edward. *Unintended Consequences: Why Everything You've Been Told about the Economy Is Wrong*. New York: Portfolio Penguin, 2012.

Ferguson, Niall. *The Ascent of Money: A Financial History of the World*. New York: The Penguin Press, 2008.

Kahneman, Daniel. *Thinking Fast and Slow*. New York: Farrar, Straus, and Giroux, 2011.

Reinhart, Carmen M., and Kenneth S. Rogoff. *This Time Is Different: Eight Centuries of Financial Folly*. Princeton, NJ: Princeton University Press, 2009.

Rickards, James. *Currency Wars: The Making of the Next Global Crisis*. New York: Portfolio Penguin, 2011.

Rickards, James. *The Death of Money: The Coming Collapse of the International Monetary System*. New York: Portfolio Penguin, 2014.

Thaler, Richard H., and Cass R. Sunstein. *Nudge: Improving Decisions about Health, Wealth, and Happiness, revised and expanded edition*. New York: Penguin Books, 2009.

Wessel, David. *Red Ink: Inside the High-Stakes Politics of the Federal Budget*. New York: Crown Business, 2012.

Wiedemer, David, Robert Widemer, and Cindy Spitzer. *Aftershock: Protect Yourself and Profit in the Next Global Financial Meltdown, revised and updated, 3rd edition*. Hoboken, NJ: John Wiley & Sons, 2014.

Zingales, Luigi. *A Capitalism for the People: Recapturing the Lost Genius of American Prosperity*. New York: Basic Books, 2012.

About the Author

Tom Anderson has his MBA from the University of Chicago and a BSBA from Washington University in St. Louis, where he achieved a double major in Finance and International Business. During his undergraduate years Tom studied abroad extensively, participating in programs at the London School of Economics and the Cass Business School at City University London, and he spent a full year at ESCP Europe on their Madrid campus.

In 2002, Tom attended the Wharton School of the University of Pennsylvania and subsequently obtained the title of Certified Investment Management Analyst® (CIMA®), sponsored by the Investment Management Consultants Association (IMCA). In addition, Tom has earned the Chartered Retirement Planning Counselor℠ (CRPC®) designations through the College for Financial Planning.

Tom worked in investment banking in New York before moving into private wealth management. He is fluent in Spanish and has lived and worked in Spain and Mexico. His extensive academic studies at some of the top schools in finance and economics, international experiences, and institutional background deliver a unique perspective on global markets and on the value of debt.

Tom has received multiple national recognitions for his wealth management accomplishments including being named four times by *Barron's* magazine as one of America's Top 1,000 advisors: State by State,[1] and was one of *On Wall Street* magazine's "40 under 40," which recognized him as one of the largest producing advisors in the industry under 40 years old. He is married and lives with his wife and three children in Chicago.

---

[1] *Barron's* "Top 1,200 Advisors," February 2014, as identified by *Barron's* magazine, using quantitative and qualitative criteria and selected from a pool of over 4,000 nominations. Advisors in the Top 1,200 financial advisors have a minimum of seven years of financial services experience. Qualitative factors include, but are not limited to, compliance record, interviews with senior management, and philanthropic work. Investment performance is not a criterion. The rating may not be representative of any one client's experience and is not indicative of the financial advisor's future performance. Neither the advisor's firm nor the advisor pay a fee to Barron's in exchange for the rating. In 2013 *Barron's* expanded the annual state-by-state listing from 1,000 advisors to 1,200 to include Registered Investment Advisors. *Barron's* is a registered trademark of Dow Jones & Company. All rights reserved.

Index